WITHDRAWN

JUN 28

DAVID O. McKAY LIBRARY
BYU-IDAHO

P9-AFZ-415

Games and Gamesters
of the Restoration

Games and Gamesters of the Restoration

THE COMPLEAT GAMESTER

By Charles Cotton, 1674

and

LIVES OF THE GAMESTERS

By Theophilus Lucas, 1714

With an Introduction by

CYRIL HUGHES HARTMANN

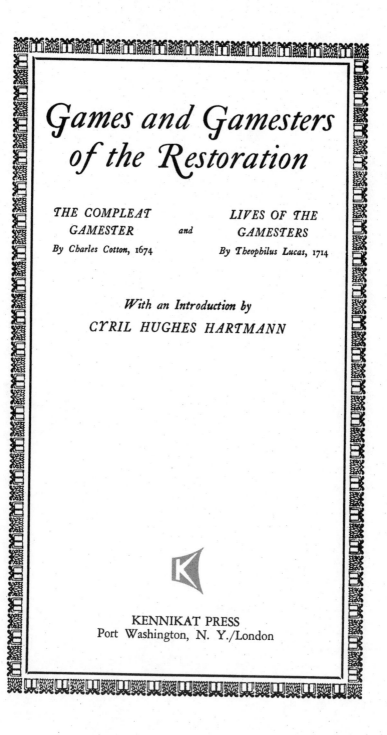

KENNIKAT PRESS

Port Washington, N. Y./London

GAMES AND GAMESTERS OF THE RESTORATION

First published in 1930
Reissued in 1971 by Kennikat Press
Library of Congress Catalog Card No: 74-118475
ISBN 0-8046-1224-2

Manufactured by Taylor Publishing Company   Dallas, Texas

CONTENTS

v

LIST OF ILLUSTRATIONS

INTRODUCTION

AFTER the upheaval of the Civil Wars, the years of Cromwell's despotic and repressive rule, and the period of confusion and anarchy which followed, it is scarcely to be wondered at that the English people should have emerged with the temporary loss of all its ideals, political, social, and moral. It might, indeed, be likened to a human body, which, weakened by wounds and exposure, is unable either to resist the latent tendencies towards disease that may be within itself or to repel the venomous attacks of alien germs. The moral aspect of the Restoration period is at least as important as the political, and the exceptional depravity of that time is traceable to deep-seated causes. It cannot be lightly attributed, as it so often is, to the influence of the King himself and a few dissolute boon-companions: the morals of the Court were not the cause but merely a symptom of the prevailing corruption, which manifested itself in excessive indulgence in all forms of pleasure.

At no time probably in the history of England has the passion for gambling reached a greater height or spread over a larger section of society than it did during the latter half of the seventeenth and the opening years of the eighteenth centuries. It is certainly true that the natural reaction against Puritanism consequent upon the Restoration was no unimportant factor in the situation; but it should not be forgotten that the gambling mania had already gripped the rest of Europe, and that the inordinate craze for games of chance which developed during the reign of Charles II received its first impulse from abroad. During their long exile in foreign countries the Cavaliers had gained an extensive and intimate

ix

acquaintance with more games of hazard and skill than they had before suspected to be in existence, and on their return they made no scruple of introducing them all into England. The seeds they scattered rapidly took root wherever they fell whether in the Court or the slums. Though Gaming is a plant for which no soil appears to be too barren, the soil of English society, having lain fallow throughout the years of the Commonwealth, was now peculiarly receptive.

That the Court at Whitehall set the worst of examples is not to be denied. " This evening, according to costome," wrote priggish John Evelyn on January 6th, 1662, " his Majesty open'd the revells of that night by throwing the dice himselfe in the privy chamber, where was a table set on purpose, and lost his 100 *l.* (The yeare before he won 1500 *l.*) The ladies also plaied very deepe. I came away when the Duke of Ormond had won about 1000 *l.* and left them still at *passage, cards,* &c. At other tables, both there and at ye Groom-porter's, observing the wicked folly and monstrous excesse of passion amongst some loosers; sorry I am that such a wretched costome as play to that excesse should be countenanc'd in a Court which ought to be an example of virtue to the rest of the kingdome."

Charles II himself was not one of the leading spirits. In his characteristically indolent way he followed the prevailing fashion, but without any real enthusiasm. It gave him some pleasure to win, but, like many another otherwise open-handed man, he was a bad loser—and he usually lost. He had no taste for cards, although during the years of his exile he had occasionally beguiled his weariness by playing with such intimates as Rochester and Sir Henry Bennet. A letter from the King to Ormonde contains a whimsical comment on his habitual ill-luck: " God sende you better lucke at pickett than I have with Harry Bennett at cribbadge." John Sheffield, Duke of Buckingham, in his *Character* of the King points out that this aversion to gambling was a somewhat unexpected trait in a man generally so careless of money. " While he sacrificed all things to his mistresses, he would use to grudge, and be uneasy at their losing a little of it again at play, tho' never so necessary for their diversion : Nor would he venture five pounds at Tennis to those servants, who might obtain as many thousands, either before he came thither, or as soon as he left off."

The phrase " tho' never so necessary for their diversion " is significant. Unless one gambled freely it was quite impossible to be accounted a gentleman, or, for that matter, a lady of fashion at the Court of Charles II. Gambling, dancing, and the theatre were almost the only occupations of the Court when it was at Whitehall, so that to show an interest in all three was actually considered an indispensable part of good breeding. Reckless play for ridiculously high stakes was by no means confined to rakes and debauchees, but was freely indulged in by persons of the highest character. One of the most extravagant players in the land was that most noble and upright of Cavalier gentlemen, the Duke of Ormonde, who, however, according to Bishop Burnet, was " decent even in his vices," a quality rare at a time when the exact opposite might well have been said of so many of his contemporaries. But Gambling, which was the natural and common practice of both sexes in all classes, was at that time scarcely regarded as a vice at all. Even the ex-Puritan Pepys was not above an occasional mild flutter, though he was suitably shocked when he discovered that the Queen and the Duchess of York actually played cards on Sunday. But he was by nature far too careful to be drawn into fashionable excesses, and he flatly refused to hazard his luck even once at the Groom Porter's. He contented himself with playing with friends, and was overjoyed when he won nine shillings and six pence, this being, as he confessed, " the most that ever I won in my life."

While the Courtiers disported themselves in the apartments of the reigning favourites or at the inner sanctuary of aristocratic Gaming, the lodging of the Groom Porter, the less privileged classes resorted to the taverns and coffee-houses, where facilities for all kinds of play were provided for them. Gambling in one form or another was rife at all hours and in all places, and even in the halls of the Inns of Court Pepys saw " dirty prentices and idle people " playing at dice. When the floor of the Middle Temple Hall was taken up in 1764 the workmen discovered nearly a hundred pairs of dice which had fallen through the crevices between the boards.

Cards and dice were only two of the many manifestations of the spirit of gambling which pervaded the whole of society like an insidious poison. Betting was another. Bets were made on every conceivable subject : nothing seemed to be too lofty or too low to be made the excuse for a wager. There is little or no exaggeration in the remark made by a character in one of Killigrew's comedies: " You see the virtue of a wager, the new, philosophical argument lately found out to decide all questions."

The astounding mania for gambling formed a favourite subject for satire in the plays of Restoration dramatists and for fulminations in the sermons of Restoration divines. Amongst the most remarkable attacks upon the fashionable vice was that of the poet, Sir John Denham, who, professing penitence for having wasted so much time and money in play, wrote a treatise against gaming so admirably thought out and so manifestly sincere that his angry father relented from his previous decision to disinherit him and left him a substantial fortune—which he promptly proceeded to dissipate at the card-table.

Not a few of those about the Court depended on their skill at cards for their very subsistence. Amongst them was the celebrated Chevalier de Gramont, whose disgust and indignation at Frances Stuart's predilection for building card-houses and so distracting his usual victims from the more orthodox uses for cards led him to brand that shrewd and level-headed woman as an inanimate fool. Many of these " professional " card-players—not excluding Gramont, who himself admitted that he "played high and loſt but seldom"—were by no means over-scrupulous in their methods, and cheating was hardly regarded as so heinous a social offence as it became in the succeeding century. In faɛt, so long as its exponents were not aɛtually caught red-handed it was regarded almoſt in the light of an embellishment to skilful play.

Cards appear to have been introduced into England some time in the fourteenth century, but for a long time card games were regarded as a pastime to be indulged in only during the twelve days of Chriſtmas. By the reign of Edward IV they had attained sufficient vogue for the Government to consider it advisable to prohibit the importation of cards from abroad in order to safeguard a rising home induſtry. The English gentry of the six-teenth century were less addiɛted to cards, though two at leaſt of the games favoured by the courtiers of the Reſtoration, Gleek and Angel-beaſt, had been played by their anceſtors in Tudor times. During the firſt half of the seventeenth century Gleek, Picquet, and, later, Cribbage were the moſt fashionable games. Sir John Suckling, the poet, who was an inveterate gameſter and was accounted the moſt skilful as well as the moſt reckless player of his time, is credited with the invention of the game of Cribbage. Playing-cards were at that time im-ported from France, and it was commonly believed that Suckling had made an arrangement with the French makers whereby all packs of cards imported into England for the use of the Court were secretly marked with distinguishing signs known only to himself. This ingenious if disreputable expedient would not have been feasible after the Reſtoration, when, owing to the un-precedented demand, cards had to be imported in far larger quantities and even once more manufaɛtured at home.

In the early years of the Reſtoration period the moſt popular game was Ombre, a game of Spanish origin, supposed to have been introduced into England by Queen

Catherine of Bragança. Probably she was no more responsible for doing so than she was for the first introduction of tea, with which she is also popularly credited in spite of the fact that it had been drunk in England for some twenty years before her arrival. But at any rate it was the game which she played with the greatest frequency and pleasure. One of the most indifferent epigrams composed by Edmund Waller was written on a card Her Majesty tore at Ombre.

About the year 1677 Ombre was temporarily displaced by Basset, the intricacies of which were first expounded in London at the apartments of the Duchesse Mazarin by another foreign adventurer, a croupier named Morin, whose dubious conduct at the tables had recently made France too hot to hold him. Despite the violent attacks in prose and verse of Sir George Etherege and Monsieur de St. Evremond, who were highly incensed that their favoured ladies preferred the thrills of the game to those of their own sprightly conversation, Basset at once attained an immense vogue in circles where really high play was possible. The royal mistresses ventured huge sums at it. Nell Gwyn once lost as much as £5000 to the Duchesse Mazarin in a single night, and the losses of the Duchesses of Cleveland and Portsmouth were even more considerable. No doubt the fortune of the game was not always against them ; there must have been times when they won ; but it is their losses that have come down to posterity, because they had to come out of the King's pocket and so are recorded in State documents, while their winnings went into their own and disappeared.

Basset never really caught on outside the Court circle owing to the enormous sums involved. So expensive and risky was this game that in France it was eventually forbidden upon severe penalties except in the houses of foreign ministers. The games most favoured by the French were Lansquenet, Picquet, and Ombre. A gentleman attached to the suite of an English ambassador to France was so impressed by Parisian society's unenviable reputation for sharp play that he thought it necessary to issue a warning to any of his fellow-country-men who might feel disposed to try their luck at cards in the French capital. " The French," he wrote, " are very adroit at cards, and therefore a Foreigner will do well to know his Men, before he engages in Play; or rather, he'll do much better not to play at all, for even the Ladies do not want Tricks to ſtrip a Bubble."

As the reign progressed Gaming proved to be no pass-ing craze: the fervour for play increased rather than diminished. In 1684 a friend at Court wrote to the Countess of Rutland: " Play is grown the predominate passion even of the ladies as well as men preferrs it to all divertions. Comette now reigns though Baſſette ſtill keeps in creditt at her Grace of Portsmouth, the Duke of Norfolk, the Lady Poltney, and Mrs. Morine— Sir Robert Thorold's daughter." Comet may have been the fashion of the moment at Court, but the day of Ombre was far from being over, and both had a formidable rival for popularity in whist, which boaſted an advantage over other games in its comparative simplicity, for, as Cotton says in his chapter on *English Ruff and Honours, and Whiſt,* " every child almoſt of eight years old hath a competent knowledg in that recreation."

Hackneyed though it may be, Evelyn's juſtly famous description of the scene that greeted his eyes at White-hall a few days before the death of Charles II cannot possibly be left out of any account of gaming in the Reſtoration period : " I can never forget the inexpres-sible luxury and prophanenesse, gaming and all dissolute-ness, and as it were total forgetfullnesse of God (it being Sunday evening) which this day se'nnight I was witnesse of, the King sitting and toying with his concu-bines, Portsmouth, Cleaveland, and Mazarine, &c. a French boy singing love songs, in that glorious gallery, whilſt about 20 of the greate courtiers and other dis-solute persons were at Basset round a large table, a Bank of at leaſt 2000 in gold before them, upon which two gentlemen who were with me made reflexions with aſtonishment. Six days after was all in the duſt!"

In the reigns of Charles II's successors the craze for gaming continued unabated, although the play at Court itself was, perhaps, not quite so high. Queen Mary II was so keen a card-player that on her marriage to the Prince of Orange she had shocked her husband's Dutch subjeéts by her persiſtence in playing on Sundays. But she was inclined to frown upon excessive gambling and insiſted upon the ſtakes being kept low whenever she herself was playing. Her excellent example evidently did not survive her, for Katherine, Countess of Rutland, writing to her husband after a visit to William III's Court in 1701, mentions that since the Queen's death the silver table had been abolished and only gold was played for.

Social critics of this time conſtantly drew attention to the extraordinary increase of gambling amongſt women. Sir Richard Steele, as St. Evremond had done before him, especially deplored the effeét of the late hours and the excitement upon their health and appearance. "The Beauties of the Face and Mind are generally deſtroyed by the same means. This Consideration should have a particular Weight with the Female World, who were designed to please the Eye, and attraét the Regards of the other half of the Species. Now, there is nothing that wears out a fine Face like the Vigils of the Card Table, and those cutting Passions which naturally attend them. Hollow Eyes, haggard Looks, and pale Complexions, are the natural Indications of a Female Gameſter. Her Morning Sleeps are not able to repair her Midnight Watchings. I have known a Woman carried off half dead from Bassette, and have, many a time grieved to see a Person of Quality gliding by me, in her Chair, at two a Clock in the Morning, and looking like a Sceptre amidſt a flare of Flambeaux. In short, I never knew a thorough paced Female Gameſter hold her Beauty two Winters together."

Pope also, in his *Rape of the Lock*, has many a tilt

against the fashionable feminine predilection for card-playing :

> Think not when Woman's transient breath is fled
> That all her vanities at once are dead :
> Succeeding vanities she still regards,
> And tho' she plays no more, o'erlooks the cards.
> Her joy in gilded chariots when alive,
> And love of *Ombre* after death survive.

At the time of the Restoration Gaming had been officially recognized by the revival of the appointment of Groom Porter, an officer of the Lord Steward's department to whom the superintendence and regulation of all matters relating to cards and dice had been committed ever since the reign of Henry VIII, if not from a still earlier date. As has been seen, the Groom Porter was the presiding genius of gambling at Court; and that his authority extended beyond its confines is shown by the following extract from the " London Gazette " for December 6–10, 1706 :

" Whereas Her Majesty, by her Letters Patent to Thomas Archer, Esqre., constituting him Her Groom Porter, hath given full power to him and such Deputies as he shall appoint to supervise, regulate and authorize (by and under the Rules, Conditions, and Restrictions by the Law prescribed) all manner of Gaming within this Kingdom. And, whereas, several of Her Majesty's Subjects, keeping Plays or Games in their Houses, have been lately abused, and had Moneys extorted from them by several ill-disposed Persons, contrary to Law. These are, therefore, to give Notice, That no Person whatsoever, not producing his Authority from the said Groom Porter, under Seal of his Office, hath any power to act anything under the said Patent. And, to the end that all such Persons offending as aforesaid, may be proceeded against according to Law, it is hereby desired, that Notice be given of all such Abuses to the said Groom Porter, or his Deputies, at his Office, at Mr. Stephenson's, a Scrivener's House, over against old Man's Coffee House, near Whitehall."

Introduction

The Groom Porter continued to preside over the Court gambling through the next two reigns; but the office was finally abolished by George III, who did not care for or approve of gambling and heartily shared his consort's desire to discourage it at Court and especially among his own household.

The two vastly different books here reprinted together give a comprehensive and representative view of gamesters and gambling in the latter half of the seventeenth century. Lucas's book is of much the same nature as the society gossip columns in twentieth-century Sunday newspapers, and exactly the same amount of credence can be given to it. Some of his anecdotes are authentic, others can boast a substratum of truth, others again are recklessly inaccurate. Nevertheless, the book as a whole does give a broad, colourful, and not too much exaggerated picture of the doings of a certain section of society. Even if some of his stories were not actually true of the persons of whom they were told, none of them is too scandalous to have been true of one or another of the dissolute characters of the period.

Charles Cotton's book, like much else of his work, was first published anonymously. A variant version of the opening chapter appeared in 1669 in the form of a pamphlet entitled *The Nicker Nicked : Or the Cheate of Gaming discovered. Leathermore's advice concerning Gaming.* The first edition of the *Compleat Gamester* was published in 1674. It was not until Richard Seymour's *Compleat Gamester* was published in 1734 that it became generally known that Cotton was the author of the anonymous work from which the second and third parts of Seymour's book were compiled. Much of Cotton's work was practically hack-work: he was, unlike most of his friends in the world of letters, a professional author, forced upon the decay of his fortunes to seek a living by his pen. Yet the *Compleat Gamester* shows little trace of being hack-work. This was probably because, as was also the case with the *Compleat Angler*, another and better-known work in the authorship of which his name is associated with that of Izaak Walton, he was dealing with subjects dear to his heart. The game of billiards must have been congenial to a man who could describe it as " the gentile, cleanly and most ingenious game at billiards." His chapter on *The Art and Mystery of Riding* can still be read with profit as well as pleasure by anyone who loves a horse. In sum, Charles Cotton wrote with taste, discrimination, and infectious enthusiasm of the accomplishments proper to the class to which he himself belonged, and his book may be held to afford as good a picture as can be obtained of the manners, habits, and pastimes of the average English gentleman of the upper classes in the days of the last Stuart monarchs.

CYRIL HUGHES HARTMANN.

Note.—Cotton's *Compleat Gamester* has been reprinted from the first edition, 1674, and Lucas's *Memoirs of the Lives*, etc., with the omission of two coarse but irrelevant anecdotes, from the first edition, 1714. Descriptions of the games of Basset, Bragg, and Primero have been added from the 1721 edition of the *Compleat Gamester*.

PLATE I

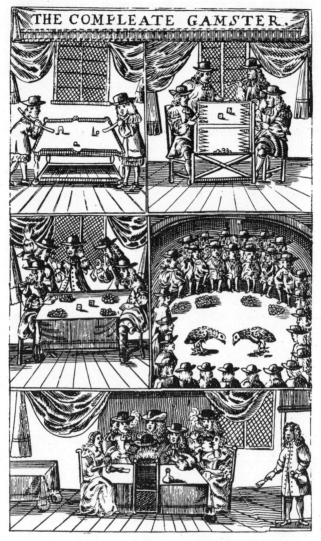

FRONTISPIECE TO C. COTTON. COMPLEAT GAMESTER

[*face p. xxi*

Billiards from Spain at first deriv'd its name,
Both an ingenious, and a cleanly game.
One gamester leads (the table green as grass)
And each like warriers strive to gain the pass.
But in the contest, e're the pass be won,
Hazzards are many into which they run.
Thus while we play on this terrestrial stage,
Nothing but *Hazzard* doth attend each age.

    Next here are *Hazzards* play'd another way,
By box and dice ; 'tis *Hazzard* is the play.
The Bully-Rock with mangy fist, and pox,
Justles some out, and then takes up the box.
He throws the main, and crys, who comes at seven ?
Thus with a dry fist nicks it with eleven.
If out, he raps out oaths I dare not tell,
Hot, piping out, and newly come from Hell.
Old-Nick o're-hearing, by a palming-trick
Secures the Gamester ; thus the Nicker's nickt.

    Now t' *Irish*, or *Back-Gammoners* we come,
Who wish their money, with their men safe home ;
But as in war, so in this subtle play,
The stragling men are ta'ne up by the way.
By entring then, one reinforceth more,
It may be to be lost, as those before.
By topping, knapping, and foul play some win ;
But those are losers, who so gain by sin.

    After these three the Cock-pit claims a name ;
A sport gentile, and call'd a Royal Game.
Now see the gallants crowd about the pit,
And most are stockt with money more than wit ;
Else sure they would not, with so great a stir,
Lay ten to one on a cocks faithless spur.

    Lastly, observe the women with what grace
They sit, and look their partners in the face.
Who from their eyes shoot Cupids fiery darts ;
Thus make them lose at once their game and hearts.
Their white soft hands (when e're the cards they cut)
Make the men wish to change the game to *Putt*.
The women knew their thoughts, then cry'd, enough,
Let's leave off *Whist*, and go to *Putt*, or *Ruff*,
    Ladies, don't trust your secrets in that hand,
    Who can't their own (to their great grief) command.
    For this I will assure you, if you do,
    In time you'l lose your *Ruff* and *Honour* too.

THE COMPLEAT

: : Gameſter : :

or,

INSTRUCTIONS

How to play at

BILLIARDS, TRUCKS, BOWLS,

and CHESS.

Together with all manner of uſual and
moſt Gentile Games either on

CARDS or DICE.

To which is added

THE ARTS AND MYSTERIES

of

RIDING, RACING, ARCHERY,

and COCK-FIGHTING.

LONDON : Printed by *A. M.* for *R. Cutler,*
and to be ſold by *Henry Brome* at the
Gun at the Weſt-end of St. *Pauls.* 1674.

THE EPISTLE TO THE READER

READER,

I was once resolv'd to have let this ensuing treatise to have ſtept naked into the world, without so much as the leaſt rag of an Epiſtle to defend it a little from the cold welcome it may meet with in its travails; but knowing that not only cuſtom expeċts but necessity requires it, give me leave to show you the motives inducing to this present publication.

It is not (I'le assure you) any private intereſt of my own that caus'd me to adventure on this subjeċt, but the delight and benefit of every individual person; delight to such who will pass away their spare minutes in harmless recreation if not abus'd; and profit to all, who by in-speċting all manner of games may observe the cheats and abuses, and so be arm'd againſt the injuries may accrue thereby.

Certainly there is no man so severe to deny the lawful ness of recreation; there was never any Stoick found so cruel, either to himself, or nature, but at some time or other he would unbend his mind, and give it liberty to ſtray into some more pleasant walks, than the miry heavy ways of his own sowr, willful resolutions. You may observe the heathen sages of the firſt world founded with their laws their feaſts, with their labours their Olympicks, with their warfare their triumphs. Nay at this day the severeſt Dionysian pedagogue will give his scholars their play-days, & breakings up with a *Horum miserere laborum, essum quies plurimum juvat.* And the moſt covetous maſters will tye their servants but to certain hours; every toyl exaċting as *ex officio*, or out of duty some time for recreation. I myself have observed in the course of many men of exceeding ſtriċt lives and conversation, to whom although severity of profession, infirmity of body, extremity of age, or such like, have taken away all actual recreation, yet have their minds begot unto themselves some habits or customs of delight, which have in as large measure given them contentment whether they were their own, or borrowed, as if they had been the sole actors of the same. Futhermore, recreation is not only lawful but necessary:

> Interpone tuis interdum gaudia curis,
> Ut possis animo quemvis sufferre laborem.

> So intermix your care with joy, you may
> Lighten your labour by a little play.

Now what recreation this should be I cannot prescribe, nor is it requisite to confine any to one sort of pleasure, since herein Nature taketh to her self an especial prerogative, for what to one is most pleasant, to another is most offensive; some seeking to satisfie the mind, some the body, and others both in a joint motion. To this end I have laid before you what variety of pastimes I could collect for the present, leaving the rest (as you like these) to be suppli'd hereafter. Mistake me not, it is not my intention to make gamesters by this collection, but to inform all in part how to avoid being cheated by them. If I am imperfect in my discoveries, impute it to my being no profest gamester, and the hatred I bear that hellish society; by whom I know I shall be laught at, and with whom if I should converse, I might sooner by my study come to be Nature's secretary, and unriddle all her *Arcana's*, than collect from them any new unpractised secret, by which they bubble ignorant credulity, and purchase money and good apparel with everlasting shame and infamy.

To conclude, let me advise you, if you play (when your business will permit) let not a covetous desire of winning another's money engage you to be losing your own; which will not only disturb your mind, but by the disreputation of being a gamester, if you lose not your estate, you will certainly lose your credit and good name, than which there is nothing more valuable. Thus hoping you will be thus advis'd, and will withal excuse my errors, I shall ever study how to serve you, and subscribe myself a well-willer to all men.

CONTENTS

TO

THE COMPLEAT GAMESTER

Contents

The Compleat Gamester

Chapter I

Of Gaming in General, or an Ordinary Described

GAMING is an enchanting witchery, gotten betwixt idleness and avarice : an itching disease, that makes some scratch the head, whilſt others, as if they were bitten by a Tarantula, are laughing themselves to death : or laſtly, it is a paralytical diſtemper, which seizing the arm the man cannot chuse but shake his elbow. It hath this ill property above all other vices, that it renders a man incapable of prosecuting any serious aćtion, and makes him always unsatisfied with his own condition; he is either lifted up to the top of mad joy with success, or plung'd to the bottom of despair by misfortune, always in extreams, always in a ſtorm; this minute the gameſter's countenance is so serene and calm, that one would think nothing could diſturb it, and the next minute so ſtormy and tempeſtuous that it threatens deſtrućtion to it self and others ; and as he is transported with joy when he wins, so losing he is toſt upon the billows of a high swelling passion, till he hath loſt sight of both of sense and reason.

I have seen some dogs bite the ſtones which boys have thrown at them, not regarding whence they were flung ; so I have seen a losing gameſter greedily gnawing the innocent box, and sometimes tearing it to pieces as an accessary to his throwing out; nor muſt the dice go unpunished for not running his chance, and therefore in rage are thrown on the ground to be kickt to and fro by every body ; and at laſt lookt upon no other than the fit companions of every saucy skip-jack.

Then fresh dice are called for, as thinking they will prove more kind than the former, or as if they believed that some were good natur'd, others bad, and that every bale produced a different disposition. If these run cross too, the box-keeper shall not go without a horrid execration, if for nothing else but that he lookt strictly to the cast, it may be conceiving that his very eyes were capable of making them turn to his disadvantage. This restless man (the miserable gamester) is the proper subject of every mans pity. Restless I call him, because (such is the itch of play) either winning or losing he can never rest satisfied, if he wins he thinks to win more, if he loses he hopes to recover. To this mans condition the saying of Hannibal to Marcellus may be fitly applied, that *nec bonam, nec malam fortunam ferre potest*, he could not be quiet either conqueror or conquered. Thus have I heard of some who with five pounds have won four hundred pounds in one night, and the next night have lost it to a sum not half so much; others who have lost their estates and won them again with addition, yet could not be quiet till they lost them irrecoverably.

And therefore fitly was that question propounded, Whether men in ships at sea were to be accounted among the living or the dead, because there were but few inches betwixt them and drowning. The same *quære* may be made of great gamesters, though their estates be never so considerable, Whether they are to be esteemed poor or rich, since there are but few casts at dice betwixt a rich man (in that circumstance) and a beggar.

Now since speculation will not be convincing, unless we shew somewhat of the modern practice; we must therefore lay our scene at an ordinary, and proceed to action: where note, an ordinary is a handsome house, where everyday, about the hour of twelve, a good dinner is prepared by way of ordinary, composed of variety of dishes, in season, well-drest, with all other accommodations fit for that purpose, whereby many gentlemen of great estates and good repute, make this place their resort, who after dinner play a while for recreation both

2

moderately and commonly, without deserving reproof. But here is the mischief, the best wheat will have tares growing amongst it, rooks and daws will sometimes be in the company of pigeons; nor can real gentlemen now-adays so seclude themselves from the society of such as are pretendedly so, but that they oftentimes mix company, being much of the same colour and feather, and by the eye undistinguishable.

It is reported of the polypus (a fish), that it will conform itself to the colour of what is nearest, for security and advantage: and so do these pretended gentlemen attire themselves in what is both gentle and fashionable, that under that disguise they may with more facility riggle themselves into the society of such worthy persons, out of whom they intend to squeize some sums of moneys by cards, dice, or otherways.

These rooks can do little harm in the day time at an ordinary, being forc'd to play upon the square, although now and then they make an advantage, when the box-keeper goes with him, and then the knave and rascal will violate his trust for profit, and lend him (when he sees good) a tickler shall do his business; but if discovered, the box-keeper ought to be soundly kickt for his pains. Such practices, and sometimes the box-keepers connivances, are so much us'd of late, that there is nothing near that fair play in an ordinary, as formerly.

The day being shut in, you may properly compare this place to those countries which lye far in the North, where it is as clear at midnight as at noonday: and though it is a house of sin, yet you cannot call it a house of darkness, for the candles never go out till morning, unless the sudden fury of a losing gamester make them extinct.

This is the time (when ravenous beasts usually seek their prey) wherein comes shoals of *Huffs, Hectors, Setters, Gilts, Pads, Biters, Divers, Lifters, Filers, Budgies, Droppers, Crossbyters*, etc., and these may all pass under the general and common appellation of *Rooks*. And in this particular, an ordinary serves as a nursery for Tyburn;

for if any one will put himself to the trouble of observation, he shall find that there is seldom a year wherein there are not some of this gang hang as pretious jewels in the ear of Tyburn. Look back and you will find a great many gone already, God knows how many are to follow.

These rooks are in continual motion, walking from one table to another, till they can discover some unexperienc'd young gentleman, casheer or apprentice, that is come to this school of virtue, being unskill'd in the quibbles and devices there practised; these they call *Lambs*, or *Colls*. Then do the Rooks (more properly called *Wolves*) strive who shall fasten on him first, following him close, and engaging him in some advantageous bets, and at length worries him, that is, gets all his money, and then the *rooks* (rogues I shculd have said) laugh and grin, saying, the lamb is bitten.

Some of these rooks will be very importunate to borrow money of you without any intention to pay you; or to go with you seven to twelve half a crown or more, whereby without a very great chance (ten to one or more) he is sure to win. If you are sensible hereof, and refuse his proposition, they will take it so ill, that if you have not an especially care they will pick your pocket, nim your gold or silver buttons off your cloak or coat; or it may be draw your silver-hilted sword out of your belt without discovery, especially if you are eager upon your cast, which is done thus; the silver buttons are strung, or run upon cats guts fastned at the upper and nether end; now by ripping both ends very ingeniously (as they call it) give it the gentile pull, and so rub off with the buttons; and if your cloak be loose 'tis ten to one they have it.

But that which will most provoke (in my opinion) any mans rage to a just satisfaction, is their throwing many times at a good sum with a *dry fist* (as they call it) that is; if they *nick* you, 'tis theirs; if they lose, they owe you so much with many other quillets: some I have known so abominably impudent, that they would snatch up the stakes, and thereupon instantly draw, saying, if you will have your money you must fight for it; for he is a gentleman and will not want: however, if you will be patient, he will pay you another time. If you are so tame to take this, go no more to the ordinary; for then the whole gang will be ever and anon watching an opportunity to make a mouth of you in the like nature. If you nick them, 'tis odds, if they wait not your coming out at night and beat you. I could produce you an hundred examples in this kind, but they will rarely adventure on the attempt unless they are backt with some *Bully-Huffs*, and *Bully-Rocks*, with others whose fortunes are as desperate as their own. We need no other testimony to confirm the danger of associating with these anthropophagi or man-eaters, than Lincolns-Inn-Fields whilst Speerings ordinary was kept in Bell-yard, and that you need not want a pair of witnesses for the proof thereof, take in also Covent-Garden.

Neither is the house itself to be exempted, every night almost some one or other, who either heated with wine, or made cholerick with the loss of his money, raises a quarrel, swords are drawn, box and candlesticks thrown at one anothers head, tables overthrown, and all the house in such a garboyl, that it is the perfect type of Hell. Happy is the man now that can make the frame of a table or chimney-corner his sanctuary; and if any are so fortunate to get to the stair-head, they will rather hazard the breaking of their own necks than have their souls pusht out of their bodies in the dark by they know not whom.

I once observed one of the desperadoes of the town (being half drunk) to press a gentleman very much (at play) to lend him a crown, the gentleman refus'd him several times, yet still the borrower persisted, and holding his head somewhat too near the casters elbow, it chanced to hit his nose, the other thinking it to be affront enough to be denied the loan of money without this slight touch of the nose, drew, and stepping back (unawares to the gentleman) made a full pass at him, intending to have run him through the body; but his drunkenness misguided his hand, so that he ran him only through the arm:

this put the house into so great a confusion and fright, that some fled thinking the gentleman slain. This wicked miscreant thought not this sufficient, but tripping up his heels, pinn'd him as he thought to the floor; and after this, takes the gentlemans silver sword, leaving his in the wound, and with a grand-jury of dammees (which may hereafter find him guilty at the great tribunal) bid all stand off if they lov'd their lives, and so went clear off with sword and liberty; but was notwithstanding (the gentleman recovering) compel'd to make what satisfaction he was capable of making, besides a long imprisonment; and was not long abroad before he was apprehended for burglary committed, condemned, and justly executed.

Fatebere tandem
Nec Surdum, nec Tiressam quenquam esse Deorum.

But to proceed on as to play: late at night when the company grows thin, and your eyes dim with watching, false dice are frequently put upon the ignorant, or they are otherwise cheated by *Topping, Slurring, Stabbing,* &c., and if you be not careful and vigilant, the box-keeper shall score you up double or treble boxes, and though you have lost your money, dun you as severely for it, as if it were the justest debt in the world.

The more subtile and gentiler sort of rooks (as aforesaid) you shall not distinguish by their outward demeanor from persons of condition; these will sit by a whole evening, and observe who wins; if the winner be bubbleable, they will insinuate themselves into his company by applauding his success, advising him to leave off whilst he is well; and lastly, by civilly inviting him to drink a glass of wine, where having well warm'd themselves to make him more than half drunk they wheadle him in to play; to which if he condescend he shall quickly have no money left him in his pocket, unless perchance a crown the rooking-winner lent him in courtesie to bear his charges homewards.

This they do by false dice, as *High-Fullams* 4, 5, 6. *Low-Fullams* 1, 2, 3. By Bristle-dice, which are fitted

6

for their purpose by sticking a hogs-bristle so in the corners, or otherwise in the dice, they shall run high or low as they please; this bristle must be strong and short, by which means the bristle bending, it will not lie on that side, but will be tript over; and this is the newest way of making a high or low *Fullam :* the old ways are by drilling them and loading them with quick-silver; but that cheat may be easily discovered by their weight, or holding two corners between your forefinger and thumb, if holding them so gently between your fingers they turn, you may then conclude them false; or you may try their falsehood otherwise by breaking or splitting them : others have made them by filing and rounding; but all these ways fall short of the art of those who make them : some whereof are so admirably skilful in making a bale of dice to run what you would have them, that your gamesters think they never give enough for their purchase if they prove right. They are sold in many places about the town; price current (by the help of a friend) eight shillings, whereas an ordinary bale is sold for sixpence; for my part I shall tell you plainly, I would have those bales of false dice to be sold at the price of the ears of such destructive knaves that made them.

Another way the rook hath to cheat, is first by *Palming*, that is, he puts one dye into the box, and keeps the other in the hollow of his little finger, which noting what is uppermost when he takes him up, the same shall be when he throws the other dye, which runs doubtfully any cast. Observe this, that the bottom and top of all dice are seven, so that if it be 4 above, it must be a 3 at bottom; so 5 and 2, 6 and 1. Secondly, by *Topping*, and that is when they take up both dice and seem to put them in the box, and shaking the box you would think them both there, by reason of the ratling occasioned with the screwing of the box, whereas one of them is at the top of the box between his two forefingers, or secur'd by thrusting a forefinger into the box. Thirdly, by *Slurring*, that is by taking up your dice as you will have them advantageously lie in your hand, placing the one a top the other, not caring

7

Charles Cotton

if the uppermost run a mill-stone (as they use to say) if the undermost run without turning, and therefore a smooth-table is altogether requisite for this purpose; on a rugged rough board it is a hard matter to be done, whereas on a smooth-table (the best are rub'd over with bees wax to fill up all chinks and crevises) it is usual for some to slur a dye two yards or more without turning. Fourthly, by *Knapping*, that is when you strike a dye dead that it shall not stir, this is best done within the tables; where note there is no securing but of one dye, although there are some who boast of securing both. I have seen some so dexterous at knapping, that they have done it through the handle of a quart pot, or over a candle and candlestick: but that which I most admired, was throwing through the same less than Ames Ace with two dice upon a groat held in the left hand on the one side of the handle a foot distance, and the dice thrown with the right hand on the other.

Lastly, by *Stabbing*, that is having a smooth box, and small in the bottom, you drop in both your dice in such manner as you would have them sticking therein by reason of its narrowness, the dice lying one upon another; so that turning up the box, the dice never tumble; if a smooth box, if true, but little; by which means you have bottoms according to the tops you put in. For example, if you put in your dice so that two fives or two fours lie a top, you have in the bottom turn'd up two two's, or two treys; so if six and an ace a top, a six and an ace at bottom.

Now if the gentleman be past that *classis* of ignoramusses, then they effect their purpose by cross-byting, or some other dexterity, of which they have variety imaginable. A friend of mine wondring at the many slights a noted gamester had to deceive, and how neatly and undiscoverably he managed his tricks, wondring withall he could not do the like himself, since he had the same theory of them all, and knew how they were done; O young man, replied the gamester, there is nothing to be attain'd without pains; wherefore had you been as laborious as my self in the practice hereof, and had

8

sweated at it as many cold winter mornings in your shirt as I have done in mine, undoubtedly you would have arrived at the same perfection.

Here you must observe, that if these rooks think they have met with a sure bubble, they will purposely lose some small sum at first, that they may engage him the more freely to bleed (as they call it) which may be at the second, if not beware of the third meeting, which under the notion of being very merry with wine and good cheer, they will make him pay for the roast.

Consider the further inconveniences of gaming as they are rank'd under these heads.

First, if the house find you free to the box and a constant caster, you shall be treated with suppers at night, and a cawdle in the morning, and have the honour to be stiled a lover of the house, whilst your money lasts, which certainly cannot be long; for here you shall be quickly destroy'd under pretence of kindness as men were by the Lamiae of old; which you may easily gather if from no other consideration than this; that I have seen three persons sit down at twelve penny *In and In*, and each draw forty shillings a piece in less than three hours, the box hath had three pound, and all the three gamesters have been losers.

Secondly, consider how many persons have been ruined by play. I could nominate a great many, some who have had great estates have lost them, others having good imployments have been forced to desert them and hide themselves from their creditors in some foreign plantation by reason of those great debts they had contracted through play.

Thirdly, this course of life shall make you liable to so many affronts and manifold vexations, as in time may breed destraction. Thus a young fellow not many years since, had by strange fortune run up a very small sum to a thousand pounds, and thereupon put himself into a garb accordingly; but not knowing when he was well fell to play again, fortune turn'd, he lost all, ran mad and so died.

9

Fourthly, is it not extreme folly for a man that hath a competent estate to play whether he or another man shall enjoy it; and if his estate be small, then to hazard even the loss of that, and reduce himself to absolute beggery; I think it madness in the highest degree. Besides, it hath been generally observed that the loss of one hundred pounds shall do you more prejudice in disquieting your mind, than the gain of two hundred pounds shall do you good were you sure to keep it.

Lastly, consider not only your loss of time which is invaluable, *Nulla major est jactura quam temporis omissio*, but the damage also the very watching brings to your health, and in particular to the eyes, confirmed by this distick.

> *Allia, Vina, Venus, Fumus, Faba, Lumen & Ignis,*
> *Ista nocent oculis, sed vigilare magis.*

> Garlick, Wine, Women, Smoak, Beans, Fire and Light
> Do hurt the eyes, but watching more the sight.

I shall conclude this character with a penitential sonnet, written by a Lord (a great gamester a little before his death) which was in the year 1580.

> By loss in play men oft forget
>   The duty they do owe
> To him that did bestow the same,
>   And thousand millions moe.
> I loath to hear them swear and stare
>   When they the Main have lost;
> Forgetting all the Byes that were
>   With God and Holy Ghost:
> By wounds and nails they think to win,
>   But truly 'tis not so;
> For all their frets and fumes in sin
>   They moniless must go.
> There is no wight that us'd it more
>   Than he who wrote this verse,
> Who cries *peccavi* now therefore,
>   His oaths his heart do pierce;
> Therefore example take by me
>   That curse the luckless time,
> That ever dice mine eyes did see,
>   Which bred in me this crime.

The Compleat Gamester

Lord pardon me for what is past,
I will offend no more,
In this most vile and sinful cast
Which I will still abhor.

The Character of a Gamester

Some say he was born with cards in his hands, others
that he will die so, but certainly it is all his life, and
whether he sleeps or wakes he thinks of nothing else. He
speaks the language of the game he plays at, better than
the language of his country ; and can less indure a solecism
in that than this : he knows no judge but the groom-
porter, no law but that of the game which he is so expert
all appeal to him, as subordinate judges to the supream
ones. He loves Winter more than Summer, because it
affords more gamesters, and Christmas more than any
other time, because there is more gaming then. He gives
more willingly to the butler than to the poors-box, and
is never more religious than when he prays he may win.
He imagines he is at play when he is at Church ; he takes
his prayer-book for a pack of cards, and thinks he is
shuffling when he turns over the leaves. This man will
play like Nero when the city is on fire, or like Archimedes
when it is sacking, rather than interrupt his game. If
play hath reduced him to poverty, then he is like one a
drowning, who fastens upon any thing next at hand.
Amongst other of his shipwracks, he hath happily lost
shame, and this want supplies him. No man puts his
brain to more use than he ; for his life is a daily invention,
and each meal a new stratagem, and like a flie will boldly
sup at every mans cup. He will offer you a quart of sack
out of his joy to see you, and in requital of his courtesie
you can do no less than pay for it. His borrowings are
like subsidies, each man a shilling or two, as he can well
dispend, which they lend him not with the hope to be
repaid, but that he will come no more. Men shun him
at length as they do an infection, and having done with
them aye as his cloaths to him, hung on as long as he could,
at last drops off.

11

Chapter II

Of BILLIARDS

THE gentile, cleanly and moſt ingenious game at *Billiards* had its firſt original from Italy, and for the excellency of the recreation is much approved of and plaid by moſt nations in Europe, especially in England there being few towns of note therein which hath not a publick Billiard-Table, neither are they wanting in many noble and private families in the country, for the recreation of the mind and exercise of the body.

The form of a Billiard-Table is oblong, that is something longer than it is broad; it is rail'd round, which rail or ledge ought to be a little swel'd or ſtuft with fine flox or cotton: the superficies of the table muſt be covered with green-cloth, the finer and more freed from knots the better it is: the board muſt be level'd as exactly as may be, so that a ball may run true upon any part of the table without leaning to any side thereof; but what by reason of ill-season'd boards which are subject to warp, or the floar on which it ſtands being uneven, or in time by the weight of the table, and the gameſters yielding and giving way, there are very few billiard-tables which are found true; and therefore such which are exactly level'd are highly valuable by a good player; for at a false table it is impossible for him to show the excellency of his art and skill, whereby bunglers many times by knowing the windings and tricks of the table have shamefully beaten a very good gameſter, who at a true table would have given him three in five.

But to proceed in the description thereof; at the four corners of the table there are holes, and at each side exactly in the middle one, which are called hazards, and have hanging at the bottoms nets to receive the balls and keep them from falling to the ground when they are hazarded. I have seen at some tables wooden boxes for

PLATE II

LOUIS XIV AT BILLIARDS

the hazards, six of them as aforesaid, but they are nothing
near so commendable as the former, because a ball struck
hard is more apt to fly out of them when struck in.

There is to the table belonging an ivory port, which
stands at one end of the table, and an ivory king at the
other, two small ivory balls and two sticks; where note
if your balls are not compleatly round you can never
expect good proof in your play: your sticks ought to be
heavy, made of Brasile, Lignum vitæ or some other
weighty wood, which at the broad end must be tipt with
ivory; where note, if the heads happen to be loose, you
will never strike a smart stroke, you will easily perceive
that defect by the hollow deadness of your stroak and
faint running of your ball.

The game is five by day light, or seven if odds be given,
and three by candle-light or more according to odds in
houses that make a livelihood thereof; but in gentlemens
houses there is no such restriction; for the game may
justly admit of as many as the gamesters please to make.

For the lead you are to stand on the one side of the
table opposite to the king, with your ball laid near the
cushon, and your adversary on the other in like posture;
and he that with his stick makes his ball come nearest the
king leads first.

The leader must have a care that at the first stroke his
ball touch not the end of the table leading from the king
to the port, but after the first stroke he need not fear to
do it, and let him so lead that he may either be in a possibility of passing the next stroke, or so cunningly lie that
he may be in a very fair probability of hazarding his
adversaries ball, that very stroak he plaid after him.

The first contest is who shall pass first, and in that
strife there are frequent opportunities of hazarding one
another; and it is very pleasant to observe what policies
are used in hindering one another from the pass, as by
turning the port with a strong clever stroke; for if you
turn it with your stick it must be set right again; but indeed more properly he that doth it should lose one;
sometimes it is done (when you see it is impossible to

pass) by laying your ball in the port, or before your adversaries, and then all he can do is to pass after you; if he hath paſt and you dare not adventure to pass after him, for fear he should in the interim touch the king and so win the end, you muſt wait upon him and watch all opportunities to hazard him, or king him; that is, when his ball lyeth in such manner that when you ſtrike his ball may hit down the king, and then you win one.

Here note, that if you should king him, and your ball fly over the table, or else run into a hazard, that then you lose one notwithſtanding.

The player ought to have a curious eye, and very good judgment when he either intends to king his adversary's ball, or hazard, in taking or quartering out juſt so much of the ball as will accomplish either; which observation muſt be noted in passing on your adversary's ball, or corner of the port. Some I have observed so skilful at this recreation, that if they have had less than a fifth part of a ball they would rarely miss king or hazard.

As this is a cleanly paſtime, so there are laws or orders made againſt lolling slovingly players, that by their forfeitures they may be reduced to regularity and decency; wherefore be careful you lay not your hand on the table when you ſtrike or let your sleeve drag upon it, if you do it is a loss. If you smoak and let the ashes of your pipe fall on the table, whereby oftentimes the cloth is burned, it is a forfeiture, but that should not so much deter you from it as the hindrance piping is to your play.

When you ſtrike a long ſtroke, hold your ſtick nearly between your two fore fingers and your thumb, then ſtrike smartly, and by aiming rightly you may when you please either fetch back your adversary's ball when he lyeth fair for a pass, or many times when he lyeth behind the king, and you at the other end of the table you may king him backward.

If you lie close you may use the small end of your ſtick, or the flat of the big end, raising up one end over your shoulder, which you shall think moſt convenient for your purpose.

Have a care of raking, for if it be not a forfeiture it is a fault hardly excusable, but if you touch your ball twice it is a loss.

Beware when you jobb your ball through the port with the great end of your ſtick that you throw it not down, if you do it is a loss, but do it so handsomly that at one ſtroke without turning the port with your ſtick you effeCt your purpose; it is good play to turn the port with your ball, and so hinder your adversary from passing; neither is it amiss if you can to make your adversary a Fornicator, that is having paſt your self a little way, and the others ball being hardly through the port you put him back again, and it may be quite out of pass.

It argueth policy to lay a long hazard sometimes for your antagoniſt, wherby he is often entrapped for rashly adventuring at that diſtance. Thinking to ſtrike your ball into the hazard, which lieth very near it, he frequently runs in himself by reason of that great diſtance.

There is great art in lying abscond, that is, to lie at bo-peep with your adversary, either subtlely to gain a pass or hazard.

Here note, if your adversary hath not paſt and lyeth up by the king, you may endeavour to pass again, which if you do, and touch the king, it is two, but if thrown down you lose. Some inſtead of a king use a ſtring and a ball, and then you need not fear to have the end, if you can pass firſt; this is in my judgment bungling play, there being not that curious art of finely touching at a great diſtance a king that ſtands very ticklishly.

For your better underſtanding of the game read the ensuing orders. But there is no better way than praCtice to make you perfeCt therein.

Orders to be observed by such who will play at Billiards

1. If the leader touch the end of the table with his ball at the firſt ſtroke he loseth one.
2. If the follower intend to hit his adversaries ball, or

pass at one stroke he must string his ball, that is, lay it even with the king, or he loseth one.

3. He that passeth through the port hath the advantage of touching the king which is one if not thrown down.

4. He that passeth twice, his adversary having not past at all, and toucheth the king without throwing him down wins two ends.

5. He that passeth not hath no other advantage than the hazards.

6. He that is a fornicator (that is, hath past through the back of the port) he must pass twice through the fore part, or he cannot have the advantage of passing that end.

7. He that hits down the port or king, or hazards his own ball, or strikes either ball over the table loseth one.

8. He that hazards his adversary's ball, or makes it hit down the king winneth the end.

9. If four play, two against two, he that mistakes his stroke loseth one to that side he is of.

10. He that after both balls plaid, removes the port without consent, or strikes his ball twice together, or that his adversaries ball touch his stick-hand, clothes, or playeth his adversaries balls, loseth one.

11. He that sets not one foot upon the ground when he strikes his ball shall lose an end, or if he lay his hand or sleeve on the cloth.

12. A stander by though he betts shall not instruct, direct or speak in the game without consent, or being first asked; if after he is advertised hereof he offend in this nature, for every fault he shall instantly forfeit two pence for the good of the company, or not be suffer'd to stay in the room.

13. He that plays a ball, while the other runs, or takes up a ball before it lie still loseth an end.

14. He that removes the port with his stick when he strikes his ball, and thereby prevents his adversaries ball from passing loseth an end.

15. All controversies are to be decided by the standers

by, upon asking judgment. Here note, that whosoever breaks the king forfeits a shilling, for the port ten shillings, and each ſtick five shillings.

16. Five ends make a game by day-light, and three by candle-light.

The Orders in Verse as I found them fram'd for a very ancient Billiard Table

1. The leading ball the upper end may'nt hit;
   For if it doth is loseth one by it.
2. The follower with the king lie even shall
   If he doth pass or hit the others ball;
   Or else lose one, the like if either lay
   Their arm or hand on board when they do play.
3. That man wins one who with the others ball
   So ſtrikes the king that he doth make him fall.
4. If ſtriking at a hazard both run in,
   The ball ſtruck at thereby an end shal win.
5. He loseth one that down the port doth fling;
   The like doth he that juſtles down the king.
6. He that in play the adverse ball shall touch
   With ſtick, hand, or cloaths forfeits juſt as much.
7. And he that twice hath paſt shall touch the king,
   The other not paſt at all shall two ends win.
8. If both the balls over the table flie,
   The ſtriker of them loseth one thereby.
   And if but one upon the board attend,
   The ſtriker ſtill the loser of the end.
9. One foot upon the ground muſt ſtill be set,
   Or one end's loſt if you do that forget:
   And if you twice shall touch a ball e're he
   Hath ſtruck between an end for him is free.
10. If any ſtander by shall chance to bet,
    And will inſtruct, he then muſt pay the set.
11. The port or king being set, who moves the same
    With hand or ſtick shall lose that end or game.
12. He that can touch being paſt, or ſtrike the other
    Into the hazard is allowed another.
13. If any ſtander by shall ſtop a ball,
    The game being loſt thereby he pays for all.
14. If any paſt be ſtricken back again,
    His pass before shall be accounted vain.
15. He that breaks anything with violence,
    King, port, or ſtick is to make good th' offence.

17

16. If any not the game doth fully know
    May ask another whether it be so,
    Remember also when the game you win,
    To set it up for fear of wrangling.
17. He that doth make his ball the king light hit,
    And holes th' other scores two ends for it.

There are several other orders which only concern the house which I omit, as impertinent to the rules of playing at billiards.

Since recreation is a thing lawful in it self if not abused, I cannot but commend this as the most gentile and innocent of any I know, if rightly used; there being none of those cheats to be plaid at this as at several other games I shall hereafter mention. There is nothing here to be used but pure art; and therefore I shall only caution you to go to play, that you suffer not your self to be over-matcht, and do not when you meet with a better gamester than your self condemn the table, and do not swear as one did playing at nine-pins, this L. N. hath put false pins upon me.

To conclude, I believe this pastime is not so much used of late as formerly, by reason of those spunging cater-pillars which swarm where any billiard-tables are set up, who making that single room their shop, kitching and bed-chamber; their shop, for this is the place where they wait for ignorant cullies to be their customers; their kitching, for from hence comes the major part of their provision, drinking and smoaking being their common sustenance; and when they can perswade no more persons to play at the table, they make it their dormitory, and sleep under it; the floor is their feather-bed, the legs of the table their bed-posts, and the table the tester; they dream of nothing but *Hazards*, being never out of them, of *passing*, and *repassing*, which may be fitly applied to their lewd lives, which makes them continually pass from one prison to another till their lives are ended; and there is an end of the game.

Chapter III

Of TRUCKS

TRUCKS is an Italian game, and is much used in Spain and Ireland; it is not very unlike Billiards, but more boisterous, and in my opinion less gentile.

It is a pastime less noted in England, wherefore the tables are rarely met withal; one I have seen at Tower-hill, but so bunglingly composed, and so irregularly form'd and fram'd, that it was fit for none to play at but such who never saw or plaid at any other than that.

A right Truck-table ought to be somewhat larger than a Billiard-table, being at least three foot longer than it is broad and covered with green cloth, but it need not be every whit so fine as the former.

It hath three holes at each end, besides the corner holes; the middle-most at one end stands directly against the *Sprigg* which stands for the king at billiards, and the other end, middle-most hole, stands exactly against the *Argolio*, which is in the nature of a port at billiards. Of each side there are ten holes, none of these have nets to receive the balls, and therefore it is a sport more trouble-some than billiards.

The *Argolio* stands as the port at billiards as aforesaid, and is made of a strong hoop of iron fastned to the table, that it cannot stirr, having a wider passage than a port, and in its bending is higher from the board.

The *Sprigg* is another piece of iron, about the thickness of a man's little finger, and is taller than the billiard king, and driven into the board, so that it is immovable.

The *Tacks* with which they play, are much bigger than billiard sticks, and are headed at each end with iron; the small end is round from the middle, or farther run-ning taper-wise, but the great end is flat beneath, though rounding a top; good gamesters play for the most part with the small end.

The balls are made of ivory, and are in bigness like tennis-balls, and require much art in their rounding, for otherwise they will never run true.

You may lead as you do at billiards, but that is lookt upon as bungling play; the best artist at this game usually bank at the fourth cushon from the end where the Argolio stands, and is commonly markt for distinction with a little chalk.

The game because it is sooner up than billiards, is nine, and sometimes fifteen, or indeed as many, or as few as you please.

He that leads must have a care he hit not the end, for that is a loss, but he may bank if he please; if the leader lie in pass, the follower must hit him away if he can, for if he pass it is ten to one but he wins the end, because he may boldly strike at the sprigg. If the leader lies not in pass, he may either strike at him, or lye as well to pass as the former, and then all the strife lyeth in trucking one another, or striving who shall pass first.

In passing here is this subtlety to be observed, if your adversary's ball lie strait before the argolio, and yours lies a little behind it, and it is your stroke, you would think it impossible to pass by reason of that obstruction; whereas it is easily done thus, take the small end of your tack, and set it sloaping behind your ball, but touch it not, for if you do, you lose the end; then bend your fist, and give your stick a smart cuff, and it will raise your ball over your adversary's through the port with much facility, this is called by artists *fulkating*; all that the follower can do to save the end, is (lying as he doth just against the sprigg) to pass and touch the sprigg at one stroke, and that is two; if he touch not the end, is the others; if in striking the sprigg too hard, he run not out of one hole or other, and then he loseth.

For the advantage of striking you may lay one hand on the table, arm, etc., without forfeiture; but you must not touch your ball with your sleeve or hand without leave first obtained under the loss of the end. As thus, you may not know which is your ball, upon this you cry,

By your leave, Sir, and then you may take it up and see by the mark whether it be yours or not.

If you truck your adversary's ball it is one, but if you do it and run out, or fly over the table, you lose one, so if you strike at your adversary's ball, and one or both fly over the table it is a loss to you.

If after you have past you truck your adversary's ball and hit the sprigg it is three; if you pass at one stroke, truck your adversary's ball and hit the sprigg, you win four; this is very rarely done, as you may well imagin, yet I have seen it done, but never done by design, but casually; there is much art in holding your tack rightly, the best way I can inform you is to hold the great end in your right hand, and level the small end over your fore-finger and thumb, leaning your left arm on the table, for the more steddy and direct guidance of your tack to transmit the ball to what part of the table you shall think most requisite, and when you intend a smart stroke let your shove be brisk.

In short I must leave this as all other games to your observation and practice; only this let me advise you, if any difference arise leave it to the judgment of the table, to decide the controversie, but end it not with your lives, by using two such clubbing arbitrators as you play with, for with one stroke (they are so strong and heavy) they are sufficient to dash out a man's brains, and by the several great mischiefs have been done thereby be advised not to fall into the like dangerous rashness.

One thing I had almost forgot, and that is, if you fulkate over hand be very careful how you strike your ball, for by carelesness or missing your ball you frequently wound the table. Now fulkating over hand, is, when you lie near the cushon for a pass, and your adversary's ball lies directly before yours, to make yours to jump over his through the argolio, you must strike a strong stroke, sloaping downwards, which will make your ball mount aloft.

Orders for a Truck-Table

1. If the leader touch the end, it is the loss of one.
2. If the follower intend to hit his adversary's ball from the pass at the firſt ſtroke he muſt ſtring his ball even with the sprigg, or loseth one.
3. He that passeth and firſt hits the sprigg wins one.
4. He that passeth twice and hits the sprigg wins two.
5. He that passeth backward (and is called a fornicator) he muſt pass twice through the fore-part, or he cannot have the advantage of passing that end.
6. He that trucks his own ball, or ſtrikes it, or his adversary's over the table, loseth one.
7. He that trucks his adversary's ball wins two.
8. He that toucheth his adversary's ball with hand, ſtick, or clothes, or ſtrikes it for his own, loseth one.
9. He that passeth and toucheth at a ſtroke, wins two.
10. He that having paſt trucks his adversaries ball and hits the sprigg with his own, wins three.
11. Lastly, he that passeth, trucketh his adversary's ball and hits with his own the sprigg, wins four.

There are other trivial orders which for brevity sake I here omit.

Chapter IV

Of BOWLING

Bowling is a game or recreation, which if moderately used is very healthy for the body, and would be much more commendable than it is were it not for those swarms of rooks which so peſter bowling-greens, bares, and bowling-alleys where any such places are to be found, some making so small a spot of ground yield them more annually then fifty acres of land shall do elsewhere about the city, and this done cunning, betting, crafty matching, and basely playing booty.

In bowling there is a great art in chusing out his
ground, and preventing the windings, hanging, and many
turning advantages of the same, whether it be in open
wide places, as bares and bowling-greens, or in close
bowling-alleys. Where note that in bowling the chusing
of the bowl is the greatest cunning. Flat bowls are best
for close alleys ; round byassed bowls for open grounds
of advantage, and bowls round as a ball for green swarths
that are plain and level.

There is no advising by writing how to bowl, practice
must be your best tutor, which must advise you the
risings, fallings and all the several advantages that are
to be had in divers greens, and bowling-alleys ; all that
I shall say, have a care you are not in the first place rookt
out of your money, and in the next place you go not to
these places of pleasure unseasonably, that is when your
more weighty business and concern require your being at
home, or some where else.

The Character of a Bowling-Alley, and Bowling-Green

A bowling-green, or bowling-alley is a place where three
things are thrown away besides the bowls, viz: time,
money, and curses, and the last ten for one. The best
sport in it, is the gamesters, and he enjoys it that looks on
and betts nothing. It is a school of wrangling, and worse
than the *Schools* ; for here men will wrangle for a hairs
bredth, and make a stir where a straw would end the
controversie. Never did mimmick screw his body into
half the forms these men do theirs ; and it is an article
of their creed, that the bending back of the body or
screwing in of their shoulders is sufficient to hinder the
over-speed of the bowl, and that the running after it adds
to its speed. Though they are skilful in ground, I know
not what grounds they have for loud lying, crying, sometimes the bowl is gone ' a mile, a mile,' etc., when it
comes short of the jack by six yards and on the contrary
crying ' short, short,' when he hath overbowled as far.
How senseless these men appear when they are speaking

sense to their bowls, putting confidence in their intreaties for a good cast. It is the best discovery of humours
especially in the losers, where you may observe fine
variety of impatience, whilst some fret, rail, swear, and
cavel at every thing, others rejoyce and laugh, as if that
was the sole design of their creation.

To give you the moral of it, is the emblem of the
world, or the worlds ambition, where most are short,
over, wide, or wrong byassed, and some few justle in to
the mistress, Fortune! And here it is as in the court,
where the nearest are the most spighted, and all bowls
aim at the other.

Chapter V

Of a Game at CHESS

CHESS is a Royal game and more difficult to be understood than any other game whatever, and will take up
sometimes in the playing so long a time that I have
known two play a fortnight at times before the game hath
been ended: and indeed I believe the tediousness of the
game hath caus'd the practice thereof to be so little used;
however since this pastime is so highly ingenious that
there is none can parallel it, I shall here lay down some
brief instructions tending to the knowledg thereof.

The first and highest is a King, the next in height is a
Queen, the cloven heads are Bishops; they who have
heads cut aslaunt like a feather in a helmet are called
Knights, the last are called Rooks, with a round button'd
cap on his head; and these signifie the country and
peasantry, the Pawns are all alike, and each nobleman
hath one of them to wait upon him.

The chess-men standing on the board, you must place
the white King in the fourth house being black from
the corner of the field in the first and lower rank, and the
black King in the white house, being the fourth on the
other side in your adversaries first rank opposite to

PLATE III

Le Jeu des Echecs.

A GAME OF CHESS IN FRANCE

[face p. 24

the white King; then place the white Queen next to the white King in a white house, which is the fourth on that side of the field; likewise the black Queen in a black house next to a black King in the same rank.

Then place on the other side of the King in the same rank, first a Bishop, because he being a man of counsel is placed before the Knight, who is a man of action or execution; the Knight after the Bishop, and after the Knight place the Rook (who is the peasant or country-man) in the last place or corner of the field: place also on the Queens side and next to her a Bishop, next a Knight and then a Rook; the Pawns take up the last place; one of which you must place before each nobleman as attendants, so that these great or noblemen fill up the first rank and the Pawns the second from one corner of the field to the other, and as many great men and Pawns as belong to the King so many hath the Queen, viz: three great men and four Pawns apiece, that is, one Bishop, one Knight, and one Rook with their Pawns.

Having thus placed and ordered your men, you must in the next place consider their march how they advance and take guard and check.

The Pawns do commonly begin first the onset, and their march is forward in their own file, one house at once only and never backward; for the Pawns alone never retreat, the manner of his taking men is side-ways in the next house forward of the next file to him on either side, where when he hath captivated his enemy, and placed himself in his seat, he proceeds and removes forward one house at once in that file, until he find an opportunity to take again.

The Pawn guards a piece of his side which stands in that place, where if it were one of the contrary party he might take it. In like manner the Pawn checks the King, viz: as he takes not as he goes, which check if the adverse King cannot shun either by taking up the Pawn himself (if the Pawn be unguarded, or occasion his taking by some of his pieces, he must of necessity remove himself out of the Pawns check) or if it lie not in his power it is

Pawn-Mate, and so the game is ended, and lost by him whose King is so Mate.

The Rook goes backward and forward in any file and cross-ways to and fro in any rank as far as he will, so that there stands no piece between him and the place he would go to. Thus he doth guard his own and check the King also, which check if the King can neither cover by the interposition of some piece of his between the checking Rook and himself, nor take the Rook, nor be the cause of his taking, he must remove himself out of that check or it is Mate, and the game is up.

The Knight skips forward, backward and on either side from the place he stands in to the next save one of a different colour, with a sideling march or a sloap, thus he kills his enemies, guards his friends, and checks the King of the adverse party, which because (like the Pawns check) it cannot be covered, the King must either remove or course the Knight to be taken (for he himself cannot take the Knight that checks him) or its Mate, and the game is up.

The Bishop walks always in the same colour of the field that he is first placed in, forward and backward asloap every way as far as he lists ; provided, that the way be clear between him and the place he intends to go to : thus he rebukes the adversary, guards his consorts, and checks the adverse King, which not being avoided as aforesaid, is Mate to him and the game is ended.

The Queens walk is more universal ; for she goes the draughts of all the aforenamed pieces, (the Knights only excepted, for her march is not from one colour to the other asloap) so far as the listeth finding the way obstructed by any piece, and thus she disturbs her adversaries, protects her subjects, and mates the King, unless (as aforesaid) he removes, covers, takes, or causes her to be taken, otherwise it is his Mate and the game is concluded.

The Kings draught is from his own to the next to him any way, that either is empty of his own subjects, or where he may surprise any unguarded enemy, or where he may stand free from the check of any of the adverse party.

Thus he confounds his foes, defends his friends, but checks not the King his enemy, who never check one another; for there must ever be one house or place at least between the two Kings, though unpossest of any other piece; and if one King be compel'd to flie for refuge to the King of the adverse party then it is Mate or a Stale, and so he that gives the first wins the game. Let this suffice for the various draughts and several walks of the Chess-men; but this is not all, I shall give you some other instructions as brief as I may, and refer the rest to your observation.

Kings and Queens have seven a piece to attend them. The King whether white or black guards five persons before he goes forth, and being once advanced into the field, though it be but into the second house, he then and afterwards in his march guards eight houses till he come again to one side or other of the field.

The five the King guards before his march, are the Queen, the Bishop, his own, his Queens, and his Bishops Pawn.

The Queen protects her King, and Bishop her Kings, her Bishops, and her own Pawn. Thus the Queen guards as many as the King before she goes forth, and after till the game be won or lost.

The Kings Bishop guards the Kings Pawn, and his Knights, the Queens Bishop guards the Queens Pawn, and her Knights guard but three houses apiece before they go forth; but after they are marched off from the side of the field, they guard as many houses as the King and Queen do. Those houses which the Knights guard ere they go out are the Kings. The Knight guards the Kings Pawn, and the third house in the front of the Kings Bishops Pawn, and the third house in the front of the Kings Rooks Pawn.

The Queens Knight guards her Pawn, and the third house in the front of her Bishops Pawn, also the third house in the front of her Rooks Pawn. The Kings Rook guards his own Pawn, and the Kings Knight and no more till he be off of the side of the field, and then he guards four houses, and the same does the Queens Rook. The Pawns likewise guard these places before they be advanced into the field, viz: The Kings Pawn guards the third house before the Queen, and the third before the Kings Bishop, the Queens Pawn guards the third house before the King, and the third before her Bishop. The Kings Bishop's Pawn guards the third house before the King, and the third before the Kings Knight. The Queens Bishop's Pawn guards the third house before the Queen, and the third before the Queens Knight. The Kings Knights Pawn guards the third house before the Kings Bishop, and the third before the Kings Rook. The Queens Knight's Pawn guards the third house before the Queens Bishop, and the third before the Queens Rook. The Kings Rooks Pawn, and the Queens Rooks Pawn guard but one house apiece, that is to say, the third house before the Knight, because they stand on the side of the field.

Next consider the value of the great men. The King exposeth not himself to danger upon every occasion, but the Queen is under him as General, and doth more service than any two great men besides; and when it happens that she is lost, her King most certainly loseth the field, unless the adversary knows not how to make use of so great an advantage. Wherefore if a King lose two or three of his best men in taking the opponents Queen, yet he hath the best of it if he can but manage his game rightly.

Next to the Queen in value is the Rook, and is as much in worth above the Bishop and Knight as the Queen is above him; so that a Rook is more worth than two Bishops or two Knights because he can give a Mate by the help of the King, which no other piece can do, unless plaid with excellent skill.

Bishops are accounted better than Knights, because they can give a Mate with a King when no other men are left to help them, with more ease than the Knights can; for they seldom or never do it: yet it is more dangerous to lose a Knight than a Bishop, because the Knights check is more dangerous than the Bishops; for the Bishop is tyed to one colour of the field out of which he cannot pass, but the Knight passeth through all the houses of the field; the Bishops check may be covered, the Knights cannot; besides if it fall out that one of the Kings hath no other men left but Bishops, and the other King none but his Knights, the Knights with their checks can take the Bishops one after another, because the Bishops cannot guard each other which the Knights can do; so that at the beginning of the game it is better to lose Bishops for the adversaries Knights than the contrary.

The difference of the worth of Pawns is not so great as that of noblemen, because there is not such variety in their walks, only thus much, the Kings Bishop's Pawn is the best in the field among the Pawns, and therefore the gamester ought to be very careful of him; for if it should happen that the black King lose his Bishop's Pawn to gain the white Kings Pawn, the black Kings loss is the greater, because he cannot after this accident make a rank of Pawns of three of a rank on that side of the field for his own security, which is a great disadvantage, so that it is better for either of the Kings to lose his own Pawn than his Bishop's.

But if you should object that the King which loseth his Bishops Pawn may relieve himself on the other side of the field, turning to his Queens Rooks quarters, where he shall have Pawns to succour him, I answer, 'tis true, he may do so, but he will be a longer time in effecting his business, because there are more pieces between him and his Queens Rooks by one draught than between his own Rook and himself; so that in playing that draught he indangers the whole game if his adversary know how to make use of advantages. The Kings Pawn is next in worth which oftentimes keeps the King from check by discovery; then the Queens Pawn is next, and after that the Knights, and last of all the Rooks Pawns, because they guard but one house apiece in the field.

The King and the Pawn have certain priviledges granted them, which none of the other chess-men have;

as for inftance, the King whose remove (as hath been already mentioned) is from the place of his ftanding at any time to the next house in file or rank of any side (that is one only ftep at once), yet if at any time his rank be empty of his men, so that no one ftands between the King and the Rook of either corner, the King may then shift or change with what Rook he pleaseth, between whom and himself the way ftands clear from other men ; and that for his better security, provided, that neither the King nor the Rook he intends to change with, hath not as yet been removed from the place of their firft ftanding; now the manner of the Kings shifting or changing with a Rook is thus :

The rank cleared as aforesaid, and neither King nor Rook having yet ftirred, he may go two draughts at once to his own Rook, and so towards his Queens Rook, causing the Rook he changeth with to change his place, and come and ftand by him on the other side ; that is, his own Rook in the Bishops place, and the Queens Rook in the Queens place, and either of these changes but for one draught. This is the Kings firft prerogative.

The second is, that whereas any man may be taken by any adversary, if he be brought so near as to come within the compass, the King cannot, but he is only to be saluted by his adversary with the word check, advising him thereby to look about him the more warily, and provide for his own safety : now if that adversary do this unguarded so near the King, he may ftep thither by his true draught, and the King may ftay him with his own hand if he judge it convenient.

As for the Pawn, the firft priviledge he hath, is, that whereas his walk is but to the next house forward in his own file at once when he marcheth, and to the next house side-long forward of the next file of either side, when he takes, I say, his priviledg is, that he may remove to the second house forward, which is the fourth rank in his own file for his firft draught, and ever after but one forward at once.

The second priviledg is greater, and that is, when any

Pawn is come so far as to the first rank of the adversary, and seats himself in any of his Noble houses, he is dignified for this fact with the name and power of a Queen, and so becomes chief of his own Kings forces if the first Queen were slain before, and if the first Queen be yet standing in the field, the Pawn coming to the rank aforesaid in any house whatsoever, may there make what piece you please which you have already lost.

Some are of opinion that chess as well as draughts may be plaid by a certain rule, indeed I am partly inclined to believe it notwithstanding that most are of a contrary opinion.

The first remove is an advantage, and therefore you must draw for who shall have the first draught, which may be done with a black and white man distributed into either hand, and offer'd the opponent which he will chuse; if he chuse his own man the first draught is her: but when a game is ended, and a Mate given, he is to have the first draught next game who gave the former Mate.

The first remove is divers according to the judgment of the gamester, as some will first remove their Kings Knights Pawn one single remove, that is to the third house in his own file, others play the Kings Rooks Pawn first a double draught; but the best way is to play the Kings Pawn first a double remove, that so if they are not prevented by their adversaries playing the like, they may still move that Pawn forward with good guard; for he will prove very injurious to the adverse King.

This Pawn I shall advise you to remove first, but not so venturously as a double remove, because if you cannot guard him cunningly, then are you like to lose him with a check to your King, by the Queens coming forth upon him to the great hazard of your Kings Rook; therefore, play your Kings Rook one single remove, that there may be way made for the coming forth of Queen one way two houses asloap, and to your Kings Bishop the other way three houses asloap, and so upon the neglect of your adversary he may be put to a scholars check, at least in danger of it: here note it is ill to play the Bishops Pawn first, and worse to play the Queens.

He that would be an artist in this noble game, must be so careful to second his pieces, that if any man advanced be taken, the enemy may be likewise taken by that piece that guards or seconds it; so shall he not clearly lose any man, which should it fall out contrarily might lose the game; he must also make his passages free for retreat, as occasion shall serve, lest he be worsted.

In defending you must also be very careful that you are as able to assault as your enemy; for you must not only answer your adversaries assault by foreseeing his design by his play, and preventing it, but you must likewise devise plots, how to pester and grieve your assailant, and chiefly how to entrap such pieces as are advanced by him, preventing their retreat, amongst which a Pawn is the soonest ensnared, because he cannot go back for succour or relief; but Bishops and Rooks are harder to be surprized, because they can march from one side of the field to the other to avoid the ensuing danger, but the Knights and Queens of all are most difficultly betray'd, because they have so many places of refuge, and the Queen more especially; where note as a great piece of policie, that if possible you constantly have as many guards upon any one piece of yours as you see your enemy hath when he advanceth to take it; and be sure withall that your guards be of less value than the pieces he encountreth you with; for then if he fall to taking you will reap advantage thereby; but if you see you cannot guard yours but must of necessity lose it, then be very circumspect and see whether you can take a far better piece of his in case he takes yours, by advancing some other piece of yours in guard; for so (as it often falls out) that yours which you had given over for lost may be saved, whereas no other way could have done it.

When an adverse piece comes in your way, so that by it all may be taken, consider with your self first whether it be equal in worth to yours; next whether it can do you any damage in the next draught, if not let it alone; for as it is best to play first, so it is to take last; unless as was said you might take the piece clear, or get a better than that you lose to take it, or at least disorder him one Pawn in his taking your man that took his; but when you have the advantage be it but of one good piece for a worse, or of a Pawn clear, then it is your best way to take man for man as often as you can; besides you are to note, that whatsoever piece your adversary plays most or best withal, be sure if it lie in your power to deprive him thereof though it be done with loss of the like, or of one somewhat better, as a Bishop for a Knight; for by this means you may frustrate your adversaries design and become as cunning as himself.

Now the chief aim at chess is to give the Mate, which is when you so check the King of the adverse party, that he can neither take the checking piece (because it is guarded) nor cover the check, nor yet remove out of it.

Your care ought to be in the interim how to deprive him of some of his best pieces, as his Queen or Rook; and the way to entrap a Queen is two-fold. First by confining her to her King, so that she may not remove from him for leaving him in check of an adverse piece; secondly, by bringing her to or espying her in such a place as a Knight of yours may check her King, and the next draught take her. In the same manner you may serve a Bishop if the adverse Queen covers her slope-wise; but if she stand not in such a posture she may be brought to it; entice her thither with some unguarded man, which she out of eagerness of taking for nothing, may indiscreetly bring her self into trouble.

But if you intend to catch the Queen with a Knight, imagine that the adverse King stands in his own place unremoved, and that the Queen hath brought her self to stand in that place where the Kings Rooks Pawn stood; first, she standing in this posture bring if you can one of your Knights to check her King in the third house before his own Bishop; and if there be no man ready to take up your Knight, immediately he will take up the Queen at the next draught.

The Rooks are also to be surprized two ways; first, by playing your Bishop into your Knights Pawns first place of standing, which Bishop shall march aslope towards the adverse Rook of the opposite corner, which if you can make uncovered of the Knights Pawn, your Bishop will then undoubtedly take clear for nothing; the other way is like that of surprizing the Queen with a Bishop or a Knight; where you must take notice that your adversaries Queens Rook is so much the easier to be taken with your Queens Knight, that that Knight at his third draught may check the King and take the same Rook at his forth draught. There are several other ways to take a Rook, which practice must inform you.

There is an ingenious way of taking a great man for a Pawn; when you espy two great men of your adversaries standing in one and the same rank, and but one house between them, then prepare a guard (if you have it not ready to your hand) for a Pawn, which bring up to the rank next to them in the middle or front of both of them, and without doubt, if he save the one your Pawn will take the other; this way of taking is called a Fork or Dilemma.

The neatest and most prejudicial trick you can put upon your adversary at chess is a check by discovery, which may be thus effected; observe when you find your adversaries King any way weakly guarded, or perhaps not all, that is, easie to be checked then before you bring that piece that can check him there to provide some other man in that course that checks him not; afterwards bring that piece of yours which will check him (your brought-piece being away) and then with all possible speed remove away for that former piece where it may most annoy him, saying withall, *Check by discovery of your last brought a piece:* which he being compelled to cover or remove, you may do him a greater prejudice with that piece you removed from between the check at the next draught thus demonstrated.

Suppose you play with the whitemen, he removes first his Kings Pawn a double draught forward, you answer him with the like play; he then plays out his Kings Knight in front of his Kings Bishop's Pawn, you do the like with yours: that Knight of his takes your Kings Pawn, and your Knight takes his likewise; he advances the Queens Pawn, and removes to chase away or to take your Knight; you play up your white Queen one remove before your King to frighten his Knight also: he thinks it better to save his Knight from your Queen, than take yours with his Queens Pawn; and therefore conveys him away into a more secure place; you play your Kings Knight in front of his Queens Bishop's Pawn, and there withall say, *Check by discovery of your Queen;* now let him cover this check by discovery as well as he can, your Knight at the next draught will assuredly take his Queen. There are several other ways to make a discovery, and a Mate given with it, which is the noblest Mate of all.

A Queen if lost indangers much the game; but if there be Pawns left on either side, there is possibility of making a new Queen, and so by consequence the renovation of the game; which ten to one was lost before. There are several ways to Mate this Queen and estate her in as great power as the former, for brevity sake, two Pawns in files next one to the other, and plaid first one forward and the other backward close together is a good way to make a new Queen, especially if any one of them be guarded underneath with a Rook, for so they will force their way before them, nor can any of them be taken without great difficulty and danger.

As to short Mates take these observations: having both placed your men and yours the first draught; suppose you advance your Kings Pawn forward one single remove, your adversary plays his Kings Pawn forward a double remove in his own file; you at your second draught come out with your Queen upon that Pawn, placing her in the house forward of your Kings Rooks file, your enemy to guard his Kings Pawn plays forth his Queens Knight into the third house of the Queens Bishops file, you (hoping that he will not spy the attempt) bring out for your third draught your Kings Bishop, which you place in the fourth house of your Queens Bishops file, he not perceiving your intention judging all secure makes for your Queen with his Kings Knight, playing it in the front of his Kings Bishops Pawn, either to chase her away or take her; you immediately upon this take up that Bishops Pawn with your Queen, and for your fourth draught give him a Mate, which is called a *Scholars Mate*; because any but young beginners may prevent it.

You may also give a Mate at two draughts if you encounter with a raw gamester, playing after this manner. First remove his Kings Bishops Pawn a single draught (which is ill play at first) you your Kings Pawn a single remove, he his Kings Knights Pawn advanced a double remove for his second draught, you bringing out your Queen into the fifth house of your Kings Rooks file give him a Mate at your second draught.

There is another called a *Blind-Mate*, and that is when your adversary gives you a check that you cannot avoid by any means, and is indeed a *Mate absolute*; but he not seeing it to be a Mate, says only to you *check*, and it is therefore called a *Blind-mate*; this should be both loss of game and stake if you before agree not to the contrary.

A *Stale* may be termed a Mate and no Mate, an end of the play but no end of the Game, because it properly should be ended with a *Check-Mate*.

The Stale is thus when his King hath the worst of the game, and brought to such a strait, that he hath but one place to flie unto, and the pursuing King is so unadvised as to bar him of that place or stop it without checking him, the distressed King being no way able to remove but in check, and having no other piece of his own that he can play, then it is a Stale and a lost game to him that gives it. Therefore he that follows the flying King gives him check as long as he hath any place to fly to; but when he hath none left to avoid his check, let him then say *check-Mate*, and both game and stake are won.

Laſtly, there is another term used in chess-playing, and that is called a *Dead-Game*, which makes (if I may say improperly) an endless end of the game, both gameſters having their ſtakes: and thus it is, when the assailant falls to take all that comes near, carelessly giving man for man, so that it happens that either King hath but one man apiece left him, the assailant following his eager pursuit takes his adversaries man, not minding that his King can take his also, so that the Kings losing all their men and they being so unable to come so near as to grapple the game is ended, but the ſtakes on both sides are saved.

I shall conclude this game with the Laws of Chess, which are these following.

1. What piece soever of your own you touch or lift from the point whereon it ſtandeth, you must play it for that draught if you can, and into what house you set your man there it muſt ſtand for that draught, according to the saying at this Game, *Touch and take, out of hand and ſtand.*

2. If you take up your adversaries man, and after think beſt to let it ſtand untaken, before you set your piece in place thereof, you muſt cry him mercy or lose the game.

3. If your adversary play a false draught, and you see it not till you play your next draught 'twill then be too late to challenge him for it.

4. If you play a false draught through miſtake, and your adversary take no notice for his advantage, and plays his next draught, you cannot recall it.

5. If you misplace your men, and so play a while, and then discover it, it lies in your adversaries power to continue or begin the game.

6. Pawns may be plaid a double remove forward for their firſt draught, but no Pawn hath that priviledg without permission, on whose next file on either side a Pawn of your adversaries is already advanced as far as your fourth rank.

7. The standing of the King ought to be certain in his shifting and not as you please to place him as some men play.

8. If your King standing in the check of any adverse piece, and you have plaid one draught or more without avoiding the check, your adversary may say, *check* to you when he listeth, and for your draught then make you avoid that check you stood in, though it may be to your great peril.

9. If any one condition by wager, that he will give Mate or win the game, and the adversary brings it to a *Dead-Game*, though he save the first stake yet he loseth the wager.

10. He that gives over the game before it is finished, without the consent of his adversary, loseth his stake.

Many more observations might be here inserted for the understanding of this noble game, which I am forced to wave to avoid prolixity.

PRINCIPAL GAMES AT CARDS

Chapter VI

PICKET

BEFORE you begin the game at picket, you muſt throw out of the pack the deuces, treys, fours, and fives, and play with the reſt of the cards, which are in number thirty and six.

The usual set is an hundred, not but that you may make it more or less; the laſt card deals and the worſt is the dealers.

The cards are all valued according to the number of the spots they bear, the Ace only excepted, which wins all other cards, and goes for eleven.

The dealer shuffles, and the other cuts, delivering what number he pleaseth at a time, so that he exceed not four nor deal under two, leaving twelve on the table between them.

He that is the elder, having lookt over his cards, and finding never a court-card among them, says *I have* a blanck, and I intend to discard such a number of cards, and that you may see mine, discard you as many as you intend; this done, the eldeſt shows his cards and reckons ten for the blanck, then taking up his cards again he discards those which he judgeth moſt fit: here note he is always bound to that number which he firſt propounded. This being done, he takes in as many from the ſtock as he laid out; and if it should chance to fall out that the other hath a blank too, the youngers blank shall bar the former and hinder his *Picy* and *Repicy*, though the eldest hands blank consiſts of the biggeſt cards.

39

Charles Cotton

It is no small advantage to the eldest to have the benefit of discarding, because he may take in eight of the twelve in the stock discarding as many of his own for them, not but that if he find it more advantageous he may take in a less number; after this the antagonist may take in what he thinks fit, acquitting his hand of the like number. Here note, that let the game be never so good the gamesters are both obliged to discard one card at least. After the discarding you must consider the *Ruff*, that is how much you can make of one suit; the eldest speaks first, and if the youngest makes no more the Ruff is good, and sets up one for every ten he can produce; as, for example, for thirty reckon three, for forty four, and so onward, withall take notice you are to count as many for thirty-five as for forty, and as much for forty-five as fifty, and so of the rest; but from thirty-five to thirty-nine you must count no more than for thirty-five, and so from thirty to thirty-four count no more than for thirty; and this rule is to be observed in all other higher numbers.

As for *Sequences* and their value after the Ruff is plaid, the elder acquaints you with his Sequences (if he have them) and they are *Tierces, Quarts, Quints, Sixiesms, Septiesms, Huictiesms* and *Neufiesms*, as thus; six, seven, and eight; nine, ten, and Knave; Queen, King, and Ace; which last is called a Tierce Major, because it is the highest. A Quart is a sequence of four cards, a Quint of five, a Sisixm of six, &c. These sequences take their denomination from the highest card in the sequence. It is a Tierce Major or a Tierce of an Ace when there is Queen, King, and Ace, a Tierce of a King when the King is the best Card; a Tierce of a Queen when there is neither King nor Ace, and so till you come to the lowest Tierce, which is a Tierce of an eight. You must reckon for every Tierce three, for a Quart four, but for a Quint fifteen, for a Sixiesm sixteen, and so upward; now what ever you can make of all you must add to your blank, and count the whole together.

Here note that the biggest Tierce, Quart, or other

40

sequence, although there be but one of them makes all the others less sequences useless unto him be they never so many; and he that hath the biggeſt sequence by vertue thereof reckons all his less sequences, though his adversaries sequences be greater, and otherwise would have drowned them.

Farther observe, that a Quart drowns a Tierce, and a Quint a Quart, and so of the reſt, so that he who hath a Sixiesm may reckon his Tierces, Quarts, or Quints, though the other may happen to have Tierce, Quart, &c. of higher value than the others are that hath the Sixiesm; trace the same method in all the other like sequences.

After you have manifeſted your sequences, you come to reckon your three Aces, three Kings, three Queens, three Knaves, or three Tens, as for Nines, Eights, Sevens, and Sixes, they have no place in this account; for every Ternary you count three, and they are in value as it is in sequences; Aces the higheſt and beſt, King next, after these Queens, then Knaves, and laſt of all Tens. The higher drowns the lower here as in the sequences. He that hath three Aces may reckon his three Queens, Knaves, or Tens, if he have them, though the other hath three Kings; and this is done by reason of his higher Ternary. Now he that hath four Aces, four Kings, four Queens, four Knaves, or four Tens, for each reckons fourteen, which is the reason they are called Quatorzes.

Now they begin to play the cards, the elder begins and younger follows in suit as at Whisk, and for every Ace, King, Queen, Knave, or Ten, he reckons one.

A card once play'd muſt not be recalled, unless he have a card of the same suit in his hand, if the elder hand plays an Ace, King, Queen, or Ten, for every such card he is to reckon one, which he adds to the number of his game before; and if the other be able to play upon it a higher card of the same suit, he wins the trick, and reckons one for his card as well as the other. Whosoever wins the laſt trick reckons two for it, if he win it with a ten, but if with any card under, he reckons but one; then they tell their cards, and he that hath the most is to reckon ten for them.

After this, each person sets up his game with counters, and if the set be not up, deal again. Now a set is won after this manner, admit that each party is so forward in his game that he wants but four of five to be up, if it so happens that any of the two have a blank, he wins the set, because the Blanks are always first reckoned; but if no Blanks, then comes the Ruff, next your Sequences, then your Aces, Kings, Queens, Knaves, and Tens, next what cards are reckoned in play, and last of all the cards you have won. If any of the gamesters can reckon, either in Blanks, Ruffs, Sequences, Aces, &c. up to thirty in his own hand, without playing a card, and before the other can reckon anything, instead of thirty he shall reckon ninety, and as many as he reckons after above his thirty, adding them to his ninety; this is known by the name of a *Repicy*.

Moreover, he that can make in like manner, what by Blank, Ruff, Sequences, &c. up to the said number, before the other hath play'd a card, or reckoned anything, instead of thirty he reckons sixty, and this is called a *Picy*. Here note, that if you can but remember to call for your Picy, or Repicy, before you deal again, you shall lose neither of them, otherwise you must.

He that wins more than his own cards reckons ten, but he that wins all the cards reckons forty, and this is called a *Capet*.

The rules belonging to this game are these. If the dealer give more cards than his due, whether through mistake or otherwise it lieth in the choice of the elder hand whether he shall deal again or no, or whether it shall be play'd out.

He that forgets to reckon his Blank, Ruff, Sequences, Aces, Kings, or the like, and hath begun to play his cards cannot recall them. So it is with him that showeth not his Ruff before he play his first card, losing absolutely all the advantage thereof.

He that misreckons anything, and hath play'd one of his cards, and his adversary finds at the beginning, middle, or end of the game, that he had not what he reckoned, for his punishment he shall be debar'd from reckoning anything he really hath, and his adversary shall reckon all he hath, yet the other shall make all he can in play. He that takes in more cards than he discardeth is liable to the same penalty.

He that throws up his cards imagining he hath lost the game, mingling them with other cards on the table though afterward he perceive his mistake, yet he is not allowed to take up his cards and play them out.

No man is permitted to discard twice in one dealing.

He that hath a Blank, his Blank shall hinder the other *Picy* and *Repicy*, although he hath nothing to shew but his Blank.

He that hath four Aces, Kings, Queens, &c. dealt him and after he hath discarded one of the four reckons the other three, and the other say to him *it is good;* he is bound to tell the other, if he ask him what Ace, King, Queen, &c. he wants.

If after the cards are cleanly cut, either of the gamesters know the upper card by the backside, notwithstanding this the cards must not be shuffled again. In like manner, if the dealer perceive the other hath cut himself an Ace, and would therefore shuffle again, this is not permitted ; and if a card be found faced, it shall be no argument to deal again, but must deal on ; but if two be found faced, then may he shuffle again.

Lastly, whosoever is found changing or taking back again any of his cards, he shall lose the game, and be accounted a foul player.

Charles Cotton

Chapter VII

The Game at GLEEK

DEUCES and Treys must be cast out as useless in this game, then lifting for dealing the least card deals. The number of persons playing must be three, neither more nor less, and most frequently they play at farthing, half-penny, or penny-Gleek, which in play will amount considerably.

The dealer delivers the cards by four till every one hath twelve, and the rest are laid on the table, for the stock, being in number eight, seven whereof are brought and the Ace is turned up; the turn'd up card is the dealers; and if it be Tiddy turn'd up is four apiece from each to the dealer.

The Ace is called Tib, the Knave Tom, the four of Trumps Tiddy, Tib the Ace is fifteen in hand and eighteen in play, because it wins a trick, Tom the Knave is nine, and Tiddy is four, the fifth Towser, the sixth Tumbler, which if in hand Towser is five and Tumbler six, and so double if turn'd up, and the King and Queen of Trumps is three.

The eldest hand bids for the stock in hopes of bettering his game, though sometimes it makes it worse: the first penny you bid is twelve, thirteen, and so on; if at sixteen they say take it, and none will venture more for it, he is bound to take it, that is taking in seven cards, and putting out seven in their stead, and must pay besides eight to one and eight to the other of the gamesters for buying, if any odd money be given, as 15, 17, or the like, the eldest hand usually claims it, or else it is given to the box; but if he have Mournival, Gleek or Tiddy in his hand after he hath taken in the stock he bates for them all, and so possibly may gain by it, if he have a good hand and pay for his buying two.

Here you must note that if Tib be turned up it is

fifteen to the dealer in reckoning after play, but he muſt not make use of it in play being the trump-card, for then 'twould make him eighteen, because it would win a trick which is three more.

Next you speak for the Ruff, and he that hath moſt of a suit in his hand wins it, unless some of the game-ſters have four Aces and then he gains the Ruff, though you have never so many of a suit in your hand. If any wins a Ruff and forgets to show it before a card plaid loseth it, and he that shews any for a Ruff after shall have it.

The first or eldest says, *I'le vye the Ruff*, the next says, *I'le see it*, and the third, *I'le see it and revie it*. *I'le see your revie*, says the firſt; because he hath as many in his hand as another: the middle probably says, *I'le not meddle with it*. Then they shew their cards, and he that hath moſt of a suit wins six pence or farthings according to the game of him that holds out longeſt, and four of the other that said he would see it, but after refused to meddle with it; but if any of the three game-ſters says he hath nothing to say as to the Ruff he pays but a farthing, half-pence, penny, according as the game is aforesaid; and if the eldest and second hand pass the Ruff the youngest hath power to double it, and then it is to be plaid for the next deal, and if any forgets to call for the double Ruff, it is to be play'd for the next deal after that.

Sometimes one of the gameſters having all of a suit in his hand bids high for the Ruff, and the other having four Aces is resolved to bid higher, so that it sometimes amounts to sixteen and more, then *I'le see it and revie*, saith one; *I'le see it and revie*, saith another, that is, eight to the winner, and all above is but two a time, as it may be they will say, *I'le see it and revie it again*, *and I'le see that and revie it again*, saith another, for which seeing and revying they reckon but two, after that it is once come to eight; but he that hath the four Aces carrieth it clearly, &c. as aforesaid.

Buying or bidding for the Ruff is when you are in

likelihood to go in for Mournival, Gleek, or increase of
Trumps, that so if you have bad cards, you may save
your buyings and your cards too, whereas otherwise
you may lose all.

If you call for either Mournival or Gleek, and have
lay'd them out in the stock, if you be taken in it, for
forfeit double what you receive.

Sometimes out of policy or a vapour they will vie
when they have not above thirty in their hands, and the
rest may have forty or fifty, and being afraid to see it,
the first many times wins out of a meer bravado, and this
is good play though he acquaint you with it hereafter.

A Mournival of Aces is eight, of Kings six, of Queens
four, and a Mournival of Knaves two a piece.

A Gleek of Aces is four, of Kings three, of Queens two,
and of Knaves one a piece from the other two gamesters.

A Mournival is either all the Aces, the four Kings,
Queens, or Knaves, and a Gleek is three of any of the
aforesaid.

Here note, that twenty-two are your cards; if you
win nothing but the cards that were dealt you, you lose
ten; if you have neither Tib, Tom, Tiddy, King, Queen,
Mournival, nor Gleek, you lose because you count as
many cards as you had in tricks, which must be few by
reason of the badness of your hand. If you have Tib,
Tom, King, and Queen of Trumps in your hand, you
have thirty by honours, that is, eight above your own
cards, besides the cards you win by them in play. If
you have Tom only, which is nine and the King of
Trumps, which is three, then you reckon from twelve,
thirteen, fourteen, fifteen, till you come to two and
twenty, and then every card wins so many half-pence,
pence, &c. as you play'd for; if you are under two and
twenty you lose as many.

Here note, that before the cards are dealt, it is requisite
to demand, whether the gamesters will play at Tiddy,
or leave it out, it being a card that is apt to be forgotten;
and know, that it is lookt upon as very foul play to call
for a Gleek of Kings, Aces, Queens, or Knaves, when the

person hath but two in his hands. If you discard wrong, i.e., lay out but 5 or 6 cards, if you call for any Gleek or Mournivals, you lose them all if it be found out that you so discard. Let this suffice for this noble and delightful game or recreation.

Chapter VIII

L'OMBRE, a Spanish Game

THERE are several sorts of this game called *L'Ombre*, but that which is the chief is called *Renegado*, at which three only can play, to whom are dealt nine cards apiece, so that by discarding the eights, nines and tens, there will remain thirteen cards in the stock; there is no Trump but what the player pleaseth; the first hand hath always the liberty to play or pass, after him the second, &c.

There are two sorts of counters for stakes, the greater and the lesser, which last have the same proportion to the other as a penny to a shilling. Of the great counters each man stakes one for the game, and one of the lesser for passing, and for the hand when eldest, and for every card taken is one counter.

There are two suits; Black and Red; of the Black there is first the *Spadillo*, or Ace of Spades; the *Mallillio* or black Deuce; the *Basto* or Ace of Clubs; the King, the Queen, the Knave, the seven, the six, the five, four, and three. Of the Red Suit there is the *Spadillo, Punto, Mallillio,* &c.

The Spadillo or Ace of Spades, is always the first card, and always Trump, and the Basto or Ace of Clubs is always third; of the Black there is 11 Trumps, of the Red 12. The Red Ace enters into the fourth place when it is Trump and it is called *Punto* then, otherwise only called an Ace.

The least small cards of the red are always best, and

the most of the Black; except the Deuce and Red Seven, which are called the *Mallillio's* and always second when Trump. The *Matadors* (or killing cards) which are the Spadillo, Mallillio, and Basto, are the chief cards, and when they are all in a hand the others pay for them three of the greater counters apiece; and with these three for foundation you may count as many Matadors as you have cards in an interrupted series of Trumps; for all which the others are to pay you one counter apiece.

He who hath the first hand hath his choice (as aforesaid) of playing the game, of naming the Trump, and of taking in as many and as few cards as he list, and after him the second, &c. having demanded whether any one will play without *taking in*, you oblige your self to take in though your game be never so good, wherefore you do well to consider it before.

If you name not the Trump before you look on the cards which you have taken in, any other may prevent you and name what Trump they please; if you know not of two suits which to name Trump first, the black suit is to be preferred before the red, because there are fewer Trumps of it. Secondly, you were best to chuse that suit of which have not the King, because besides your three Trumps you have a King which is as good as a fourth. When you have the choice of going in three Matadors, or the two black Aces with three or four other Trumps, if the stakes be great you are to chuse this last, as most like to win most tricks; if it be but a simple stake you are to chuse the first, because the six counters you are to receive for the three Matadors more than countervail the four or five you lose for the game.

He that hath the first hand is never to take in nor play, unless he have three sure tricks in his hand at least; to understand which the better, know the end of the game is to win most tricks, whence he that can win five tricks of the nine hath a sure game; or if he win four and can so divide the tricks as one may win two, the other three, if not it's either *Codillio*, or *Repuesto*, so the player loseth and maketh good the stakes.

It is called Codillio when the player is bested, and another wins more tricks than he, when this takes up the ſtakes and the other makes it good.

Here note, although the other two always combine to make him lose yet they all do their beſt (for the common good) to hinder any one from winning, only ſtriving to make it Repueſto, which is when the player wins no more tricks than another, in which case the player doubles the ſtake without any ones winning it, and remains so for the advantage of the next player.

Here note that Kings of any suit are accounted as good Trumps, mean while all other cards but Kings and Trumps are to be discarded.

The player having taken in, the next is to consider the goodness of the game, and to take in more or less for the beſt advantage of his game; neither is any for the saving a counter or two to negleƈt the taking in, that the other may commodiously make up his game with what cards he hath left, and that no good cards may lie dormant in the ſtock, except the player playeth without taking in, when they may refuse to take in, if they imagine he hath all the game.

When one hath a sure game in his hand, he is to play without taking in, then the others are to give him each one of the great counters as he is to give them, if he play without taking in a game that is not sure and loseth it ; if you win all the tricks in your hand or the *Voll*, they likewise are to give you one counter apiece, but then you are to declare before the fifth trick that you intend to play for the Voll, that so they keep their beſt cards, which else, seeing you win five tricks (or the game) they may carelesly caſt away.

If you renounce you are to double the ſtake, as also if you have more or fewer cards than mine, to which end you must carefully count you cards in dealing and taking in before you look on them; besides according to the rigour of the game if you speak any thing tending to the discovery thereof, either in your own hand or anothers (excepting *Gagno*) or *play so*, to hinder the

49

making of Repuesto or Codillio, you are not fit to play.

Observe, that in playing Trumps, if any plays an ordinary one, and you have only the three best cards or Matadors singly or jointly in your hands, you may refuse to play them without renouncing, because of the priviledge which these cards have, that none but commanding cards can force them out of your hand.

You are to say nothing when you play your card, but *I pass* or *play*, or *gagno*, or *gagno del Re* when you play your Queen to hinder them from taking it with the King.

Now since it is impossible to provide against all accidents in the game, only take notice of these general rules.

First, never win more than one trick if you cannot win more than two, because of the advantage you give the player by it, in dividing the tricks.

Secondly, you are to win the trick always from the player if you can, unless you let it pass for mere advantage, where the second is to let pass to the third if he have the likelier game to beast the player, or if he be likelier to win it. There may be diverse advantages in refusing to take the players trick; but the chief is, if you have the *Tenaces* in your hand, that is two cards, and if you have the leading, you are sure to lose one of them; if the player lead to you, you are sure to win them both. For example, if you have Spadillio and Basto in your hand, and he have the Mallillio and another Trump, if you lead you lose one of them; for either you play your Spadillio, and he plays the lesser trump upon it and wins your Basto the next trick with his Mallillio and so the contrary; whereas if he leads he loseth; for if he leads his Mallillio you win it with your Spadillio, and with your Basto win the other Trump, &c.

If you are not sure to win five tricks, having only three Matadors, and Kings your auxiliary cards; if you have the leading, play first a Matador or two before you play your Kings to fetch out his Trumps which might have trumped them, and if you have three Matadors

with two other Trumps, your best way is to play your
Matadors first to see where the Trumps lie; if both
follow, you are sure if the Trump be red there remains
only one Trump in their hands, if black none at all.

Lastly, if the players have but a weak game, they are
to imitate cunning Beast-players in dividing the tricks,
and consulting to play their cards. To conclude, lay
your tricks angle-wise, that you may the more facilely
compute them.

Chapter IX

The Game at CRIBBIDGE

AT *Cribbidge* there are no cards to be thrown out, but
all are made use of; and the number of the set is sixty-
one.

It is an advantage to deal, by reason of the Crib, and
therefore you must lift for it, and he that hath the least
card deals.

There are but two players at this game, the one
shuffles and the other cuts, the dealer delivers out the
cards one by one, to his antagonist first and himself last,
till five apiece be dealt to one another; the rest being
set down in view on the table, each looketh on his game,
and ordereth his cards for the best advantage.

He that deals makes out the best cards he can for his
Crib, and the other the worst, because he will do him as
little good as he can, being his Crib; which Crib is
four cards, two a piece, which they lay out upon the
table, not knowing nor seeing one anothers cards, and
then they turn up a card from the parcel that was left of
dealing, and each of them may make use of that card to
help them on in their game in hand, and when they have
play'd out their three cards, and set up with counters
their games in their hands, the crib is the others the next
deal, and so they take it by turns.

The value of the cards is thus. Any fifteen upon the

Charles Cotton

cards is two, whether nine and six, ten and five, King and five, seven and eight, &c.

A *Pair* is two, a *Pair-Royal* six, a double *Pair-Royal* twelve, *Sequences of three* is two, *Sequences of four* is four, *of five* five, &c. and so is a *Flush of three*, three; *of four*, *four*, &c. *Knave Noddy* is one in hand and two to the dealer; that is, if you have a Knave of that suit which is turned up, it is *Knave Noddy*. A pair of Aces, Kings, Queens, Knaves, Tens, &c. is two; Three Aces, Kings, Queens, &c. is a *Pair-Royal*; a double *Pair-Royal* is four Aces, four Kings, four Queens, &c. and is twelve games to him that hath them.

Having lookt on your cards, you count your game after this manner. Suppose you have in your hand a nine and two sixes, after you have laid out two cards for the Crib, that makes you six games, because there is two fifteens and a pair, by adding your nine to the two sixes, and if a six chance to be turn'd up, then you have twelve games in your hand; for though you muſt not take the turn'd up card into your hand, yet you may make what use you can of it in counting, so that the three sixes makes you six, being a *Pair-Royal*, and the nine added to every six makes three fifteens, which six more added to the former, make twelve, which you muſt set up with counters or otherwise, that your opponent may know what you are, though you muſt not see his cards, nor he yours; if you think he plays foul by reckoning too much, you may count them after the hand is play'd.

Thus you have set up your twelve, your opposite it may be hath four, five, and six in his hand; that is two, because of *Sequences of three*; then it is two more because it is four, five and six; again, taking in the counting six that is turn'd up, that is in all four, then there is fifteen and fifteen, four and five is nine, and six is fifteen, and then with the six turn'd up 'tis fifteen more, which makes eight games, this he likewise sets up, keeping his cards undiscovered. Here note, he that deals not sets up three in lieu thereof.

Having thus done, he that dealt not plays firſt, suppose

it a six, if you have a nine play it, that makes fifteen, for which set up two, the next may play a four which makes nineteen, you a six twenty five, and he a five that is thirty, you being not able to come in, having a six in your hand, he sets up one (for it is one and thirty you aim at in playing the cards), because he is moſt, and two for Sequences four, five, and six, which were his four after the fifteen, your five and his six ; and that doth not hinder them from being Sequences, though the six was play'd between the four and the five; but if an Ace, Nine, King, Queen, or the like, had been play'd between, they had been no Sequences, so the two for the Sequences, and the one for thirty being most (as at one and thirty) makes him three, which he muſt set up to the reſt of his game, and in this playing of the cards you may make *Pairs, Sequences, Flush, Fifteens, Pair-Royals*, and double *Pair-Royals*, if you can, though that is rarely seen.

Laſtly, you look upon your Crib, that is the two cards apiece laid out at firſt, which is the dealers ; if he find no games in them, nor help by the card that was turn'd up, which he takes into his hand, then he is bilkt, and sometimes it so happens that he is both bilkt in hand and crib. Thus they play and deal by turns till the game of sixty one be up.

Here note, if you get the game before your adversary is forty five (forty four will not do it) you must then say, I have *lurkt* you, and that is a double game for whatever you play'd with six shilling, or a greater summ.

Chapter X

A Game at ALL-FOURS

All-Fours is a game very much play'd in Kent, and very well it may, since from thence it drew its first original ; and although the game may be lookt upon as trivial and inconsiderable, yet I have known Kentish gentlemen and others of very considerable note, who have play'd great sums of money at it, yet that adds not much to the worth of the game, for a man may play away an estate at *One and Thirty*; as I knew one lose a considerable sum *at most at three throws*.

This game I conceive is called All-Fours from *Highest*, *Lowest*, *Jack*, and *Game*, which is the set as some play it, but you may make from seven to fifteen, or more if you please, but commonly eleven.

There are but two can play at it at a time, and they must lift for dealing, the highest Put-card deals, who delivers to his adversary three cards, and to himself the like, and the like again, and having six apiece, he turns up a card which is Trump; if Jack (and that is any Knave) it is one to the dealer.

If he to whom the cards were dealt after perusal of his game like them not, he hath the liberty of begging one; if the dealer refuse to give him one, then he deals three apiece more, but if he then turns up a card of the same suit, he deals further till he turns up a card of another suit.

Here note, that an Ace is four, a King is three, a Queen is two, a Knave one, and a Ten is ten.

Now you must play down your cards, but to what advantage I cannot here prescribe, it must be according to the cards you have in your hand managed by your judgment to the best advantage.

Having play'd your cards you reckon, if you are highest and lowest of what is Trumps, you reckon two; if you are only highest but one, and the like of Jack and Game; sometimes you are Highest, Lowest, Jack, and Game, and then you must reckon four; the game is he that tells most after the cards are play'd, and therefore a Ten is a very significant card, which crafty gamesters know so well that they will frequently take out of a pack two Tens, and hide them contrary to the knowledg of the other, which is a great advantage to this foul player, if he play of the same suit of these Tens he hath absconded, for it must of necessity secure him from losing the game.

Here note, that he that wins Jack wins one also ; and furthermore observe that for advantage reneging is allowable if you have Trumps in your hand to trump it.

There is another sort of All-fours called *Running-All-Fours*, at which they play one and thirty up, and in this game the dealer hath a great advantage, for if he turn up an Ace it is four, a King three, a Queen two, and a Knave one, and these are the same also in play. A Ten is the beſt card for making up.

Chapter XI

English RUFF AND HONOURS, *and* WHIST

Ruff and Honours (alias *Slamm*) and *Whiſt*, are games so commonly known in England in all parts thereof, that every child almoſt of eight years old hath a competent knowledg in that recreation, and therefore I am unwilling to speak any thing more of them than this, that there may be a great deal of art used in dealing and playing at these games which differ very little one from the other.

In playing your cards you muſt have recourse altogether to your own judgment or discretion, ſtill making the beſt of a bad market ; and though you have but mean cards in your own hand, yet you may play them so suitable to those in your partners hand, that he may either trump them, or play the beſt of that suit on the board.

You ought to have a special eye to what cards are play'd out, that you may know by that means either what to play if you lead, or how to trump securely and advantagiously. Reneging or renouncing, that is, not following suit when you have it in your hand, is very fowl play, and he that doth it ought to forfeit one, or the game upon a game, and he that loseth dealing loseth one, or a trick as you make it.

At Ruff and Honours, by some called Slamm, you

have in the pack all the Deuces, and the reason is, because four playing having dealt twelve a piece, there are four left for the ſtock, the uppermoſt whereof is turn'd up, and that is Trumps, he that hath the Ace of that, *Ruffs;* that is, he takes in those four cards, and lays out four others in their lieu; the four Honours are the Ace, King, Queen, and Knave; he that hath three Honours in his own hand, his partner not having the fourth sets up eight by cards, that is two tricks; if he hath all four, then sixteen, that is four tricks; it is all one if the two partners make them three or four between them, as if one had them. If the Honours are equally divided among the gameſters of each side, then they say Honours are split. If either side are at eight Groats he hath the benefit of calling *Can-ye*, if he hath two Honours in his hand, and if the other answers one, the game is up, which is nine in all, but if he hath more than two he shows them, and then it is one and the same thing; but if he forgets to call after playing a trick, he loseth the advantage of Can-ye for that deal.

All cards are of value as they are superiour one to another, as a Ten wins a Nine if not Trumps, so a Queen, a Knave in like manner; but the leaſt Trump will win the higheſt card of any other card; where note the Ace is the higheſt.

Whiſt is a game not much differing from this, only they put out the Deuces and take in no ſtock; and is called Whiſt from the silence that is to be observed in the play; they deal as before, playing four, two of a side, (some play at two handed, or three handed Whiſt; if three handed, always two ſtrive to suppress and keep down the rising-man). I say they deal to each twelve a piece and the Trump is the bottom card. The manner of crafty playing, the number of the game Nine, Honours and dignity of other cards are all alike, and he that wins moſt tricks is moſt forward to win the set.

He that can by craft over-look his adversaries game hath a great advantage, for by that means he may partly know what to play securely; or if he can have some petty

The Compleat Gamester

glimpse of his partners hand. There is a way by winking, or the fingers to discover to their partners what Honours they have, as by the wink of one eye, or putting one finger on the nose or table, it signifies one Honour, shutting both the eyes, two; placing three fingers or four on the table, three or four Honours. They have several ways of securing an Honour or more in the bottom when they deal, either to their partners or selves; if to their partner they place in the second lift next the top, 1, 2, 3, or four Aces, or Court-cards all of a suit, according as they could get them together in the former deal, and place a card of the same suit in the bottom, when the cards are cut they must use their hand so dexterously as not to put the top in the bottom, but nimbly place where it was before.

If they would secure Honours to themselves when dealing, they then place so many as they can get upon their lap or other place undiscerned, and after the cards are cut, then clap them very neatly under. But the cleanliest rooking way is by the *breef*, that is take a pack of cards and open them, then take out all the Honours, that is as aforesaid, the four Aces, the four Kings, etc., then take the rest and cut a little from the edges of them all alike, by which means the Honours will be broader than the rest, so that when your adversary cuts to you, you are certain of an Honour, when you cut to your adversary cut at the ends, and then it is a chance if you cut him an Honour, because the cards at the ends are all of a length, thus you may make breefs end-ways as well as side-ways.

There are a sort of cunning fellows about this city, who before they go to play will plant half a dozen of these packs (nay sometimes half of score) in the hands of a drawer, who to avoid being suspected will call to their confederate drawer for a fresh pack of cards, who brings them as from a shop new, and some of these packs shall be so finely markt, whereby the gamester shall plainly and certainly know every card therein contain'd by the outside, although the best of other eyes shall not discern where any mark was made at all; and this done with that variety that every card of every suit shall have a different diftinguishable mark.

Some have a way to slick with a slick-ftone all the Honours very smooth, by which means he will be sure to cut his partner an Honour, and so his Partner to him again, and that is done by lying a forefinger on the top indifferent hard, and giving a slurring jerk to the reft which will slip off from the slickt card.

It is impossible to shew you all the cheats of this game, since your cunning gamefter is always studying new inventions to deceive the ignorant.

Chapter XII

FRENCH-RUFF

At *French-Ruff* you muft lift for deal, moft or leaft carries it according to the agreement of the gamefters.

You may play either two, four or six of a side, dealing to each five a piece, either two firft at a time, or three, according to pleasure, and he that deals turns up Trumps; the King is the higheft card at Trumps, and so it is higheft in all other cards that are not Trumps, the Queen is next, the Knave next, and next to that the Ace, and all other cards follow in preheminency according to the number of the pips, but all small Trumps win the higheft of any other suit.

Having turn'd up Trumps, he that hath the Ace muft take the Ace turn'd up, and all other Trumps which immediately follow that, if so agreed among the gamefters, laying out so many cards as he took up in lieu thereof.

After this they play, to win two tricks signifies nothing, to win three or four wins but one, but to win five is the winning of five.

If you play at *forsat* (that is the rigour of the play) he that deals wrong loseth one and his deal. You are bound to follow suit, and it you renounce or renege you lose the whole game, if you so make it, otherwise but one or two according to agreement.

He that plays a card that is trumped by the follower, if the next player hath none of the former suit he must trump it again, although he hath never a trump in his hand that can win the former trump, and so it must pass to the last player.

All the players round are bound to win the highest trump play'd if they can. Here note, that he who playeth before his turn loseth one, unless it be the last card of all

Chapter XIII

FIVE-CARDS

Five-Cards is an Irish game, and is as much play'd in that Kingdom, and that for considerable sums of money, as All-fours is play'd in Kent, but there is little analogy between them.

There are but two can play at it, and there are dealt five cards a piece. The least of the black, and the most of the red wins. The Ace of Diamonds is the worst of the whole pack, unless it prove to be Trump.

The five fingers (alias five of Trumps) is the best card in the pack; the Ace of Hearts is next to that and the next is the Ace of Trumps, then the Knave, and the rest of cards are best according to their value in pips, or as they are trumps.

Before you play ask whether he will *five it*, if he speaks affirmatively turn up the next card of the pack under that first turn'd up, and that must be trumps; if not, play it out: he that wins most cards wins five, but he that wins all, wins ten.

Observe, that the Ace of Hearts wins the Ace of Trumps, and the Five-fingers not only wins the Ace of Trumps, but also all other cards whatever.

Chapter XIV

Of a Game called COSTLY-COLOURS

THIS game is to be play'd out only by two persons, of which the eldeſt is to play firſt as in other games. You muſt deal off three a piece, and turn up the next card following; then the eldeſt is to take his choice whether he will *Mogg* (that is change a card or no) and whosoever refuseth is to give the other one chalk or hole, of which generally threescore and one makes the game. Then muſt the eldeſt play, and the other if he can muſt make it up fifteen, for which he shall set up as many holes or chalks as there are cards upon the table; so likewise for five and twenty, and also as many cards as are play'd to make up thirty, no more nor less, so many chalks may be set up who play'd laſt, to make up one and thirty, and if one and thirty be not made, then he that play'd laſt and is neareſt one and thirty without making out muſt set up one, which is called setting up one for the latter.

This being done, the eldeſt muſt show how many chalks he hath in his hand to set up, and after him the youngeſt, which they muſt reckon in this manner, taking notice both of the colour and number of pips upon the card turn'd up as those in their hands ſtill, reckoning as many for all the fifteen and five and twenty as there go cards to make the number; and if you have it by chance in your hand, and with the card turned up one and thirty, then you muſt set up four for that. You muſt also set up if you have them in your hands or can make them so in the card turn'd up as followeth; two for a pair, be they either Coat-cards, or others; two for a Knave, and if a Knave of the same colour and suit of the card turn'd up, then you muſt set up four; and so for a Deuce four, if it be of the same colour turn'd up: if you have three of a sort, either three fours, five sixes, or Coat-cards, you must set up nine, and this is called a *Pair-Royal*; now if they are all either Hearts, Diamonds, or the like, then you must set up six for *Costly-Colours*. If you have three of a colour you can reckon but two for Colours.

Whosoever dealt, if he turn'd up either Deuce or Knave, he must set up four for it; as for example, imagine you had dealt your adversary three cards, viz: the five of Hearts, four of Hearts, and eight of Hearts; to yourself the Deuce of Hearts, seven of Clubs, and nine of Hearts. Lastly, you turn up a card, which is the Knave of Hearts, for which you must set up four; then because he will not ask you to change one, he gives you one, which you must set up, and then he plays, suppose it be his five of Hearts, you then play your seven of Clubs, which makes twelve, then he plays his eight of Hearts, which makes twenty; then you play your nine of Hearts, which makes twenty nine, and because he cannot come in with his five of Hearts, you must play your Deuce of Hearts, which makes you one and thirty. For your five you must set up five, then he must set up what he hath in his hand, which you will find to be but six, for he hath nothing in his hand but Costly-Colours. Then must you set up your games, which first are two, for your nine of Clubs, and nine of Hearts which make fifteen, then that fifteen and the Knave turn'd up makes five and twenty, for which set up three; then for your Deuce of Hearts which is the right, set up four, and three for Colours, because you have three of a sort in your hand with that turn'd up, now these with the five you got in playing for thirty one makes you this deal with the Knave turn'd up and the cards in your hand just twenty. Many other examples I might give you, but that it is needless since this one is sufficient to direct you in all others. And thus much for Costly-Colours.

Charles Cotton

Chapter XV

BONE-ACE

THIS game you may look on as trivial and very inconsiderable, and so it is by reason of the little variety therein contein'd, but because I have seen ladies and persons of quality have plaid at it for their diversion, I will briefly describe it, and the rather because it is a licking game for money.

There are seven, or eight (or as many as the cards will permit) play at it at one time. In the lifting for dealing the least deals, which is a great disadvantage; for that makes the dealer youngest hand:

The dealer deals out two to the first hand, and turns up the third, and so goes on to the next, to the third, fourth, fifth, etc. He that hath the biggest card carries the *Bone*, that is one half of the stake, the other remaining for the game; now if there be three Kings, three Queens, three Tens, &c., turn'd up, the eldest hand wins it. Here note that the Ace of Diamonds is *Bone-Ace*, and wins all other cards whatever: thus much for the Bone; afterwards the nearest to one and thirty wins the game, and he that turns up or draws to one and thirty wins it immediately.

Chapter XVI

Of PUTT and the High-Game

Putt is the ordinary rooking game of every place, and seems by the few cards that are dealt to have no great difficulty in the play, but I am sure there is much craft and cunning in it; of which I shall show as much as I understand.

If you play at two-handed Putt (or if you please you may play at three hands) the beſt Putt-card deals. Having shuffled the cards, the adversary cuts them, then the dealer deals one to his antagoniſt, and another to himself till they have three apiece : five up or a Putt is commonly the game. The eldeſt if he hath a good game, and thinks it better than his adversaries, puts to him, if the other will not or dare not see him, he then wins one, but if he will see him they play it out, and he that wins two tricks or all three wins the whole set; but if each win a trick and the third tyed, neither win, because it is trick and tye.

Sometimes they play without putting, and then the winner is he that wins moſt tricks. Here note that in your playing keep up your cards very close ; for the leaſt discovery of any one of them is a great advantage to him that sees it.

This game consiſts very much in daring ; for a right gameſter will put boldly upon very bad cards sometimes, as upon a five, seven and a nine ; the other thinking he hath good cards in his adversaries hand, having very indifferent ones in his own dares not see him, and so by going to ſtock loseth one. Here note that he that once hath the confidence to put on bad cards cannot recal his putting, by which means he frequently pays for his bravado.

The beſt Putt-cards are firſt the Trey, next the Deuce, then the Ace, the reſt follow in preheminence thus ; the King, the Queen, the Knave, the Ten, and so onwards to the four, which is the meaneſt card at Putt.

Some of the cheats at Putt are done after this manner. Firſt, for cutting to be sure of a good Putt-card, they use the *Bent*, the *Slick*, and the *Breef* ; the Bent is a card bended in play which you cut, the Slick is when beforehand the gameſter takes a pack of cards, and with a slickſtone smooths all the Putt-cards, that when he comes to cut to his adversary with his forefinger above and his thumb about the middle, he slides the reſt of the cards off that which was slickt, which is done infallibly with much facility; but in this there is required neatness and dexterity for fear of discovery, and then your confidence in this contrivance will be vain and of no effect.

Lastly, the Breef in cutting is very advantagious to him that cuts, and it is thus done. The cheat provides beforehand a pack of cards, whereof some are broader than others; under some of which he plants in play some good Putt-cards, which though they shuffle never so much they shall rarely separate them; by which means he that cuts (laying his fingers on the broad card) hath surely dealt him a Putt-card.

In dealing these rooks have a trick they call the *Spurr*, and that is, as good cards come into their hands that they may know them again by the outside (and so discover the strength or weakness of their adversaries game) I say some where on the outside they give them a gentle touch with their nail.

Now when they intend to bleed a *Col* to some purpose whom they have set before, they always fix half a score packs of cards before (as I have related in Whist) by slicking them or spurring them, that is, giving them such marks that they shall certainly know every card in the pack, and consequently every card that is in his adversaries hand, an advantage that cannot well be greater.

But if they are not furnished with such cards, and cannot accomplish their ends by the former indirect means without palpable discovery, then they have accomplices who standing by the innocent Col look over his Game, and discovers what it is to his adversary: and to strengthen their interest by cheating, they frequently carry about them Treys, Deuces, Aces, &c. in their pockets, which they use as need requires, or if not, they will steal them out of the pack whilst they are playing, which is the securest way and freest from discovery.

Lastly, they have one most egregious piece of roguery more, and that is playing the *High-game* at Putt; and this is to be done but once at a set-meeting; and therefore on this depends the absolute overthrow of the Col that plays, or the Col that is a ſtander by.

This High-game at Putt is thus performed: the rook whilſt playing singles out the Deuces and Treys for the laſt game, and placeth them thus in order, hiding them in his lap or other covert, firſt a Deuce, then a Trey, next a Deuce, then a Trey, then a Trey and a Trey; now ſtooping letting fall a card or some other way as he shall think fit, he claps these cards fac'd at the bottom, having shuffled the cards before, and bids his adversary cut, which he nimbly and neatly with both his hands joyns the divided cards, and then the bottom fac'd cards are upwards, and then he deals, and leſt there should be a discovery made of the facing, he palms them as much as he can, nimbly passing the laſt card.

Now do the gameſters smile at the goodness of each others game, one shows his to one, the other, his to another; and cries 'Who would not put at such cards?' The other in as brisk a tone, says, 'Come if you dare.' 'What will you lay of the game?' says the Rook. 'What you dare,' says the Col; then pausing a while the rook seems to consult with his friends, who cry, they know not what to think on't. 'Five pound,' cries a rooking confederate on this gentlemans side. The Col encouraged hereby, cries ten pound more: and thus the rook holds him in play till there be a good sum of money on the board; then answers the Putt of the now ruin'd Cully. They now play; the Col begins with a Deuce, the rook wins that with a Trey; the rook then plays a Deuce, and the Col wins it with his Trey; then he plays his Deuce which is won with a Trey; thus the rook wins the day. This game may be plaid otherways according to fancy: let these and the former cheats be a sufficient warning.

Chapter XVII

WIT AND REASON, a Game so called

Wit and Reason is a game which seems very easie at first to the learner, but in his practice and observation shall find it otherwise. It is a game something like one and thirty, and is plaid after this manner.

Two playing together, the one hath all the red cards, and the other hath the black: then they turn up cross or pile who shall lead; for the leader hath a great advantage over the other, as shall be demonstrated.

You are not to play a ten first; for if you do you shall certainly lose; for one and thirty being the game he that first comes to it wins. Now should the leader play a ten the follower will play another ten, that makes twenty; let the leader then play anything next, the follower will be sure to make it up one and thirty.

He that hath the lead if he play a nine may certainly win the game, if he look about him; ever remembring to get first to twenty, without spending two of the one sort, as two Deuces, two Treys, two Quaters, &c. otherwise you will lose. As, for example, you play a nine first, your adversary plays a Deuce that makes eleven, you then play a nine again, and that makes twenty; thus you have plaid out both your nines, wherefore your antagonist plays a Deuce, now you can play no card but he wins; for if you play an eight (for you cannot come in with your ten) and you have never a nine, then he hath an Ace for one and thirty; so if you play a seven, which makes nine and twenty, he hath a Deuce remaining to make up one and thirty, and so you may observe in the rest of the cards.

Take this for a general rule, that you have a very great advantage in fetching out by play any two of a number, as aforesaid; as two fives, two sixes, two sevens, &c. wherefore you must not play rashly, but with due consideration arithmetically grounded to make up a certain game of one and thirty. To conclude, he that hath the art of playing well at one and thirty without cards, that is by naming such a number at firſt, and prosecuting it by such addition of others, that your adversary cannot think of any number but what shall be your game; I say such a man is fitteſt to play at this game called Wit and Reason.

Chapter XVIII

A Pastime called THE ART OF MEMORY

THIS *Art of Memory* is a sport at which men may play for money, but it is moſt commonly the way to play the drunkard. It is beſt when many play at it; for with few it is no sport at all. For example, as many persons as do play so many cards trebled muſt be thrown down on the table with their faces upwards; which every one muſt take notice of and indeavour to regiſter them in his memory. Then the dealer muſt take them all up, and shuffling them after cutting deals to every one three apiece.

The firſt it may be calls for a King, which muſt be laid on the table with his face downwards by him that hath it in his hands; the next it may be calls for a ten of the Spades, which muſt be laid down in like manner, and so it goes round; now if any one calls for what is already laid down, if they play for liquor, he muſt then drink a glass; if for money, he muſt then pay a farthing, half-penny, or the like.

This sport wholly depends on the memory; for want of which a man may lose at this sport his money or his underſtanding.

Chapter XIX

A Game called PLAIN-DEALING

He that deals hath the advantage of this game; for if he turn up the Ace of Diamonds he cannot lose; to his adversary he delivers out nine and but three to himself; then are the cards plaid as at Whiſt, the beſt of Trumps or other cards wins, and but one to be gotten at a deal. I cannot commend this paſtime for its ingenuity, and therefore only name it, because we treat of games in general.

Chapter XX

A Game called QUEEN NAZAREEN

There may as many play at it as the cards will allow of; five cards are dealt to every player. The Queen of Diamonds is *Queen Nazareen*, and he that hath it demands three apiece of every player. The Knave of Clubs is called *Knave Knocher*, and he that hath it challengeth two apiece. If women play among men, it is cuſtomary for Knave Knocher to kiss Queen Nazareen.

Laſtly, he that lays down a King the laſt card that is plaid challengeth one, and begins again; and he that hath firſt plaid away his cards demands as many counters as there are cards in the hands of the reſt.

Chapter XXI

LANTERLOO

Lanterloo is a Game may be plaid several ways, but I shall insiſt on none but two; the firſt way is thus.

Lift for dealing, and the beſt Put-card carries it; as

many may play as the 'cards will permit, to whom muſt be dealt five apiece, and then turn up Trump. Now if three, four, five, or six play, they may lay out the threes, fours, fives, sixes, and sevens to the intent they may not be quickly Lood; but if they would have the Loos come faſt about then play with the whole pack.

Having dealt set up five scores or chalks; and then proceed forwards in your game. He that is eldeſt hand hath the priviledg of passing by the benefit thereof, that is, he hath the advantage of hearing what every one will say, and at laſt may play or not play according as he finds his game good or bad. If the eldeſt saith he passeth, the reſt may chuse whether they will play or no.

You may play upon every card what you please, from a penny to a pound. Trumps as at Whiſt are the beſt cards, all others in like manner take their precedency from the higheſt to the loweſt.

You muſt not revoke, if you do you pay all on the table. If you play and are *Loo'd* (that is, win never a trick) you muſt lay down to the ſtock so much for your five cards as you plaid upon every one of them.

Every deal rub off a score, and for every trick you win set up a score by you till the firſt scores are out, to remember you how many tricks you have won in the several deals in the game.

All the chalks for the game being rub'd out, tell your own scores, and for so many scores or tricks which you have won, so much as they were valued at in the game so much you muſt take from the ſtock; thus muſt every one do according to the number of tricks he hath won.

Here note, that he who hath five cards of a suit in his hand Loos all the gameſters then playing, be they never so many, and sweeps the board; if there be two Loos he that is eldeſt hand hath the advantage.

As there is cheating (as they say) in all trades, so more particularly intolerable in gaming; as in this for example. If one of the gameſters have four of a suit and he want a fifth, he may for that fifth make an exchange out of his own pocket if he be skil'd in the cleanly art of

conveiance; if that fail, some make use of a friend, who
never fails to do him that kind office and favour. There
are other cheats to be performed, which I shall omit, since
it is not my business to teach you how to cheat, but so
to play as not to be cheated.

LANTERLOO ANOTHER WAY PLAID

Lift for dealing as aforesaid, and the beſt Put-card
deals five to every one apiece. The dealer for his five
cards muſt lay down so many sixpences, shillings, and
so forth, as they conclude upon and agree for every card,
or so many counters being valued at either six-pence,
or twelve-pence, more or less. After this all muſt play;
if any be Lood he muſt lay down so much for his Loo
as his five cards amount to. If any next dealing be Lood
he muſt lay down as much for his dealing, and as much
more for his Loo.

If after this the eldeſt hand pass, the reſt may refuse
to play, or play if they think they can win a card.

Here note, if there be never a Loo the money may be
divided by the gameſters according to the number of
their tricks, if there be a Loo the winners muſt take
up the money, and he that is Loo'd muſt lay down as
much money on the board as every one had laid down
before, be it never so great a summ, besides the like
quantity for dealing, if he that was Loo'd dealt.

Chapter XXII

A Game called PENNEECH

Having dealt seven cards apiece, turn up a card, and
that is Trumps. The Ace and Coat-Cards of Trumps
are thus reckoned, the Ace is five, the King four, the
Queen three, and the Knave two.

Having play'd, he that wins the firſt trick turns up

another card, and that is Trumps; and so every trick
produceth a fresh Trump, till all the seven be play'd.
Now if it so happen, that what is turn'd up proves an
Ace or Coat-card, that is a great advantage to him who
won the laſt trick; for if it be an Ace turn'd up then he
reckons five, if a King four, if a Queen three, as aforesaid.

After all the seven cards be play'd (which at firſt are
dealt one by one) he that won the laſt trick turns up a
card, and if it prove Ace, King, Queen, or Knave, he
reckons for it accordingly as aforesaid.

If the Seven of Diamonds be turn'd up, that is *Penneech*, and is reckon'd fourteen turn'd up, but it is but
seven in hand, and not that neither unless Diamonds
be Trumps; if it be Trump it is the higheſt card and
wins all others; if it be not trump it wins all Diamonds.

Laſtly, having play'd out all the fourteen cards betwixt ye, count how many cards you have more than your
own seven at firſt dealt you, and for every card reckon
one, and so you muſt reckon on with the value of your
Coat-card Trumps, with Penneech turn'd up or in hand,
till you come to sixty one, which is the game.

Here note, if you have neither Ace nor Face, you may
throw up your game and deal again.

Chapter XXIII

POST and PAIR

Poſt and Pair is a game on the cards very much play'd
in the Weſt of England, as All-fours is play'd in Kent,
and Fives in Ireland.

This play depends much upon daring; so that some
may win very considerably, who have the boldness to
adventure much upon the Vye, although their cards are
very indifferent.

You muſt firſt ſtake at Poſt then at Pair; after this
deal two cards apiece, then ſtake at the Seat, and then

deal the third card about. The eldest hand may pass and come in again, if any of the gamesters vye it; if not, the dealer may play it out, or double it.

The Ace of Trumps, as at Ruff and Honours, is the best card of all, and so of the rest in order. At *Post* the best cards are one and twenty, viz. two Tens and an Ace, but a Pair-Royal wins all, both Post, Pair, and Seat. Here note, that he who hath the best Pair or the best Post is the winner. A *Pair* is a pair of any two, as two Kings, two Queens, &c. A *Pair-Royal* is of three, as three Kings, three Queens, &c. The *Vye* is what you please to adventure upon the goodness of your own hand; or if it be bad, and you imagine your adversaries is so likewise, then bid high couragiously, by which means you daunt your antagonist, and so bring him to submission. If all the gamesters keep in till all have done, and by consent shew their cards, the best cards carry the game. Now according to agreement those that keep in till last, may divide the stakes, or shew the best card for it.

Observe, where the cards fall in several hands of the same sort, as a Pair or Pair-Royal, and so forth, the eldest hand carries it.

Chapter XXIV

BANKAFALET, a Game on the Cards so called

THE cards must be cut into as many heaps as there are players, or more if you please, and every man lays as much money on his own card as he thinks fit, or on the supernumerary heaps. So many as the dealers card is inferior to, so many he pays; so many as his card is superior to, so many he wins from.

The best card is the Ace of Diamonds, the next to that the Ace of Hearts, thirdly the Ace of Clubs, and lastly the Ace of Spades, and so the rest of these suits in order, according to their degree. The cheat lies in securing an Ace or any other good sure winning card; and if you mark the cards aforehand, so as to know them by the backside, you know how to make your advantage.

Chapter XXV

BEAST

It is called by the French *La Bett*, and is play'd by them after this manner. The best cards are King, Queen, and so forwards. They make three heaps, the *King*, the *Play*, and the *Triolet*.

To every one is dealt five cards (there may play three, four, five, or more) as at French Ruff, with the same rigour. Before the cards are dealt, every one stakes to the three heaps. He that wins most tricks takes up the heap that is called the Play; he that hath the King takes up the heap so called; and he that hath three of any sort, that is, three fours, three fives, three sixes, and so forth takes up the Triolet.

GAMES WITHIN THE TABLES

Chapter XXVI

Of IRISH

Irish is an ingenious game, and requires a great deal of skill to play it well, especially the After-game. It is not to be learn'd otherwise than by observation and practice, however I shall lightly touch hereon.

The men which are thirty in number are equally divided between you and your adversary, and are thus placed, two on the Ace point, and five on the Sice of your left hand table, and three on the Cinque, and five on the Ace point of your right hand table, answer'd on the like points by your adversaries men with the same number; or thus, two of your men on the Ace point, five on the double Sice, or Sice Cinque point, three on the Cinque point in your own tables, and five on the Sice point at home, and all these pointed alike by your adversary.

In your play have a care of being too forwards, and be not too rash in hitting every blot, but with discretion and consideration move slowly but securely; by which means though your adversary have fill'd his tables, but withal blots, and you by hitting him enter, you may win the game; nay sometimes though he hath born his men all to a very few.

'Tis the part of a prudent commander as he leads out his men to bring them home as safe as he may; so must you have a care of your men as you are bringing them home that they are not pickt up by the way.

Have a special care that your adversary double not the Trey, Ace-point with his men, and so make what

74

convenient haste you can to fill up your own tables, and beware of blotting ; that done, bear as fast as you can.

For an After-game I know not what instructions to give you, you must herein trust to your own judgment and the chance of the Dice, and if they run low for some time it will be so much the better.

Chapter XXVII

Of BACK-GAMMON

YOUR men are placed as at Irish and *Back-Gammon* differs but very little from it, but in Doublets which at this game is plaid fourfold, which makes a quicker dispatch of the game than Irish.

Be sure to make good your Trey, Ace-points, hit boldly and come away as fast as you can, to which end if your Dice run high, you will make the quicker dispatch.

When you come to bearing have a care of making when you need not, and Doublets now will stand you most in stead.

If both bear together he that is first off without Doublets wins one.

If both bear and one goes off with Doublets he wins two.

If your tables be clear before your adversaries men be come in, that's a *Back-Gammon*, which is three ; but if you thus go off with Doublets it is four.

False dice are much used at Irish and Back-Gammon for the benefit of entring, wherefore have a special care that you have not Cinque-Deuces and Quater-Treys put upon you, you may quickly perceive it by the running of the dice.

The person that is cunning at play has great advantage of a novice or innocent man, which is commonly by topping or knapping, which by its often practice may be suspected by his adversary. Then he has recourse to dice, which runs particular chances for his purpose, which the other being ignorant of, is almost an equal advantage with the former. For example, he provides dice that runs 6, 5, 4, 'tis his business to secure those points, so that if he happens to surprize any of your men coming home, as 'tis two to one but he does, he does without a kind of miracle win the set.

'Tis possible sometimes they may make use of 3, 2, which are the low chances; but that they seldom do for this reason, the high or forward points being supplied, you must enter if at all upon the low points which keeps you backwards and gives him advantage. The advantage of this game is to be forward if possible upon safe terms, and to point his men at that rate that it shall not be possible for you to pass, though you have entred your men, till he gives you liberty, having two to one the advantage of the game.

Chapter XXVIII

Of TICK-TACK

ALL your men must stand on the Ace-point, and from thence play forward, but have a care of being too forward, or so at leastwise that Doublets reach you not.

Secure your Sice and Cinque-point whatever you do, and break them not unless it be when you have the advantage of going in, which is the greatest advantage you can have next to a hit; for your adversaries eleventh point standing open you have it may be the opportunity of going in with two of your men, and then you win a double game. A hit is but one, and that is, when you throw such a cast that some one of your men will reach your adversaries unbound, but sometimes though it hits it will not pass by reason of a stop in the way, and then it is nothing. Sometimes it is good going over into your adversaries tables, but it is best for an After-game.

76

Playing close at home is the securest way, playing at length is both rash and unsafe, and be careful of binding your men when you lie in danger of the enemy. Moreover, if you see you are in danger of losing a double game give your adversary one; if you can it is better doing so than losing two.

Here note, if you fill up all the points of your second table with your own men you win two, and that you may prevent your adversary from doing so (if you are in danger thereof) if you can, make a vacant point in his tables, and it is impossible for him to do it.

This is the plain game of *Tick-Tack*, which is called so from *touch*, and *take*, for if you touch a man you must play him though to your loss; and if you hit your adversary and neglect the advantage, you are taken with a *Why not*, which is the loss of one. Likewise if you are in, and your cast is such that you may also go into your adversaries eleventh point by two other men, and you see it not, either by carelessness or eager prosecution of a hit which is apparent before your eyes, you lose two irrecoverably. Besides, it is a very great oversight as your men may stand not to take a point when you may do it.

Now some play this game with *Toots*, *Boveries*, and *Flyers*. Toots is, when you fill up your table at home and then there is required small throws, for it you get over with a Sice you have no benefit of Toots.

Boveries is when you have a man in the eleventh point of your own tables, and another in the same point of your adversaries directly answering.

Flyers is, when you bring a man round the tables before your adversary hath got over his first table, to the effecting of which there is required very high throwing of your side, and very low throwing of his.

Much more might be said as to the craft of the play, which cannot be so well discovered as from observation in your own or others playing.

There are several foolish pastims to be plaid in the Tables which are ridiculous to treat of, wherefore I shall only mention these three, Viz.

Chapter XXIX

DUBBLETS

AT *Dubblets* the fifteen men are thus placed; upon Sice, Cinque and Quater there are three men apiece, upon Trey, Deuce, Ace, but two apiece.

He that throws moſt hath the benefit of throwing firſt, and what he throws he lays down; and so doth the other what the one throws and hath not the other lays down for him to his own advantage; and thus they do till all the men are down, and then they bear, but not till they are down; he that is down firſt bears firſt, and will doubtedly win the game if the other throws not Dubblets to overtake him; now he that throws Dubblets apace is certain to win, for as many as the Dubblets are, so many he lays down, or bears; for example, if two fours, he lays down, or bears eight, and so for the other Dubblets; and therefore he that can either nap, top, or hath high runners about him hath a great advantage herein.

Chapter XXX

SICE-ACE

FIVE may play at *Sice-Ace* with six men apiece, they one load another with Aces, sixes bears only, and Dubblets drinks and throws again, so often some I have seen that for the lucre of a little money have resolved rather to lose themselves than a penny. It is commonly agreed the laſt two, or the laſt out shall lose, and the reſt go free.

Chapter XXXI

KETCH-DOLT

At *Ketch-Dolt* the firſt throws and lays down from the heap of men without the tables, what is thrown at it may be Sice Deuce, if the other throw either Sice or Deuce, and draw them not from his adversaries tables to the same point in his own, but takes them from the heap, and lays the Ace down, he is Dolted and loseth the game, or if he but touch a man of the heap and then recall himself, the loss is the same. Some by frequent praċtice will never be Dolted, and then they ſtrive who shall fill up their tables firſt; which done, he that bears them off firſt hath won the game. And so much for play within the tables.

GAMES WITHOUT THE TABLES

Chapter XXXII

Of INN AND INN

Inn and Inn is a game very much used in an ordinary, and may be play'd by two or three, each having a box in his hand. It is play'd with four dice. You may drop what you will, six-pences, shillings, or guinneys. Every Inn you drop, and every Inn and Inn you sweep all; but if you throw out, if but two plays, your adversary wins all; if three play, that *Out* is a Bye between the two other gamesters, which they may either divide or throw out for it. Here you are to observe that Out is when you have thrown no Dubblets on the four dice; Inn is when you have thrown two Dubblets of any sort, as two Aces, two Deuces, two Kings, &c. Inn and Inn is, when you throw all Dubblets, whether all of a sort or otherwise, viz. four Aces, four Deuces, or four Cinques, or two Aces, two Deuces, two Treys, two Quaters, or two Cinques, two Sixes, and so forth.

Your Battail may be as much and as little as you will, from twenty shillings to twenty pounds, and so onward to a thousand, which Battail is not ended till every penny of that money agreed upon for the Battail be won; and it is but requisite, for it is frequently seen that in a Battail of ten pound a gentleman hath been reduced to five shillings, and yet hath won at last the Battail.

For a gamester that would win without hazarding much his money, dice that will run very seldom otherwise but Sixes, Cinques, Quaters, &c., are very necessary. If those instruments are not to be had, a Taper-box will not be amiss, that as the Dice are thrown in may ſtick by the way, and so thrown to advantage. I have heard of one, who having spent the major part of his patrimony in good fellowship, and such pastims as the heat of blood with vigorous youth moſt prosecute, at length consider'd how he should live hereafter, and finding but small encouragements at home, and lesser abroad, thought if he could contrive a way to win a considerable sum at play (having been a great loser himself) that should be the basis of his future settlement. After various consultations within himself he at length contrived this ſtratagem. He caused a box to be made, not as they are usual screwed within, but smooth, and procured it to be so well painted and shadowed within that it lookt like a screw'd box; now this box was but half board wide at top, and narrow at bottom, that the dice as aforesaid might ſtick, and the box being smooth would come out without tumbling. With this box he went and play'd at Inn and Inn, by vertue whereof and his art of taking up and throwing in his dice into the box, he got the firſt night a thousand pound, and the next night two hundred a year, with a coach and six horses, which coach and horses (being very valuable) he sold, but the eſtate he lives on to this day with great improvements, and never would handle a dye since, well knowing how many worthy families it hath ruin'd.

Chapter XXXIII

Of PASSAGE

Passage is a game at dice to be play'd at but by two, and it is performed with three dice. The caſter throws continually till he hath thrown doublets under ten, and then he is out and loseth, or doublets above ten, and then he passeth and wins. High runners are moſt requisite for this game, such as will rarely run any other chance than four, five, or six, by which means if the caster throws doublets he scarcely can throw out. There is the same advantage of the smooth-taper-box aforesaid in this game, as at Inn and Inn; with the like benefit of the dice, whether by palming, topping, slurring, or knapping.

Chapter XXXIV

Of HAZZARD

Hazzard is a proper name for this game; for it speedily makes a man or undoes him; in the twinkling of an eye either a man or a mouse.

This game is play'd but with two dice, but there may play at it as many as can stand round the largest round table.

There are two things chiefly to be observed, that is, *Main* and *Chance*; the Chance is the casters, and the Main theirs who are concerned in play with him. There can be no Main thrown above nine and under five; so that five, six, seven, eight and nine are the only Mains and no more which are flung at Hazzard. Chances and *Nicks* are from four to ten, thus four is a Chance to nine, five to eight, six to seven, seven to six, eight to five; and nine and ten a Chance to five, six, seven and eight: in short, four, five, six, seven, eight, nine and ten are Chances to any Main, if any of these Nick it not. Now Nicks are either when the Chance is the same with the Main, as five and five, six and six, seven and seven, and so on, or six and twelve, seven and eleven, eight and twelve; where note, that twelve is out to nine, seven, and five; and eleven is out to nine, eight, six, and five; *Ames-Ace*, and Deuce-Ace, are out to all Mains what ever.

That I may the better illustrate this game, it will not be amiss to give one example for your better information. Seven's the Main, the caster throws five, and that's his Chance, and so hath five to seven; if the caster throw his own Chance he wins all the money was set him, but if he

throw seven which was the Main, he muſt pay as much
money as is on the board. If again seven be the Main,
and the caſter throws eleven, that is a Nick, and sweeps
away all the money on the table; but if he throw a
Chance, he muſt wait which will come firſt; Laſtly, if
seven be the Main, and the caſter throws Ames-Ace,
Deuce-Ace or twelve, he is out, but he throw from four to
ten he hath a Chance, though they are accounted the
worſt Chances on the dice, as seven is reputed the beſt
and easieſt Main to be flung; thus it is in eight or six, if
either of them be the Main, and the caſter throw either
four, five, seven, nine, or ten, this is his Chance, which
if he throw firſt, he wins, otherwise loseth; if he throw
twelve to eight, or six or the same caſt with the Main, he
wins; but if Ames-Ace or Deuce-Ace to all he loseth; or
if twelve when the Main is either five or nine. Here note,
that nothing Nicks five but five, nor nothing nine but nine.

Four and five to seven is judged to have the worſt on't,
because four (called by the tribe of Nickers little Dick-
Fisher) and five have but two Chances, Trey Ace and two
Deuces, or Trey Deuce and Quater Ace, whereas Seven
hath three Chances, Cinque Deuce, Six Ace, and Quater
Trey; in like condition is nine and ten, having but two
Chances, six Trey, Cinque and Quater, or six Quater and
two Cinques.

Now six and eight one would think should admit of no
difference in advantage with seven, but if you will
rightly consider the case, and be so vain to make trial
thereof, you will find a great advantage in seven over six
and eight. 'How can that be,' you will say, hath not six,
seven and eight eight equal chances? For example, in
six, Quater Deuce, Cinque Ace, and two Treys; in eight,
six Deuce, Cinque Trey, and two Quaters, and hath not
seven three as aforesaid? It is confeſt; but pray consider
the disadvantage in the doublets, two Treys and two
Quaters, and you will find that six Deuce is sooner
thrown than two Quaters, and so consequently Cinque
Ace or Quater Deuce sooner than two Treys: I saw an
old rook once take up a young fellow in a tavern, upon this

83

very score : the bargain was made that the rook should have seven always and the young gentleman six, and throw continually ; agreed to play they went, the rook got the firſt day ten pound, the next day the like sum ; and so for six days together losing in all three-score pounds ; notwithſtanding the gentleman, I am confident, had square dice, and threw them always himself. And farther to confirm what I alledg'd before, not only this rook, but many more have told me that they desir'd no greater advantage than to have seven always and the caſter to have six. Here note, it is the opinion of moſt that at the firſt throw the caſter hath the worſt on't.

Certainly Hazzard is the moſt bewitching game that is plaid on the dice ; for when a man begins to play he knows not when to leave off ; and having once accuſtom'd himself to play at Hazzard he hardly ever after minds any thing else. I have seen an old man about the age of seventy play at an ordinary when his own eyes were so defeÆive, that he was forced to help them with a pair of speÆacles ; and having an opportunity one day to speak to him, how a man of his years could be so vain and boyish ſtill to mind play ; insiſting withall upon the folly of that aÆion to hazzard his money when he had not sight enough remaining to discern whether he had won or loſt. ' Besides Sir,' said I, ' you cannot but hear how you are derided every time you come to the ordinary ; ' one says, ' here comes he that cannot reſt quiet, but will cry without the rattle of the dice ; ' another cries, ' certainly such a one plays by the ear ; for he cannot see to play.' ' Let them talk what they will,' said the gentleman, ' I cannot help it, I have been for above forty years so us'd to play, that should I leave it off now, I were as good ſtop those issues about me, which have been inſtrumental in the preservation of my life to this length of time.'

To conclude, happy is he that having been much inclined to this time-spending-money-waſting game, hath took up in time, and resolved for the future never to be concerned with it more ; but more happy is he that hath never heard the name thereof.

84

Chapter XXXV

The Art and Mystery of RIDING, Whether the Great-Horse or any other

As an introduction to the art of riding, I think it requisite to treat of the taming of a young colt. In order thereunto, observe, that after your colt hath been eight or ten days at home, and is reduced to that familiarity that he will indure currying without showing aversion thereunto, and will suffer his keeper to handle and stroke him in what part of the body he thinkest best, then it is time to offer him the saddle; first laying it in the manger that he may smell to it, and thereby grow acquainted with it, using all other means that he may not be afraid either at the sight thereof or at the noise of the stirrops. Having gently put on the saddle, take a sweet watring-trench washt and anointed with honey and salt, and so place it in his mouth, that it may hang directly about his tush, somewhat leaning thereon. Having so done, which must be in a morning after dressing, then lead him out in your hand and water him abroad, then bring him in, and after he hath stood rein'd a little upon his trench an hour or thereabout, then unbridle and unsaddle him, and give him liberty to feed till evening, and then do as before; having cherished him, dress and cloath him for the night.

The next day do as you did before, and after that put on him a strong Musrole, or sharp Cavezan and Martingal, which you must buckle at that length, that he may only feel it when he jerketh up his head; then lead him forth into some new plow'd land or soft ground, and there having made him trot a good while about in your hand to take him off from wantonness and wild tricks, offer to mount, which if he refuse, then trot him again in your hand, then put your foot in the ſtirrup, and mount half way and dismount again. If he seem diſtaſted at it, about with him again, and let him not want correction ; but if he take it patiently, cherish him, and place your self in the saddle, but ſtay there a very little while, then cherish him again and give him bread or grass to feed on ; then having seen all things fit and ſtrong without offence to your self and horse, remount him, placing your self even in the saddle, carrying your rod inoffensively to his eye, then let some person having in his hand the chaff-halter, lead him a little way, then make him ſtand, and having cherisht him, let him forward again. Do this seven or eight times, or so often till you have brought him of his own accord to go forward, then muſt you ſtay and cherish him, and having brought him home, alight gently, then dress and feed him well.

Observe this course every day till you have brought him to trot, which will be but three at the moſt, if you observe to make him follow some other horseman, ſtopping him now aʌd then gently, and then making him go forward, remembring his seasonable cherishings, and not forgetting his due corrections as often as you find him froward and rebellious ; and when you ride him abroad, return not the same way home, that you may make him take all ways indifferently : and by these observations you will bring him to underſtand your will and purpose in less than a fortnights time.

Having brought your horse to receive you to his back, trot foreright, ſtop and retire with patience and obedience, be never unmindful of your helps, corrections and cherishings, which consiſt in the Voice, Bridle, Rod, Calves of the Legs, and Spurs ; the laſt of which is chief for correction, which muſt not be done faintly but sharply when occasion shall require it.

Cherishings may be comprehended within three heads, the voice delivered smoothly and lovingly, as *so, so boy, so ;* then the hand by clapping him gently on the neck or buttock: lastly the rod by rubbing him therewith upon the withers or the main, in which he very much delights.

The next that you are to regard, is the Musrole or Cavezan and Martingale; this is an excellent guide to a well-disposed horse for setting of his head in due place, forming of his rein, and making him appear lovely to the eye of the spectator; and withall this is a sharp correction when a horse yerketh out his nose, disorders his head, or endeavours to run away with his rider.

The manner of placing it, is thus : let it hang somewhat low, and rest upon the tender grissel of the horses nose, that he may be the more sensible of correction; and let it not be strait, but loose, whereby the horse may feel, upon the yeelding in of his head, how the offence goeth; from and by that means be made sensible, that his own disorder was his only punishment.

You must carefully observe how you win your horses head, and by those degrees bring his Martingale straighter and straighter, so as the horse may ever have a gentle feeling of the same, and no more, till his head be brought to its true perfection, and there stay.

When you have brought your horse to some certainty of rein, and will trot forth-right, then bring him to the treading forth of the large rings. If your horses nature be sloathful and dull, yet strong-trot him first in some new plow'd field; but if agil, and of a fiery spirit, then trot him in some sandy ground, and there mark out a spacious large ring, about a hundred paces in circumference. Having walkt him about it on the right seven or eight times, you must then by a little straitning of your right rein, and laying the calf of your left leg to his side, making a half circle within your ring, upon your right hand down to the center thereof, and then by straitning a little your left rein, and laying the calf of your right leg to his side, making another semi-circle to your left hand from the center to the outmost verge; which two semi-circles contrary turn'd, will make a perfect Roman S within the ring; then keeping your first large circumference, walk

your horse about in your left hand, as oft as you did on
your right; and then change within your ring as you
did before, to your right hand again; and then trot
him firſt on the right hand, then on the left, as long as
you shall think convenient, either one, two, or three
hours, to perfeͨt him in his lesson; and this muſt be
done every morning and evening too, if you find your
horse sloathful and dull; otherwise you need not take so
much pains with him.

Having taught him to trot the large rings perfectly,
which will not require above four or five days; then in
the same manner and changes make him gallop the same
rings, making him take up his feet so truly and loftily,
that no falshood may be perceived in his ſtroke, but
that his inward feet play before his outward, and each
of a side follow the other so exactly, that his gallop
may appear the best grace of all his motions.

Here note, you muſt not enter him all at once to gallop
this great ring, but by degrees; first a quarter, then a
half quarter, &c. ever remembring, not to force him
into it with the spur, but by the lightness and cheerful-
ness of your body let him pass of his own accord into a
gallop.

Helps, correͨtions, and cherishings in the ring-turn,
are as aforesaid the elevation of the voice, and the threatning of the rod, and ſtraitning of the bridle, are good
helps, which you muſt use as you muſt the spur, rod,
and leg, for timely due correͨtions: neither muſt you
ever cherish without desert.

Having made your horse gallop as well as trot the
large ring, then teach him to ſtop fair, comely, and
without danger, after this manner: Firſt, having cherisht
him, bring him into a swift trot forward about fifty
paces: then draw in your bridle-hand ſtraightly and
suddenly, which will make him gather up his hinder
and fore-legs together, and thereby ſtand still: then
ease your hand a little, that he may give backward;
which if he doth, give him more liberty, and cherish
him: having given a little respit, draw in your bridle-

hand, and make him go back three or four paces, at which if he strike, instantly ease your hand, and draw it up again, letting him come and go till he yeeld and go backward: but if he refuse it, let some person standing by, put him back, and then cherish him, that he may know your intention. Thus every time you stop, make him retire, till you have perfected him in these two lessons at one time.

Have a care that the ground be not slippery where you stop, but firm and hard, lest the horse apprehensive of the danger of falling, refuse to stop as you would have him.

When your horse can stop well, and retire, you must then teach him to advance before, when he stoppeth; a lesson that carrieth much grace and comeliness therein. It is performed in this manner. After you have stopped your horse without giving your hand any ease, lay the calves of both your legs hard to his sides, shaking your rod, and crying, *Up, up;* which though he understand not at first, yet by frequent practice, with helps, cherishings, and corrections as aforesaid, he will come to understand your meaning. But be sure you look narrowly to the comeliness of the advancing, which consists in taking up his legs both even together, bending them inward to his body; next, his advance must not be too high, for fear of his coming over upon you; but let him couch his hinder-loins close to the ground, but by no means suffer him to sprawl or paw with his feet forward. Lastly, he must not advance for his own pleasure (for that is a great fault) but for yours, according to your will and command.

If in advancing he rise too high, ready to come over, or sprawl, or paw; give him not only your spurs both together, but lash him twice or thrice with your rod between his ears, and if he advanceth of his own accord, then jerk him over the knees, doing so as often as he commits those faults.

Now the use of advancing is this; it not only graceth all his other lessons, but makes his body agil and nimble, and fits him for ready turning; it is most used at stopping, and then very gracefully.

In the next place you must teach your horse to yerk out behind, after this manner. As soon as you have made him stop, presently give him a good jerk under his belly, near his flank, which will make him understand you in time, though not presently. At first doing, cherish him much, and having let him pawse, make him do it again, till he will do it as often as you will have him: but withall, look to the comeliness of his yerking, for it is not graceful for him to yerk out his hinder-legs till his forelegs be above the ground; and see that he yerk not one leg farther out than the other, but both even together, and not too high, or one leg out whilst the other is on the ground.

Helps in yerking, are the constant staying of his mouth on the bridle, the stroke of the rod under his belly, or a gentle touch thereof on his rump.

If he refuse to yerk, or doth it disorderly, then a single spur on that side that is faulty: and lastly, continual diseasing him till he hath done it.

Now to teach him to turn readily on both hands, is first to bring his large rings into a narrower compass, that is about four yards in circumference, walking your horse therein with all gentleness, and at his own pleasure, till he is acquainted therewith. After this, carry your bridle-hand constant, and somewhat straight, the outmost rein straighter than the inmost, making the horse rather look from the ring, than into it; and thus trot him about, first on the one side, then on the other, making your changes as aforesaid. Thus exercise him an hour and half, then stop and make him advance three or four times together, then retire in an even line, afterwards stand still and cherish him. Having pawsed a while to recover breath, exercise him as aforesaid, still endeavouring to bring his trot to all the swiftness and loftiness possible, making him do his changes roundly and readily, and causing him to lap his outmost leg so much over his inmost leg, that he may cover it more than a foot over:

and thus exercise him seven or eight days, every morning at least three hours, and suffer him only to practice his former lessons once in a morning; in this manner you teach your horse three lessons together, the *Terra a Terra*, the *Incavalere*, and the *Chambletta*.

The turn *Terra a Terra* in the outmost circle of the straight ring, and the *Incavalere* and *Chambletta* in the changes, wherein he is forced to lap one leg over another, or else to lift up the inmost leg from the ground, whilst he brings the outmost over it. This lesson is so difficult, that a compleat horseman should think his horse hath never perfectly learn'd it; and therefore he must continually practice his horse in trading, trotting, and galloping these narrow rings; and from thence to pass them about in ground-salts, as from taking up his fore-legs from the ground both together, and bringing his hinder feet in their place, and so passing the ring as often as the strength of your horse and your own reason will allow of.

Thus you see the perfecting your horse in the large ring will easily introduce him into the knowledg of the straight ring, and that brings him to turn perfectly, and stopping begets retiring, and retiring advancing.

Having brought your horse to this perfection, take off his Musrole and Trench, and in their stead put on his head a gentle Cavezan, in such manner that it lye on the tender grissel of his nose somewhat near the upper part of his nostrols; put in his mouth a sweet smooth cannon-bit, with a plain watering chain, the cheek being of a large size, let the Kirble be thick, round, and large, hanging loosly upon his neather lip, so that it may entice him to play therewith.

Having so done, mount, casting the left rein of your Cavezan over the horses right shoulder, and bear it with your thumb with the reins of the bit in your left hand; let the right reins of the Cavezan be cast over his left shoulder, and bear it with your rod in your hand, and so trot him forth the first morning about two miles in the high-way, making him now and then stop and retire, and gather up his head in its due place; the next day bring him to his former large rings, and perfect him therein with the bit as you did with the snaffle in all the foregoing lessons, which is more easily done by reason the bit is of better command and of sharper correction.

The next thing we shall speak of (to avoid every thing that is not very pertinent to our purpose) is the Turning-post, which must be smooth and strong, and very well fixt in the center of the straight ring, then causing some person to stand at the post, give him the right rein of your Cavezan to hold about the post, and so walk or trot your horse about the same as oft as you think fit on your right hand; then change your right rein for your left, and do as before; continue thus doing till your horse be perfect in every turn. Having so done, teach him to manage (the proper posture for a sword) which is thus performed. Cause two rods to be prickt in the earth, at what distance as you shall think fit from one another; then walk your horse in a straight ring about the first on your right hand, passing him in an even furrow down to the other rod, and walk about that also in a narrow ring on your left hand, then thrust him into a gentle gallop down the even furrow, till you come to the first rod, and there make him stop (as it were) and advance without pawse or intermission of time; thrust him forward again, beat the turn Terra a Terra about on your right hand; then gallop forth right to the other rod, and in the same manner beat the turn about on the left hand; do this as often as you shall think convenient. Though there are many sorts of Manages, yet I hold but two necessary and useful, and that is this already described, called Terra a Terra, and Incavalere or Chambletta, discoursed afore-going. As for the Career, I need not speak much thereof; only this, when you run him forth-right at full speed, stop him quickly, suddenly, firm and close on his buttock, and mark that you make not your Career too long, nor too short; the one weakens, and the other hinders the discovery of his true wind and courage; therefore let not the length of your Career extend above six-score yards; and be sure you give him some little warning by your bridle-hand, before you ſtart him, and then ſtop him firmly and ſtrongly.

Thus much for the War-horse or great Saddle.

Of the Horse of Pleasure

If you will make your horse to bound aloft, you muſt firſt trot him about fifteen yards, then ſtop him, and when he hath advanced twice, ſtreigthen a little your bridle-hand, and then give him the even ſtroke of both your spurs together hard, which at firſt will only amaze him, but if he have good mettle and courage, he will at length rise from the ground by often doing it; if he doth it, though but little, cherish him very much, then let him pause and give him your spurs again, and if he acts according to your desire, cherish him again, make him do thus three or four times a day, till he is so perfect that he will do it at any time at your spurs command.

Next, teach him to corvet thus. Hollow the ground a horse's length, where two walls join together, then place a ſtrong smooth poſt by the side of the hollowness of a horse's length likewise from the wall, then over againſt the poſt faſten an iron ring at the wall; this done, ride your horse into the hollow place, and faſten one of the reins of the Cavezan to the ring, and the other about the poſt; then having firſt cherished your horse make him advance by the help of the calves of your legs, twice or thrice together, then let him pause; after this (cherishing him again) advance him half a score times together, and daily encrease his advancings, till you perceive he hath got such a habit therein, that he will by no means go forward, but keeping his ground certain, advance both before and behind of an equal height, and keep juſt and certain time with the motions of your legs; and if he raise his hinder legs not high enough, you muſt have some body behind, who having a rod, muſt gently jerk him on the fillets, to make him raise his hinder parts. By taking this course, in a few days you will so teach your horse to corvet, that without any helps at any time and place, you may make him corvet at your pleasure.

I need not speak of the Capriole, since it is the same manner of motion as the Corvet, only it is done forward, gaining ground in the salt, raising his hinder parts as high or higher then the foremost.

If you would have your horse go side-long on any hand, you must draw up your bridle-hand straight, and if you would have him go on the right hand, lay your left rein close to his neck, and the calf of your leg close to his side, making him put his left leg over his right, then turning your rod rackward, gently jerking him on the left hinder thigh, make him bring his hinder parts to the right side also, and stand in an even line as at the first, then make him remove his fore-parts more than before, so that he may as it were cross over the even line, and then make him bring his hinder part after, and stand in an even line again, and this do till by practice he will move his fore-parts and hinder parts both together, and go side-long as far as you please; and if you would have him go on the left hand, do as before.

To conclude, these are the most material lessons requisite to be taught any horse whatever, either for service or pleasure, which if taught your horse with care and patience, you may conclude your horse perfect and compleat. But be sure you observe this, that whatsoever lesson your horse is most imperfect in, with that lesson ever when you ride begin and end with it; repeating every one over, more or less, lest want of use breed forgetfulness, and forgetfulness absolute ignorance.

Chapter XXXVI

Of RACING

For the compleating a gentlemans delight in the art of Racing, he is to take special cognizance of these subsequent rules and orders.

First, he is to consider what is the moſt convenient time to take his horse from grass, which is about Bartholomew-tide, the day being dry, fair, and pleasant. As soon as he is taken up, let him ſtand all that night in some convenient dry place to empty his body; the next day put him into a ſtable, and feed him with wheat-ſtraw, but no longer; for though the rule be good in taking up horses bellies after this manner, yet if you exceed your time in so doing, this ſtraw will ſtraighten his guts, heat his liver, and hurt his blood; therefore what you want in ſtraw let it be supplied by riding him forth to water morning and evening, airings, and other moderate exercise. And for his food, let it be good old sweet hay, and clothe him according to the weather and temper of his body; for as the year grows colder, and thereby you find his hair rise and ſtare about his neck, flanks, or other parts, then add a woollen cloth, or more if need require, till his hair fall smooth. Where note, that a rough coat shews want of cloth, and a smooth coat cloth enough.

A race-horse ought to be dreſt in his reſting days twice a day, before his morning and evening waterings; and muſt be done after this manner. Curry him from the tips of his ears to the setting on of his tail, all his body entirely over with an iron-comb, his legs under the knees and gambrels excepted; then duſt him and curry him high again all over with a round brush of briſtles, then duſt him the second time, and rub all the loose hair off with your hands dipt in fair water, and continue rubbing till he is as dry as at firſt, then rub every part of him with a hair-cloth, and lastly rub him all over with a white linnen cloth; then pick his eyes, nostrils, sheath, cods, tuel, and feet very clean, then cloath him and stop him round with wisps.

There is no better water for a race-horse, then a running river or clear spring, about a mile and half from the stable, near some level ground, where you may gallop him afterwards. Having scop'd him a little, bring him to the water again, then scope him and bring him again, so often till he refuse to drink more for that time; after this, walk him home, clothe and stop him up round with great soft wisps, and having stood an hour upon the bridle, feed him with sweet sound oats, either dryed by age or art. If your horse be low of flesh, or hath a bad stomach, add one third of beans to two parts of oats, and that will recover both.

The next food you shall give him shall be better and stronger, and it is bread, which you must make after this manner. Take two bushels of beans, and one of wheat, and grind them together, then boult through a fine range the quantity of half a bushel of pure meal, and bake it in three loaves, and the rest sift through a meal-sieve, and knead it with water and good store of barm, and bake it in great loaves; with the courser bread feed your runner in his resting days, and with the finer against the days of his exercise and greatest labour.

The times of his feeding, upon the days of his rest, must be after his comming from water in the morning, an hour after mid-day, after his evening watering, and at ten a clock at night; but upon his labouring days, two hours after he is throughly cold, outwardly and inwardly, afterwards as aforesaid.

Let his hay be dry and short; if it be sweet no matter how course it is, for if it be rough it will scowre his teeth. As for the proportion of his food, I need not prescribe a quantity, since you must allow him according to the goodness and badness of his stomach.

His exercise ought to be thrice a week, and it must be more or less according to the condition of his body; for if it be foul, exercise him moderately to break his grease; if clean, you may do as you think fit, having a care that you discourage him not, nor abate his mettle; and after every exercise give him that night, or the next morning, a scouring. The best I know to purge a horse from all grease, glut, or filth whatever, is this, take three ounces of Anniseeds, six drams of Cummin-seeds, a dram and half of Cathamus, two drams of Fen-greek-seed, and of Brimstone an ounce and half; beat all these to a fine powder, and searse them, then take of Sallet-oyl somewhat more than a pint, a pound and half of honey, and a pottle of white wine, then with fine white meal knead it well into a strong paste, and keep it by you, it will last a long time; when you use it, dissolve a ball thereof in a pail of fair water, and give it him to drink after exercise, in the dark, lest discolouring the water, the horse refuse to drink. This is an excellent scouring, and a remedy for all internal distempers.

Now after exercise, cool him a little abroad before you bring him home, then house him and litter him well, rubbing him with dry clothes till there be never a wet hair about him, then clothe and wisp him round.

Here note, before you air your horse, it will be requisite, to break a raw egg into his mouth, for it will add to his wind. If he be fat, air him before sunrise and after sunset; but if lean, let him have as much comfort of the sun as you can. Coursing in his clothes sometimes to make him sweat is not irrequisite, so it be moderately done; but when without his clothes, let it be sharp and swift. Let his body be empty before he course; and to wash his tongue and nostrils with vinegar, or to piss in his mouth e're you back him, is wholesom; having courst him, clothe him, after he hath taken breath, and ride him home gently.

To be short, what is here defective in the right ordering of a race-horse, your own judgments may easily supply. All that you have to do, is to be careful when to take him up, how to clothe him and dress him, when and how to feed and water, what and how much exercise is requisite either by airing or by coursing, and his ordering after exercise, and what scowrings are most requisite ; and that I may add a little more to your knowledg, and conclude this subject, take these general rules and instructions.

1. Course not your horse hard at least four or five days before you run your match, lest the soarness of his limbs abate his speed.

2. Except your horse be a foul feeder muzzle him not above two or three nights before his match, and the night before his bloody courses.

3. As you give your horse gentle courses, give him sharp ones too, that he may as well find comfort as displeasure thereon.

4. Upon the match-day let your horse be empty, and that he take his rest undisturbed till you lead him out.

5. Shoo your horse ever a day before you run him, then the pain of the hammers knocks may be out of his feet.

6. Saddle your horse on the race-day in the stable before you lead him forth, and fix both the pannel and the girths to his back and sides with shoo-makers wax, to prevent all dangers.

7. Lead your horse to his course with all gentleness, and give him leave to smell to other horses dung, that thereby he may be enticed to stole and empty his body as he goes.

8. Lastly, when you come to the place where you must start, first rub his limbs well, then uncloath him, then take his back, and the word given, start him with all gentleness and quietness that may, lest doing any thing rashly, you choak him in his own wind.

A race-horse ought to have all the finest shapes that may be, but above all things he must be nimble, quick, and fiery, apt to fly with the least motion. Long shapes are tolerably good, for though they shew weakness, yet they assure sudden speed. The best horse for this use is the Arabian Barbary, or his Bastard ; not but Gennets are good, but the Turks much better.

Having laid you down all these advantages for ordering your racer, from his taking up, to the day of his running, I hope you will make such good use of them, that if upon an equal match you should lay your money on the heels of your horse thus ordered, he shall be so far from kicking away his maſters ſtake, that the nimbleness of his feet shall make it double.

I might here insert the many subtilties and tricks there are used in making a match, the craft of the betters, with the knavery of the riders, but that they are now too generally known by the woful experience of too many racing-losers.

Chapter XXXVII

Of ARCHERY

Archery, as it is a recreation, so it hath been heretofore, and is ſtill in some parts of the world very useful in military affairs, but now quite laid aside by English men for fighting, there being found out more dextrous and speedy ways to kill and deſtroy one another.

Yet it is not so laid aside, but that it is used by some for paſtime, either at Buts or Rovers, and should not be forgotten by citizens, as appears by the continuance of that ancient cuſtom for every Lord Mayor to see the prize performed by shooting annually with the pound arrow.

Certainly this shooting in the long bow is very healthful for the body, by extending the limbs, and making them pliant; and it hath been necessary for a commonwealth, in the defence and preservation of the country; but since it is so little used now adays, I shall abreviate my discourse.

There are these rules to be observed for shooting in the long-bow.

Firſt, he muſt have a good eye to behold and discern his mark; and knowing judgment to underſtand the diſtance of ground, to take the true advantage of a side-wind, and to know in what compass his arrow muſt fly;

99

and a quick dexterity, to give his shaft a strong, sharp, and sudden loose.

Secondly, he must in the action it self stand fair and upright with his body; his left foot a convenient stride before his right, both his hams stiff, his left arm holding his bow in the midst, stretcht strait out, and his right arm with his first three fingers and his thumb drawing the string to his right ear, the notch of his arrow resting between his fore-finger and middle-finger of his right hand, and the steel of his arrow below the feathers upon the middle knuckle of his fore-finger on his left hand; he shall draw his arrow close up to the head, and deliver on the instant, without hanging on the string.

The best bow is either Spanish or English Yew; the best shaft is of Burch, Sugar-chest, or Brazel, and the best feathers gray or white.

There are three Marks to shoot at, *Buts*, *Pricks*, or *Rovers*.

The first is a level mark, and therefore you must have a strong arrow with a broad feather.

The second is a mark of some compass, yet most certain in the distance, therefore you must have nimble strong arrows, with a middle feather, all of one weight and flying.

The last, which is the Rover, is uncertain, sometimes longer, sometimes sharper, and therefore requires arrows lighter or heavier, according to the distance of shooting.

If you want strength, by debilitation in the arm or back, you may reap the same pleasure by using the cross-bow, with which you may shoot at Buts, Pricks, or Rovers.

Chapter XXXVIII

Of COCK-FIGHTING

COCKING is a sport or pastime so full of delight and pleasure, that I know not any game in that respect is to be preferred before it, and since the Fighting-Cock hath gain'd so great an estimation among the gentry, in respect to this noble recreation I shall here propose it before all the other games of which I have afore succinctly discoursed; that therefore I may methodically give instructions to such as are unexperienced, and add more knowledg to such who have already gain'd a competent proficiency in this pleasing Art, I shall as briefly as I can give you information how you shall chuse, breed, and diet the Fighting-Cock, with what choice secrets are thereunto belonging, in order thus.

Of the Choice of the Fighting-Cock

In the election of a Fighting-Cock there are four things principally to be considered, and they are Shape, Colour, Courage, and Sharp-heel.

First, as to his Shape, you must not chuse him neither too small, nor too large; the first is weak and tedious in his fighting, and the other unweildy and not active, and both very difficult to be matched; wherefore the middle-siz'd cock is the proper choice for your purpose, being easily matcht, and is both strong and nimble.

His head ought to be small, with a quick large eye, and a strong back, and (as Mr. Markham observes) must be crookt and big at the setting on, and in colour suitable to the plume of his feathers, whether black, yellow or reddish, &c. The beam of his leg must be very strong, and according to his plume, blew, gray, or yellow, his spurs rough, long, and sharp, a little bending and looking inward.

Secondly, his Colour ought to be either gray, yellow, or red, with a black breast; not but that there are many other colour'd pyles very excellent good, which you must find out by practice and observation, but the three former by the experience of most found ever the best, the pide pyle may pass indifferently, but the white and dun are rarely found good for any thing.

Here note, that if your cocks neck be invested with a scarlet complexion it is a sign he is strong, lusty and couragious; but on the contrary, if pale and wan, it denotes the cock to be faint, and in health defective.

Thirdly, you may know his courage by his proud upright standing, and stately tread in walking, and if he croweth very frequently in the pen, it is a couragious demonstration.

Fourthly and lastly, his narrow-heel or sharpness of heel is known no otherways than by observation in fighting, and that is, when upon every rising he so hits that he extracts blood from his opponent, gilding his spurs continually and every blow threatning immediate death to his adversary.

Here note, that it is the opinion of the best Cock-Masters, that a sharp-heel'd cock though he be somewhat false, is better than a true cock with a dull heel; and the reason is this, the one fights long but seldom wounds, the other carrieth a heel so fatal that every moment produceth an expectation of the battails conclusion; and though he is not so hardy as to endure the utmost hewing, so commonly there is little occasion for it, being a quick dispatcher of his business; now should your cock prove both hardy and narrow-heel'd, he is then the best cock you can make choice of.

To conclude, make your choice of such a one that is of Shape strong, of Colour good, of Valour true, and of Heel sharp and ready.

How to Breed a Cock of the Game

Whatever you do, let your hen be of a good complexion, that is to say, rightly plumed, as black, brown, speckt, gray, grissel, or yellowish; these are the right and proper colours for a hen of the game; and if she be tufted on the crown it is so much the better, for that argues courage and resolution, and if she have the addition of weapons they conduce very much to her excellency.

Let her body be large and well poked behind for the production of large eggs; you will do well to observe how

she behaveth her self to her chickens, whether friendly
or frowardly, and take especial notice of her carriage and
deportment among other hens. If she will receive abuses
from them without revenge, or show any thing of
cowardice, value her not, for you may assure your self
her chickens will be good for nothing.

By the way take this observation, confirmed by the
opinions of the beſt Cock-Maſters both ancient and
modern, that a right hen of the game from a dunghill-
cock will bring forth very good chickens, but the beſt
cock from a dunghill-hen will never get a bird that's fit
for the game, where if you intend to have a good breed
get perfeĉt cocks for your perfeĉt hens.

The beſt season for breeding is from the encrease of
the moon in February, to the encrease of the same in
March. Let her neſt be so placed that she may not be
diſturbed by the sight of any other fowl, which frequently so raiseth her choler that the eggs are in greater
danger; let the composure of her neſt be made of soft
sweet ſtraw, and let it ſtand in some warm place, for she
is a bird that is very tender.

The next thing that you are to observe is, whether she
turn her eggs often or not. If she is remiss therein, you
muſt supply her duty, but if she save you the labour,
prize her more than ordinary. And that she may not
ſtraggle too far from her eggs being necessitated to seek
abroad for food, and so cool her eggs, it will be altogether
necessary for you to set by her such necessary food as
you shall think fit with some fair water; and that she may
bathe and trim her self at her pleasure: in the place
where she sitteth let there be sand, gravel and ashes
finely sifted.

The hen hatcheth her chickens commonly after one
and twenty days; observe in the hatching to take those
newly hatched, and wrapping them in wool keep them
warm by a fire side till the reſt are disclosed; being all
hatcht put them under the hen, and be sure to keep her
warm, and suffer not your hen and chickens to ſtraggle
abroad till they are above three weeks old; and let the

room wherein they walk be boarded, for all other flours are either too moist or too cold.

Let their walk be in some grass-court or green-place, after they are a month old, that they may have the benefit of feeding on worms, and now and then to scowre themselves with grass and chick-weed, but be careful they come not near puddles or filthy places, for they engender in birds of this nature venemous distempers, which commonly prove fatal; for the prevention of such maladies by way of antidote give them every morning before they range abroad, the blades of leeks chopt or minced small and mingled among their usual diet; also it will be requisite to perfume their room with burnt Penyroyal or Rosemary.

Observe to take this course till their sexes are distinguishable; as soon as the comb or wattels are discernable, or plainly visible to the eye, cut them away, and anoint the fore place with sweet butter, till it be whole. The reasons why their combs or wattles should be cut so soon, are these. First if you let them grow till they arrive to their full bigness, and then cut them, there will follow a great flux of blood, and the least loss of blood in feather'd fowl is very dangerous; if much, frequently mortal; moreover to let them grow thus causeth gouty thick heads, with great lumps; whereas if you take them off betime as aforesaid, they will have heads finely small, smooth and slender.

The time of the separation of the cock-chickens is when they begin to fight with and peck one another, till which time you may let them walk with the hen promiscuously together, but afterwards let their walks be apart, and that walk is best where he may securely and privately enjoy his hens without the disturbance and annoyance of other cocks, for which purpose walks at Wind-mills, Water-mills, Grange-houses, Lodges in Parks, and Coney-Warrens, are very good walks, but that the later is somewhat dangerous, being too frequently haunted with polecats, and other vermin.

Let the place of feeding be as near as you can on soft

dry ground, or on boards if the place is harder, as on paved earth, or floors plaiſter'd, it will so weaken and blunt their beaks, that they will be unable to hold faſt.

Here note, that any white corn is good for a cock in his walk, and so are white-bread toſts ſteeped in drink, or man's urine, which will both scowre and cool them inwardly.

Let not above three hens walk with your cock, for should you suffer more they will tread too much by reason of the heat of their nature, and by often treading they will consume their ſtrength, and become so debilitated, that though they have courage enough, yet they have not ſtrength to perform their parts as they ought to do in a battel.

Observe the crowing of your chickens; if you find them crow too soon, that is before six months old, or unseasonably, and that their crowing is clear and loud, sit them as soon as you can for the pot or spit, for they are infallible signs of cowardise and falshood; on the contrary the true and perfect cock is long before he obtains his voice, and when he hath got it observes his hours with the beſt judgment.

Suffer not your cock to fight a battel till he is compleat and perfect in every member, and that is when he is two years old; for to fight him when his spurs are but warts comparatively, is no sign of discretion, for you may then probably know his valour and courage, but you cannot know his worth and goodness.

In especial manner take care that your cocks rooſting-perch be not too small in the gripe, or so ill placed that he cannot sit without ſtradling, or if it be crooked it is bad, for by these means, a cock will be uneven heel'd, and consequently no good ſtriker; and know that a perch either maketh or marreth a cock; to remedy or prevent such faults, is to have in your rooſt a row of little perches about eight inches in length, and ten inches from the ground, that the cock may with more facility ascend, and being up, is forced to keep his legs near together; and here take notice of this maxim amongſt the beſt cock-breeders, that the cock which is a close sitter, is ever a narrow striker.

Let the footstool of the perch be round and smooth about the thickness of a mans arm, or if you will have the best form for a perch, go visit the houses of the most skilful cock-masters, and from them all gather what is most necessary for your purpose by making inspection into their feeding-pens and other places; and let the ground underneath the perch be soft, for otherwise when he leaps down, he will be apt on a rough and hard ground to hurt his feet, insomuch they will grow knotty and gouty.

Of Dieting and Ordering a Cock for Battel

In the dieting and ordering of a cock for battail consisteth all the substance of profit and pleasure; and therefore your cunning cock-merchants are very cautious of divulging the secrets (as they call them) of dieting, for on that depends the winning or losing of the battel, they knowing very well that the best cock undieted is unable to encounter the worst that is dyeted; let others be as niggardly as they please of their experience and observations, for my part I shall be free and scorn to conceal any thing that may tend to the propagation of the art and mystery of cock-fighting; wherefore as to the dyeting and ordering of fighting cocks take these instructions following.

The time of taking up your cocks is about the latter end of August, for from that time till the latter end of May cocking is seasonable and in request, the summer season being improper by reason of its great heat.

Having taken them up, view them well, and see that they are sound, hard feather'd, and full summ'd, that is having all their feathers compleat, then put them into several pens, having a moving perch therein, so set it at which corner of the perch you think most convenient; the fashion and form of these pens you may have at the house of any cocker, and therefore I shall give you no directions how to make them; only be advised to keep your pens clean, and let not your cocks want either meat or water.

For the first four days after your cock is pend, feed him with the crumbs of old manchet cut into square bits about a handful at a time, and feed him thrice a day therewith, that is at sun-rising, when the sun is in his meridian, and at sun-setting, and let his water be from the coldest spring you can get it.

Having fed your cock thus four days, or so long till you think he hath purg'd himself of his corn, worms, gravel, and other coarse feeding, then in the morning take him out of the pen and let him sparr a while with another cock. Sparring is after this manner. Cover each of your cocks heels with a pair of Hots made of bombasted rolls of leather, so covering the spurs that they cannot bruise or wound one another, and so setting them down on straw in a room, or green-grass abroad, let them fight a good while, but by no means suffer them to draw blood of one another; the benefit that accrues hereby is this, it heateth and chafeth their bodies, and it breaketh the fat and the glut that is within them, and adapts it for purgation.

Having sparred as much as is sufficient, which you may know when you see them pant and grow weary, then take them up, and taking off their Hots give them a Diaphoretick or sweating after this manner. You must put them in deep straw-baskets made for the purpose, or for want of them take a couple of cocking-bags and fill these with straw half ways, then put in your cocks severally, and cover them over with straw to the top, then shut down the lids and let them sweat; but do not forget to give them first some white sugar-candy, chopt Rosemary, and butter mingled and incorporated together, let the quantity be about the bigness of a walnut, by so doing you will cleanse him of his grease, increase his strength, and prolong his breath.

Towards four or five a clock in the evening take them out of their stoves, and having lickt their eyes and head with your tongue, put them into their pens, and having filled their troughs with square-cut-manchet, piss therein, and let them feed whilſt the urine is hot; for this will cause their scouring to work, and will wonderfully cleanse both head and body.

After this, diet your cocks with a bread made after this manner. Of wheat-meal, and oat-meal flower, take of each a gallon, and knead them into a ſtiff paſte, with ale, the whites of half a score eggs, and some butter; having wrought the dow very well, make it into broad thick cakes, and when they are four days old, cut them into square pieces. I will not advise you to use (as some imprudently do) Liquorish, Anniseeds, or rather hot spices among your foresaid ingredients; for they will make a cock so hot at the heart, that upon the concluding of the battel, he will be suffocated and overcome with his own heat. In short, that food is beſt which is moſt consentaneous to his own natural feeding.

The second day after his sparring, take your cock into a fair green close, and having a dunghill-cock in your arms, show it him, and then run from him, that thereby you may intice him to follow, you permitting him to have now and then a blow, and thus chace him up and down about half an hour; when he begins to pant, being well heated, take him up and carry him home, and give him this scouring; take half a pound of fresh butter, and beat it in a mortar with the leaves of Herb of Grace, Hysop and Rosemary till they all look like a green salve, give him thereof a piece as big as a walnut, and then ſtove him as aforesaid till evening, and then feed him according to former prescription.

The next day let him feed and reſt, and spar him the next day after; thus do every other day for the firſt fortnight, either sparring or chasing, and after every heat a scowring, which will keep him from being faint and pursie.

Feed him the second fortnight as you did the firſt, but you muſt not spar him or chase him above twice a week, observing ſtill, that if you heat him much, you muſt ſtove him long and give him a greater quantity of scowring. When well in breath, slight heats, small scowrings, and little stoving will serve the turn.

The third fortnight (which is a time sufficient for ordering a cock for the battel) you must feed him as aforesaid, but you must not spar him at all for fear of making his head sore, but you may moderately chase him twice or thrice in that time as aforesaid, then give him his scowring rolled well in brown sugar-candy which will prevent the scowring from making the cock sick; now may you let him fight, having first let him rest four days, observing that he come empty into the Pit.

The Right Way of Cock-Matching

Of all things have a special care how you match your cock; for should you feed your cock with ever so much circumspect care and prudence, it will avail nothing if your cock be over-matcht.

In matching, take notice of these two things; first, the length of cocks, secondly, the strength of cocks; for the length, if your adversaries cock be too long, yours shall hardly catch his head, so be incapable of indangering eye or life; and if he be the stronger, he will overbear your cock, and not suffer him to rise or strike with any advantage.

The length you may judg of by the eye, when you gripe the cock by the waste, and make him shoot out his legs, in which posture you shall see the utmost of his height, and so compare them together, being herein governed by your judgment, his strength is known by the thickness of his body. Take this for a Rule, that a cock is ever held the strongest which is the largest in the garth.

You shall know the dimension of the garth by the measure of your hands, griping the cock about from the points of your great finger to the joynts of your thumbs, and either of these advantages by no means give your adversary; if you doubt loss in the one, be sure to gain in the other; for the week long cock will rise at more ease, and the short strong cock will give the surer blow.

How to Prepare Cocks for Fight

Since all cocks are not cast in one mould, the advantages on either side must be reconciled by matching; and having made an equal match as near as you can, you must thus prepare him to fight.

First, with a pair of fine cock-shears cut all his main off close unto his neck, from the head to the setting on of the shoulders. Secondly, clip off all the feathers from the tail close to his rump, the redder it appears the better is the cock in condition. Thirdly, take his wings and spread them forth by the length of the first rising feather, and clip the rest slope-wise with sharp points, that in his rising he may therewith endanger an eye of his adversary. Fourthly, scrape, smooth, and sharpen his spurs with a pen-knife. Fifthly and lastly, see that there be no feathers on the crown of his head for his adversary to take hold of; then with your spittle, moistning his head all over, turn him into the pit to move his fortune.

How to Order Cocks after Battel, and how to Cure Wounds

The battel being ended, immediately search your cocks wounds, as many as you can find, suck the blood out of them, then wash them well with warm urine, and that will keep them from ranckling; after this give him a roll or two of your best scowring, and so stove him up as hot as you can for that night. In the morning, if you find his head swell'd, you must suck his wounds again, and bathe them again with warm urine, then take the powder of Herb Robert, and put it into a fine bag, and pounce his wounds therewith; after this give him a good handful of bread to eat out of warm urine, and so put him into the stove again, and let him not feel the air till the swelling be fallen.

If he hath received any hurt in his eye, then take a leaf

or two of right Ground Ivy, that which grows in little tufts in the bottom of hedges, and hath a little rough leaf. I say, take this ivy and chew it in your mouth, and spit the juice into the eye of the cock, and this will not only cure the present malady, but prevent the growth of films, haws, warts, or the like, destructive to the eye-sight.

If after you have put out your wounded cocks to their walks, and visiting them a month or two after, if you find about their heads any swollen bunches hard and blackish at one end, you may then conclude in such bunches there are unsound cores, which must be opened and crusht out with your thumbs; and after this, you must suck out the corruption, and filling the holes full of fresh butter, you need not doubt a cure.

Cures for some Distempers in a Cock, Chick, or Hen o' th' Game

The *Pip* is a white thin scale growing on the tip of the tongue, by which means poultry in general cannot feed, it is very visible to the eye, and proceedeth from foul feeding or want of water; it is cured by pulling off the scales with your nail, and rubbing the tongue with salt.

The *Roup* is a filthy byle or swelling on the rump of the cock, hen, &c. and will corrupt the whole body. It is known by the staring and turning back of the feathers. For the cure, you must pull away the feathers, and open the sore to thrust out the core, then wash the place with water and salt, the cure is effected.

If your cock or hen have the flux which hapneth by eating too much moist meat, you may cure them by giving them scalded pease-bran; but if they cannot *mute*, anoint their vents, and give them corn steept in mans urine.

Lice is a common infirmity among them, proceeding from corrupt food, or for wanting of bathing in sand, ashes or the like. This malady you must cure by taking pepper beaten to powder, and mixing it with warm water, wash them therewith. If they are troubled with sore eyes, take a leaf or two of Ground Ivy, and chawing it well in your mouth, spit the juice thereof into their eyes, and it will presently heal. What other infirmities are incident to these birds of game I shall leave, and their cures, to your own practice and observation.

An excellent and elegant Copy of Verses upon two
COCK'S FIGHTING, by Dr. *R. Wild*

Go you tame gallants, you that have a name,
And would be accounted cocks of the game ;
That have brave spurs to shew for't, and can crow,
And count all dunghill breed, that cannot show
Such painted plumes as yours, which think on't vice
With cock-like lust to tread your cockatrice ;
Though Peacocks, Woodcocks, Weathercocks you be
If y'are not fighting-cocks, y'are not for me.
I of two feather combatants will write,
And he that means to th' life to express their fight,
Must make his ink the blood which they did spill,
And from their dying wings must take his quill.
No sooner were the doubtful people set,
The match made up, and all that would had bet,
But straight the skilful judges of the play
Brought forth their sharp heel'd warriors ; and they
Were both in linnen bags, as if 'twere meet,
Before they dy'd to have their winding-sheet.
Into the pit they're brought, and being there
Upon the stage, the Norfolk Chanticleer
Looks stoutly at his ne're before seen foe,
And like a challenger began to crow,
And clap his wings as if he would display
His warlike colours, which were black and gray.
Mean time the wary Wisbich walks and breathes
His active body, and in fury wreathes
His comely crest ; and often looking down,
He beats his angry beak upon the ground.
This done, they meet, not like that coward-breed,
Of Aesop's ; these can better fight than feed.
They scorn the dunghil ; 'tis their only prize,
To dig for pearls within each others eyes.
They fought so nimbly that 'twas hard to know
To th' skilful whether they did fight or no,

If that the blood which dy'd the fatal floar
Had not born witness of 't. Yet fought they more,
As if each wound were but a spur to prick
Their fury forward. Lightning's not more quick
Or red, then were their eyes ; 'twas hard to know
Whether 'twas blood or anger made them so,
I'm sure they had been out, had they not ſtood
More safe, being wall'd in each others blood
Thus they vy'd blows ; but yet, alas at length,
Although their courage were full try'd, their strength
And blood began to ebb. You that have seen
A watery combat on the sea, between
Two angry roaring boiling billows, how
They march and meet, and dash their curled brow,
Swelling like graves, as though they did intend
T' intomb each other, ere the quarrel end ;
But when the wind is down, and bluſtring weather,
They are made friends, and sweetly run together,
May think these champions such ; their blood grows low,
And they which leapt but now, now scarce can go,
For having left th' advantage of the heel,
Drunk with each others blood, they only reel,
And yet they would fain fight ; they came so near
Methought they meant into each others ear
To whisper wounds ; and when they could not rise,
They lay and lookt blows int' each others eyes.
But now the tragick part ! After this fit
When Norfolk cock had got the beſt of it,
And Wisbich lay a dying, so that none,
Though sober, but might venture seven to one ;
Contraſting, like a dying taper, all
His ſtrength, intending with the blow to fall,
He ſtruggles up, and having taken wind,
Ventures a blow, and ſtrikes the other blind.
And now poor Norfolk having loſt his eyes,
Fights, guided only by antipathies.
With him, alas, the proverb is not true,
The blows his eyes ne're saw, his heart muſt rue.
At laſt by chance he ſtumbling on his foe,
Not having any ſtrength to give a blow,
He falls upon him with his wounded head,
And makes his conquerors wings his feather-bed.
His friends ran in, and being very chary,
Sent in all haſte to call a pothecary ;
But all in vain, his body did so bliſter,
That 'twas not capable of any cliſter.

Physick's in vain, and 'twill not him restore
Also poor cock he was let blood before.
They finding himself weak, op'ning his bill
He calls a scrivener, and thus makes his will :
Imp. first of all, let never be forgot.
My body freely I bequeath to the pot.
Decently to be boil'd, and for its Tomb
Let it be buried in some hungry womb.
Item, For Executors I'le have none,
But he that on my side laid seven to one,
And, like a gentleman that he may live,
To him and to his heirs, my comb I give,
Together with my brains, that all may know,
That oftentimes his brains did use to crow.
Item. For comfort of those weaker ones,
Whose wives complain of, let them have my stones
For ladies that are light, it is my will,
My feathers make a fan. And for my bill
I'le give a taylor : but faith 'tis so short
I am afraid he'l rather curse me for't.
And for that worthy doctors sake, who meant
To give me a clister, let my rump be sent.
Lastly, because I find my self decay,
I yeild and give to Wisbich cock the day.

FINIS

PLATE IV

A GAMING TABLE

(Frontispiece to T. Lucas.   Lives of the Gamesters)

MEMOIRS

OF THE

LIVES, INTRIGUES,

AND

Comical Adventures

Of the most Famous

GAMESTERS

AND

Celebrated SHARPERS

In the Reigns of

CHARLES II.⎱ ⎰WILLIAM III.
AND
JAMES II. ⎰ ⎱Queen ANNE.

Wherein is contain'd

The Secret History of GAMING, discovering all the most sharping Tricks and Cheats (us'd by slight of Hand) at *Piquet, Gleek, Lanterloo, Bankafalet, Basset, Primero, Cribbage, Verquere, Tick-tack, Grand-Tricktrack;* and all the *English, Dutch, French, Spanish,* and *Italian* Games, play'd with *Cards, Dice, Tables,* or otherwise.

The whole calculated for the Meridians of *London, Bath, Tunbridge,* and the *Groom-Porters.*

By THEOPHILUS LUCAS Esq;

London, Printed for *Jonas Brown* without *Temple-bar,* and *Ferdinando Burleigh* in *Amen-Corner.* 1714.

A TABLE

OF ALL THE MEMORABLE PASSAGES
CONTAINED IN

THESE MEMOIRS

A Table

The Preface

Since gaming is become a trade, and the adventurers thereat do not all play upon the square, my design in publishing these Memoirs is to deteſt the several cheats which the sharpers use in all sorts of games on cards or dice: And tho' I have here shew'd the true way of playing the chief games in use among us, whether they be English, French, Dutch, Spanish or Italian, yet I would not have the reader think my intention is to make gameſters, but only to inform people how they may avoid being cheated by 'em.

I am sensible, the diversion and entertainment of gaming is the great excuse which gentlemen have for losing their money: Every-body pleads privilege for recreation; which is but a frivolous excuse; for if pleasure be all, why is the ſtake so high? Why is it pursu'd like business, and with all the eagerness of trade? Is the titulation of throwing seven or eleven worth so many pounds as are commonly thrown away at Hazard? Does the gameſter always sit easie? And is he never in pain for a deal or a caſt? Certainly he can have nothing of human nature about him who's cheated with this pretence.

By these memoirs of all the moſt famous sharpers living in the reign of King Charles the Second, K. James the Second, K. William the Third, and Queen Anne, our British nobility, and others, may see how they have been impos'd on by their cheating tricks; but yet young heirs will often throw off a good eſtate before they come at it, and ſtake their honour to ruin their fortunes. No argument has force enough to ſtop the hand that is turn'd to the box and dice. The mischief of gaming does not, as in moſt cases, bring the aſtor to repentance;

but this foolish passion commonly increases with the loss and injury which the gamester suffers : He fancies that the same way he lost, he may win ; and the hopes of a lucky hit that may redeem all, stifles his reflection upon a multitude of unhappy throws : Thus the nearer he is to ruin, the more eager is he to be undone.

However, to preserve gentlemen as much as may be from those cheats and abuses which are too frequently put upon 'em by sharpers, they are not only here taught how to be arm'd against their injuries ; but also (for fear of any imposition) the true manner of playing upon the square at Gleek, l'Ombre, Lanterloo, Banka-falet, Beast, Basset, Bragg, Piquet, Primero, Verquere, Tick-tack, Grand Trick-track, Back-Gammon, Passage, Inn and Inn, Chess, Hazard, and other games ; and if recreation is a gamester's plea, I do then advise all persons of quality never to play for more than they might throw away on any other diversion ; and those of a lower rank not to lose more at a time than they can bear, without any detriment to their affairs.

But considering how dextrously common sharpers can cheat men to their faces, the publication of this book was chiefly to discourage them from gaming ; because it is an enchanting witchcraft, begotten by those devils, avarice and idleness. It so infatuates a man, that it renders him incapable of prosecuting his more serious business, and makes him quarrel with his condition, tho' ever so good. If he wins, the success so elevates him, that his mad joys carry him to the height of all excesses ; but if he loses, his misfortune plunges him into the lowest abyss of wild despair. Besides, how common is it for a man at a bad throw to cast up his eyes, as if he meant to call Heaven to an account for the injustice done him, in not giving him the cast which he desired ! And at other times it is as frequent for game-sters to use such profane expressions, which carry too much horror in them to be repeated here.

It was the wholesome admonition of that great man Sir Matthew Hale, once Lord Chief-Justice of this Kingdom,

Do not play, if given to covetousness or passion; for as the first of those vices is a temptation to utter ruin and destruction, so the other being a constant attendant on gaming, frequent quarrels too often happen at cards or dice: for if a man should play ever so fair upon the square, and happen to win any thing considerable, he'll be suspected by the losers to have put a trick upon 'em by changing the cards or dice; and then right or wrong they'll quarrel with him, more for vexation at their loss, than any just ground of complaint that they have against him; and if he don't fight it out immediately, yet he shall have affronts enough to engage him to meet his adversary in the field next morning, to give him satisfaction for a meer trifle, which he calls a punctilio of honour: and if a man tamely puts up with the insults he meets with, he must never expect to go to that gaming-house again, without being pull'd by the nose, or kick'd and cane'd. Therefore, these being the many inconveniences which attend gaming, it is my advice, that all honest men would leave it off, to the great mortification of thousands of sharpers, who live by cards and dice in this nation, ; and from whom I must look for many a hearty curse, for this discovery of their unaccountable villany; but I wou'd have them to know that I slight their anger as much as I abhor their infamous conversation.

It is an old proverb in this countrey, *Give the loser leave to speak.* I'm sure, for the loss of 2000 l. per ann. at gaming, I have cause enough to exclaim against all sharpers; and though it is now too late for me to curse my fate, yet having a son who is the very next heir to 1500 pounds per ann. by the death of an uncle, I have also upon his account publish'd this uncommon piece of tricking and sharping, whereby he may shun the snares of the destroying locusts, who are lurking at Tunbridge, Bath, the Groom-Porters, and in all gaming houses in London, to ruin young gentlemen, whose honest simplicity thinks so much villany, as does, cannot be shrouded under the diversion (as they vainly think the games they are at) of cards and dice. But in case my son's inclination will, by way of inſtinct from his unfortunate father, descend to gaming, I have laid down such general rules, without any exception, for shewing the true grounds of all games now in use here, that he may easily avoid the imposition which old gameſters too frequently put on young ones.

Indeed I do not only blush with confusion and shame at my own juvenile folly, but horror and amazement runs through my wither'd veins, to see the fascination which ſtill deludes persons of quality and men of distinction, ruin themselves and families by gaming, when they have seen how many good eſtates have been shipwreck'd in that ocean of moſt immense profuseness.

However, if people will not early see this deſtructive madness, by taking my advice, but will persue their inevitable poverty, I shall conclude in the words of Cardinal Caraffa, who, when the people flock'd about him as making his entrance through Paris, in the quality of Legate from the Pope, to crave his blessing; making, inſtead of the usual form of episcopal benediction, or imposition of the hand on the head, several crosses, he bleſt the honeſt vulgar Frenchmen in these Words; *Quandoquidem iſte populus vult decipi, decipiatur*; that is to say, *If this people will be gull'd, or deceiv'd, let 'em be deceiv'd.*

THEOPHILUS LUCAS.

Memoirs of Gamesters, &c.

Major CLANCY, *a Sharper*.

THIS man was born in the County of Clare in Ireland, but the Rebellion, which broke out in that Kingdom in 1641, putting his parents to very hard shifts, they were incapacitated from doing for their only son, as they once thought, when they were in prosperity. When these disorders and commotions first arose among the Irish, the chief ringleaders of them held their place of residence at Kilkenny, where they were constantly visited by, and courted from abroad, particularly from Rome by the Pope's Nuncio; from Spain by Don Diego le Torris, and from France by Mons. Monery, a person so accomplish'd, and so obligingly civil, that all men coveted his company, insomuch that there seldom was a meeting or design of merriment intended, or contrived by any person of quality, but Mons. Monery must be one, who as often return'd their kindness in their own way.

Now Major Clancy being a very fine lively brisk boy, Mons. Monery took him for a sort of a page; in which office he was very diligent, and continued so, not only during his masters stay in Ireland, but for some years after his coming into France, where he had all the convenient opportunities for his education as could be wish'd for, which he neglected not, but made so good use of his time, that he improv'd it to the full, by acquiring the French tongue perfectly, and all that he could gather both from his Latin and dancing-master, or what else the academy could afford; which so pleased Monery,

that he took great delight in Clancy, to whose breaſt he
durſt commit the greateſt secret; nor was he maſter of
that thing in the world with which he could not truſt
his servant, as appears upon an occasion of his maſter's
being oblig'd to travel into some remote part, from whence
he should not return in a long time, and accordingly
leaving him (over other servants) in his house at Paris,
to have a particular care of his trunks, wherein there lay
some papers of concern, good apparel, and some money,
he proceeded on his journey.

In the mean time Clancy diligently discharg'd his
truſt every day, by airing his maſter's cloaths, sorting
his papers, and sometimes fingering his money, only
to please himself with the sight of such a sum in his own
cuſtody, which he could hardly believe, altho' hourly
at the sport of telling. One day Major Clancy being at
his exercise of brushing, he locks the chamber-door,
lays apart each suit of cloaths, with all that belong'd to
it, and putting on the fineſt of them, ſtruts up and down
like a crow in a gutter, then goes to the looking-glass,
where he was so ſtartled at firſt that he ſtept back,
hardly knowing who it was in such a habit; but finding
at laſt, after part of his wonder was over, that it was himself, he begins to propose to himself how happy and
how fortunate should he be if he could order matters so
as to keep all this finery by which he was so alter'd, that
he might appear to all others, as to himself in the glass.
Shortly after, Clancy tells the people he will remove these
trunks to his maſter's country house, where he is commanded to wait his coming: in order to which, carts
are prepar'd, the goods pack'd up, and this faithful
Irishman upon his road, accompany'd by several of his
comrades that went in compliment to see him part of
his way. They no sooner took their leaves of him, but
he ſteer'd his course another way, and bended towards
the sea-side; where meeting a ship ready to set sail for
Wexford in Ireland, agrees with the owner, puts his
goods aboard, and soon arriv'd in his own country. He
was receiv'd by the people of the aforesaid town as a

person of quality. The show he made by his equipage, and the number of his attendance, with his bounty to the captain of the ship, and his seamen, who were not sparing to give a very large character of him, confirm'd the inhabitants of Wexford that he muſt be a great man.

He had not been many months there, when there chanced to arrive out of Spain into the same harbour a nobleman of Scotland, by name the Earl of Crawford. The townsmen resolving to receive and entertain him as became them, made suit to Major Clancy to countenance them in this matter ; who discharged his truſt so well, that his Lordship made a suitable return of thanks, to the satisfaction of 'em all. The Major desir'd the E. to do him the honour to make use of his lodgings till his own were in readiness, which he willingly accepted of, and wherein was prepar'd for his reception a very handsome treat, to which were invited, to keep his Lordship company, the beſt of the town ; then so soon as his Honour's quarter's were ready, they all waited upon his Lordship thither ; and all took their leave, only Clancy, with whose conversation the Earl was so well pleas'd, that he was unwilling to part so soon, tho' sufficiently weary after a tedious voyage. The day following one Mr. Cheevers, a man of note, dwelling about two miles from Wexford, invited the Earl of Crawford and Major Clancy to dine at his house, where much time was spent in feaſting ; and the Major was much taken with the beauty of Mr. Cheevers's eldeſt daughter, to whom he bends all his addresses, with so much earnestness, as if he had resolv'd to dedicate his whole life and fortune to her service. The young gentlewoman retaliating his passion with a promise of marriage, she reveal'd her mind to her father, who said, My child, have a little patience till I make a further enquiry into the matter, and in case I find him to be the son and heir of Mr. Clancy of Eneſtmian, as he says, I will provide him such a portion as he deserves. Furthermore, advising his daughter from matrimony a little, for fear she should run headlong to her own deſtruction, by marrying a man that for ought he knew might prove a counterfeit, she having contracted so great a friendship with her beloved, that she could conceal nothing from him, not so much as her father's advice: Her sweetheart so heinously resented the word counterfeit, that he told her, that if it was not for her sake, that was dearer to him than all other considerations, he would expect satisfaction from any that should have an ill suspicion of his honour.

Now Major Clancy fearing some other discoveries, resolves to remove from Wexford, acquainting his dear friend the Earl with the intention occasion'd by Mr. Cheevers, and finding how apt people were to censure him, he would endeavour to prevent the like for the future, by making known that he was the son of such a father as he professes, and no counterfeit, as Mr. Cheevers took the liberty to term him. Being at dinner with his Lordship, and in a pretty pitch of jollity, the Major calls his trusty servant privately, gives him orders to be gone to a place call'd Ross, and thither to carry his trunks and cloak-bags, with all the goods he had there, to take lodgings, and wait his coming. The Major then had nothing to do but entertain his friends; afterwards calling for boxes and dice, and for his servant to bring him money, whom he knew to be some miles from thence, which his Lordship observing, lent him fifty broad pieces of gold out of his purse, which the Major made use of a while, then left one in his place, as if call'd upon in haste, took horse, and with all speed follow'd his servant. The Earl and the company at play wonder'd at the Major's stay, then calls for a glass, and drank his health, giving commendations by the dozen, till at last the company began to grow weary, and call'd for their servants to attend 'em to their several homes; but before they parted the master of the house appears with a long bill of fare in his hand, which the Earl and those with him seeing, ask'd him what he meant by it; he told 'em, he knew not who to call to for his money; that the Major had been in his house a good while, and never gave him a penny yet; nor did he now know where he was, or what became of him, therefore he hoped his Lordship and the rest of the gentlemen would not see him undone. The gentlemen looking one upon another, were all struck dumb with wonder; however, the Earl was so generous as to pay off Major Clancy's debt of thirty pounds, and then the company parted.

Major Clancy being now at Ross, he there continued his hospitable course of life, by which he purchas'd the character of the bravest man, and best companion that ever came into that town. All the inhabitants there were so desirous to be linked by some title or tye of friendship to the Major; one calls him uncle; another his brother, and another his patron; by which every body is entitul'd not only to a greater interest in him, but also to a large and fair pretence to good drinking. Among this new acquaintance, he was very great with one Mr. White, whom one day taking aside, quoth he to him, You have been no stranger, Sir, to my manner of living since my coming into this place, which I must confess is the same I have ever us'd in all my travels, and is chiefly the occasion of my begging a favour of you, which I hope will prove advantageous to you in the end. My constant expenses have exhausted my stock of money, which you must supply with the sum of 60 Pounds to carry me to Twomond, where my estate lies. I am told that my mother is marry'd to the Lord of Inchiquien's brother, Mr. Christopher O Bryan, and what provision is made for me, or how things may be imbezled I know not, by reason I was sent abroad very young; and for this great kindness I will bestow a farm of 50 pounds per ann. upon you rent-free, during your life: And for your better security for the present, I will leave in your custody one of my trunks, which I must intreat your care of till I return you your money, which I intend to bring you within two months. Mr. White was in no small trouble at this request, not knowing well how to deny or grant it, being but newly marry'd, and that without the consent of either his wife's parents, or his own;

nor did he know what money his wife had, and therefore desir'd the Major's excuse till he went home and spoke with her. She made many denials, but at laſt, being by her husband importun'd with much earnestness, consented, and deliver'd him 50 pieces of gold, which he carry'd to the Major, who no sooner receiv'd it, but he orders a trunk to be deliver'd to his good friend Mr. White. Now the Major proceeded on his journey, but not hearing from him in two months as he promis'd, nor in half a year, Mr. White and his wife broke open the trunk; the firſt thing they laid their hands on was a piece of blue sattin, under which to the very bottom there was nothing but brickbats and clods of earth. The wife seeing her self thus cheated, without any manner of hope ever to be reliev'd, falls a railing at her husband, and from railing she went to fighting with him, insomuch, that the neighbours had enough to do to part 'em.

Major Clancy was no sooner arriv'd at Twomond, but his old acquaintance and friends very much admir'd to see the greatness of his change, both in apparel and education. The gentlemen of that country are extreamly taken with his conversation, especially one Mr. Mac Nemarro of Ralahim, and Mr. Butler, with which laſt person going to Limerick, where spending 8 to 10 days together in good fellowship among their acquaintance, one morning as they were breaking their faſt, the Major's man, according to his maſter's directions, came into the room, and told him, that several of his tenants were coming to make their complaints to him about having so many of the Lord Inchiquien's soldiers quarter'd in their houses, that they were not able to maintain 'em. The Major bids him go to them and forbid 'em to enter the city, and to tell 'em he would immediately go to the commissioners and see them redreſt; with this seeming resolution he rises from the table, borrows Mr. Butler's scarlet cloak, rounded with gold-lace, his fine embroider'd belt and silver-hilted sword, goes down stairs, takes horse and rid quite away.

From hence he went to Galway, where one Mr.

Fanning, a Commissioner of the Revenue, was so taken
with Clancy's company, that he could not be one meal
without him; and in token of his extraordinary satisfaction, desir'd him to command his trunks to his house,
where he should be very welcome. The Major return'd
him hearty thanks, accepted his very kind offer, and
immediately came with his retinue to Mr. Fanning's
house; where he so insinuated himself with the master,
mistress, and servants, that whatever he would have done
was perform'd, and approv'd of by all. Now Mr.
Fanning being upon a purchase of a parcel of land from
one Mr. O Bryan in the County of Clare, he had appointed a meeting at that gentleman's house, upon a
certain day, to conclude the bargain by paying 100
pounds; in order hereto, setting out for his journey with
Major Clancy and other company, as they rid along, the
Major observing the man that had orders to follow Mr.
Fanning with the 100 pounds was not come up to them
as yet, he slacken'd his pace, and waits for him, being
prepar'd with a colourable, plausible story, with which
he accosts the servant, telling him, Your master is angry
and impatient for your long stay; whereupon he sent
me back with orders for your return to Galway with all
speed you can make, tho' you are forced to take a fresh
horse; there you must go into his closet, where you
shall find behind the right-hand leaf of the window,
in a piece of paper, 20 pounds in gold, which he intended
to bring in his own pocket to give to Mr. O-Bryan;
you are likewise to deliver me the 100 pounds to lighten
your carriage, that you may come the sooner to Mr.
O Bryan's house, where your master and we shall all
expect you. The servant not farther questioning the
matter, delivers him the 100 pounds, and rides back to
Galway, whilst Major Clancy went another way. But
not long after Mr. Fanning apprehending this spark at
Cork, where he had lost all his money at play, he pinion'd
him so fast on horseback behind one of his servants,
that he left him no hopes of escaping; then bringing
him to Galway, he there put him into a dungeon, with

orders to the jaylor to use him rigorously: Here is he kept so close under a great weight of irons, and with such slender fare, and so long, that he absolutely despairs ever to escape that imprisonment till he's carry'd to his grave.

However, the jaylor taking pity and commiseration on the Major's afflictions, he allow'd him some ease, by taking off part of his tormenting irons, and relieving him sometimes with bread and meat; and one day desiring the jaylor to fetch one Father Delahyde, the Superiour of the Franciscans, to make his confession to him, he made all the haste he could, lest the prisoner should die before he return'd. The reverend Father came in haste, who is no sooner enter'd the prison, but is struck with wonder at the sight of the Major, whose durance, hardship and pain had reduc'd him to the most lamentable spectacle in the world; he was a meer anatomy or perfect ghost, with so little breath, as was believ'd would only serve for this short time of confession; which the Major begins, having examin'd the whole course of his life, from the beginning to that hour, with such uncounterfeited zeal, so much seeming sanctity, and strong resolution of amendment in case he liv'd with so hearty a repentance, that the reverend Father admired him as the truest penitent he ever met with, and pronounced absolution. Furthermore, he prevail'd with Mr. Fanning to restore Major Clancy to his liberty; then taking him to the monastery he there became a profess'd fryer, in the order and habit of St. Francis, and chamber-fellow to Father Delahyde, who is sometimes disappointed of his rest, by the continual exercise of mortification practis'd by Brother Clancy, who every night to torment and cool that wanton body of his, pulls off his habit and rouls himself upon the cold ground, and whenever he hears the cock to crow, falls a whipping his naked body, till commanded by the reverend Father to forbear thus rigorously to torment himself, assuring him, that to preserve himself, were it but for example, would do much more acceptable service to God, than to make himself away. Moreover, this good Father daily continu'd giving every where attributes of praise to Brother Clancy, who is very well vers'd in the several ways both of the Clergy and Laity. One thing he observ'd particularly in the rules of the monastery, in not reserving for the next meal, yet being dispensed with because of the war, they of that monastery had got a little stock of money together from their charitable neighbours, which Brother Clancy knew of; and finding an opportunity by the absence of Father Delahyde, he goes to one Brother Spencer, who was then their cash-keeper, and told him, that Father Delahyde being with the commissioners, they had promised to do them a very kind piece of service, which was to employ their own servants at the Fair of Mullingar to buy lean cattel for the winter provision, and would give them grass till they were fit to be eaten, to which end Father Delahyde sent me for that little money, to deliver to the Commissioners for that use. Father Spencer believing all this to be true, delivers him the money, being 80 pounds; he no sooner had it but he carries it to a private lodging, where he puts off S. Francis's habit, puts on other cloaths, and bids adieu to his benefactor Father Delahyde, and all the rest of his dearly-beloved brother-fryers; and as soon as Father Delahyde came in, his first enquiry was for Brother Clancy, who being always very tender of him, ask'd how he did, and where he was: Truly, (says Father Spencer) he eat his dinner heartily; but for my part I have not seen him since he brought me a message from you. From me a message! What do you mean by a message? for I have not seen him this day: Are you sure you do not mistake? I am sure, Sir, he brought me your order to deliver him our little stock of money, to be carry'd to the Commissioners, who promised to send their own servants to the Fair at Mullingar, to buy lean cattel, and that they would bestow grass to feed 'em till they were fit for us to eat. God bless us (says old Father Delahyde) I am afraid you are drunk, or have left your senses. How should I be drunk that have tasted no manner of liquor this day? What then? what makes you talk at random thus of the Commissioners, of Mullingar Fair, of servants, of lean cattel, and God knows what? Sir, I know no more, I do but repeat his own words, he may give you a better account, which I suppose he will do when he comes in. But have you given the money in earnest? Yes, truly have I. And do you not know where he is? No, in good faith, not I. Why then I'm afraid we are all undone, for I'm sure we shall never see him again.

Now Major Clancy conceiving it not safe to make any ſtay in this part of the country, where he had play'd lately a great many pranks, he went to Cork, where telling the Governor of that place, that he was a person that had a small command amongſt those gentlemen that could not but be troublesom to him, he would take them away upon good conditions, which were to have safe and free quarter for them and their horses during their ſtay here, a good ship well man'd and victualled, to transport them to their design'd harbour beyond sea, with some money in their purses to serve them upon their arrival at the place whither they went, and which he left to his discretion. Quoth the Governor, Truly Captain I can't but commend your care of your men, and as your demands are not unreasonable, I grant all you desire. The conditions were written, sign'd, seal'd, and deliver'd by the Governor to Clancy, who going with 'em to the mountains, where several gentlemen of good rank, and of great courage and resolution were put to so much hardship, that unavoidably they muſt be very burthensome to the country, and troublesome enough to the neighbouring Garrisons, as having no pay or otherways to live, but by what they muſt take by force from their enemies, their friends not able to relieve them. Now these mountaineers being sadly hunger-bitten, as soon as they saw what articles Clancy had brought from the Governor of Cork, threescore and eight of them call him Captain, and march along with him thro' the countries very safely, till they came to the gates of Cork, where they are receiv'd, and provided for by the Governor, who appoints each one his quarter, where they are to stay till the wind serv'd, there being no other lett, the ship being in readiness, and the money that was articled for, paid to the Captain. Soon after this, the wind serv'd fair for their voyage, the Governor sees all clear, and aboard, waits upon Captain Clancy, wishing him a good passage. The Captain having civilly return'd his thanks, set sail, of whom we hear no more, till his coming with his troop into Flanders: Where some of them asking him for the share of their money given him by the Governor of Cork for their use, he told them that what money was given him was for his own use, and not theirs. But they, not satisfy'd with this answer, resolv'd to have it out of his bones, and so highly threaten'd him, that he was glad to get from them by stealth, and leave his troop to shift for their living; who, not knowing where to follow him, dispers'd several ways to seek their fortunes apart.

The Major returning now again to England, he had not been here before he was committed to the Marshalsea Prison for debt; however, by his cunning insinuations with the Keeper, whose daughter was up to the ears in love with Clancy, he trusted him to go daily out of the goal about his own affairs, and he as punctually came in every night, when to be sure he would not omit the least opportunity of making his address to the Keeper's daughter, to whom he was privately marry'd in a little time; and shortly after, his creditors knowing he went every day abroad, they therefore resolv'd to sue him to an execution to confine him a close prisoner. He declar'd to his wife his intention of making an escape, who had so absolutely settled her affections on her husband, that she would never decline nor forsake him, her fidelity was seal'd with a kiss, the hour appointed for meeting at Gravesend, and he went thither as fast as he could, whilst she went home to rob her father and mother; for they going that afternoon to Camberwel, and leaving her to take care of all their concerns at home, she, in their absence, broke open a chest of drawers, in which she found a couple of purses, fill'd each with 100 broad pieces of gold, which she carry'd ſtrait to Gravesend, and deliver'd to her husband, who, thinking it not safe to be there, fled with his spouse to Holland, where they spent their time merrily, as long as their ſtock laſted: but at laſt the purses being quite empty'd by their extravagancy, he sent his dearly beloved wife home to her parents again, as big as she could tumble, who in a little while dy'd in child-bed.

Major Clancy having turn'd off his wife, is now at liberty, free from any apprehension of danger or imprisonment, travels into Italy, where personating the Earl of Ormond he decoy'd the Great Duke of Tuscany out of 1000 Dollars. Then coming into England with a sham Bill drawn upon one Sir William Rider, for 500 Pounds, a merchant, at whose house he lodg'd, lent him 200 Pounds upon it. Another time as the Major was courting a mistress he had in St. Martin's Lane, and looking out of the street-window, he saw a fellow sitting upon the joyner's stall, whom knowing to be a Bayliff, and suspecting his being there to wait for him, he calls his man, bids him go over the way and fetch the joyner's prentice to him, whom he saw knocking of nails in some work. When he came, honest lad, says the Major, do you see yonder fellow with a leather belt, how it hangs across the stall, here's a crown for you, if you'll go and nail him to it. The prentice undertakes the jobb, goes over to his shop, falls a knocking of some nails, as before, of which the Bayliff taking no notice, he nail'd his belt and a lappit of his coat to the stall. Then the Major taking coach at the door, the Bayliff seeing him come out, leaps off the ſtall in great haſte, and gives it such a pull, that down comes the ſtall, boxes, childrens coffins, and all other things upon it; the fellow tumbles to the ground, with the stall at his heels, so that the aforesaid lumber with hammer and nails made such a clutter, that he was frighted out of his wits, thinking the Devil had been at his back: Out came the neighbours to see what was the matter, they disintangled the fellow, and carry him into a house till he recover'd his wits again : And by this contrivance the Major escap'd the Bayliff's clutches.

One day Clancy went into a woollen-draper's shop in St. Paul's Churchyard, takes up so many yards of cloth to make new liveries, has it carry'd into a coach, tells the draper he has not money enough about him, but send one of his prentices along with him, and he would pay him. The Major rides away, a prentice follows the coach, he knows not whither ; but instead of going to his lodgings, goes into a barber's house, into one of his upper rooms, to be trim'd ; and being shav'd, gives the barber 5 shillings, saying to him, do not think that I give you so much money for your pains you took in triming me ; no, for I have a greater charge to give you, in which I must entreat your care and diligence, for which you shall be well rewarded ; that is, as soon as I am gone, you must call up a young youth that waits on me, he's a little bashful, and you'll hardly persuade him to confess his infirmity, till you force him ; therefore lock him in with as much privacy as you can, and search him, and if you find things be amiss which I suspect you will, pray apply such medicines for his recovery as you think most expedient, and I will pay you well for your trouble. The Barber-Surgeon promises to be mindful of the lad, and so soon as the Major went into the coach, he bid the young man go along with the barber, and he would do his business : The prentice makes a handsome leg and bow, and goes along with the barber, who leads him into a private room, locks the door, begins to preach to the boy, in telling him what a pure stick of wood he was, to follow whoring so early : The lad thought the fellow mad, and blush'd to hear him : Come, come, (says the barber) your pretended modesty must not serve your turn, your master has told me your tricks, I must see how you are. The lad thought the devil had possest the fellow, ask'd him what the matter was, or what he would be at ; that he came for his master's money for cloth. The barber reply'd, I must follow your master's orders ; I am to search you for the pox, and as I am hir'd to

cure you, I will do my duty. The lad vow'd and swore
he had no pox, that his master liv'd in St. Paul's Church-
yard, and sent him with the gentleman he had shav'd,
for money for his cloth. All this would not serve the
barber's turn, but he must be true to his trust, and will
search, so that the dispute ended in some cuffs betwixt
'em ; but in the end, the barber being too hard for his
patient, forc'd down his breeches, and search'd him,
whom he found to be as clear and sound as any creature
could be. The barber satisfy'd himself that he had done
his part ; but the poor lad much troubled for this abuse,
goes home to his master, tells him the whole story,
how that instead of money, he had a good threshing
bout, and a long encounter with a barber, who search'd
him for the pox ; but the master not knowing how to help
himself, could not choose but smile at the passage, and
contentedly sat himself down with his loss.

Besides committing all these notorious cheats, Major
Clancy was a very great sharper at most games, in which
dice are us'd, and to this end he never went without
Fullums in his pocket. The high ones would run 4, 5,
and 6 ; the low Fullums 1, 2, and 3, by drilling the holes,
loading them with quicksilver, and stopping the holes,
with pitch ; or else he would file the corners of 'em a
little, and make 'em run what number he pleas'd ; so
were they very useful either at Tables or Hazard, for
taking of points, entering, or throwing a main. But if
he had none of these artificial helps about him, why then
his hand supply'd those wants by palming the die ;
that is, having the box in his hand, he nimbly takes up
both the dice as they are thrown, within the hollow of
his hand, and puts but one into the box, reserving the
other in the palm, and observing with a quick eye what
side was upward, he accordingly conforms the next
throw to his purpose, by delivering that in the box and
the other in his hand smoothly together.

He sometimes us'd Topping ; which is, by pretending
to put both dice into the box, but still holding one of
'em betwixt his fingers, which he would turn to his

advantage. He was not ignorant in Knapping, which is, striking one die dead, and let the other *run a Milstone*, as the gamester's phrase is, either at Tables or Hazard. And he was very dexterous at Slurring, which is, throwing the dice so smoothly on a table, that they turn not; for which, the smoothest part of the table must be chose; and some are so expert at this, that they'll slur a die a yard in length without turning. Major Clancy in less than two years had won 6500 Pounds at gaming, but at last his long continu'd base practices had brought him to that pass, that few or none would come near him, as dreading his having some ill design upon them; whereby he was necessitated to play at small games, rather than stand out: For debauching a servant-wench where he lodg'd, at a barber's house in Kingstreet in Westminster, and afterwards persuading her to rob her master, which she did of 100 broad pieces of gold, and 30 Pounds in silver, he was committed to Newgate, and hang'd at Tyburn, in 1666, aged 39 Years.

Sir JOHN JOHNSON, *a Gamester*.

THIS unfortunate gentleman was born at Kirkcaldy in Fyfeshire in Scotland, and going into the army when very young, to raise his fortune, which was much diminish'd by his father's too generous way of living, the regiment to which he belong'd being at the Siege of Maestricht, commanded by the Duke of Monmouth, the valour and courage which he there exerted against the enemy advanc'd him to the dignity of a Captain: however, his virtue being not equivalent to his martial prowess, he ravish'd a young woman at Utretcht in Holland; and committed, when he came into England, another rape at Chester, for which he had been call'd to an account, if he had not had good friends to have made up the matter, without coming under the censure of the law.

Sir John Johnson's extravagant way of living keeping him poor, insomuch that he could scarce subsist on his small estate of about 80 Pounds per annum, and his Captain's Commission; he was often upon the product of bettering his low circumstances by marriage; but tho' he was descended of a very good family, yet having not wherewith to turn over for a joynture to a wife that could bring him a great portion, rich people were not willing to bestow their daughters on one that had nothing: Thus being unsuccessful in his amours for want of money, it was his resolution, when he was once in Ireland, to steal a fortune, which was one Mr. Magrath's daughter at Ennis in the County of Clare, worth above 10000 Pounds at the death of her father. The gentleman having a great respect for Sir John, whose conversation was very taking in company, he often invited him to dinner to his house, where privately addressing himself to his daughter, she in a modest way made suitable returns to his passionate expressions, which gave him a perfect assurance that she was really in love with him. Her father at last having some hints given him of their courtship, took an opportunity one day of examining his daughter, with a strick charge not to conceal any part of the truth from him: To which she said, that she would sooner hazard her being for ever unhappy, than once displease him, and that she never intended to dispose of herself without his knowledge and consent. However, the young gentlewoman's father not believing her, he kept her for the future under lock and key, and was as watchful over her as Argos over Io. Now she look'd upon herself as the most miserable and most unfortunate creature in the world, to be confin'd from the sight of Sir John, whom she lov'd even to distraction; but at last she writes a letter to let him know how unquiet her life is, and that if he would come to such a place, at such an hour, on such a day in the evening, she would be ready to meet him, by some contrivance of privately breaking out of her prison. This letter she gave to a cozen, with promises of a large reward for her care in delivering it: The cozen thinking to curry favour with her uncle, delivers it not where she was directed, but to Mr. Magrath, who read it over and over; and so believing he could make some use of it, looks upon the superscription as if he had read it in mistake, and tells her, This letter is not for me, go and deliver it to him it is directed to; whereupon she goes to Sir John's lodgings, about a mile out of town, and gave him the letter, which he receiv'd with a great deal of joy and satisfaction, and writing an answer, dispatches the messenger: Next he prepar'd for the day and hour appointed; nor was he more diligent and careful in his preparation for this meeting than Mr. Magrath, so that when Sir John was come to the place, expecting his mistresses there, he meets a company of clubbatiers, who lay in ambush to wait his being on foot. No sooner did he alight than they laid hold on him, and where he expected ravishing embraces and sweet kisses, they pay'd him with buffets and crab-tree sticks, making him in such a pickle, as never was any poor knight in the like sad condition. They carry him to Mr. Magrath's house, who believ'd himself sure of this booty, and therefore prepar'd to receive him, not as heretofore with a good dinner, but with a pair of stocks, which he had placed in his common hall, purposely to be in the sight of all, both men and women. Here Sir John sat with his legs thro', his cloths torn, his face bruis'd, and his head broken; but the sight was so displeasing to Mr. Magrath's wife, that she desir'd her husband to mitigate part of this rigour, or rather tyranny; for her part she was not able to endure to see a gentleman thus us'd like a beast in her house, and that he might find other means to prevent the harm he apprehended, without enfringing the laws and rules of gentility. These words did in some measure mollifie the unreasonableness of Mr. Magrath's passion, so that he turn'd towards Sir John, and told him how much it was against his inclination to use any gentleman this; and that if he would pass his parole never to proceed farther in this matter, nor give him any farther trouble in it, he was ready to restore him first his liberty, and then his horse and pistols, and all that had been taken from him. Quoth Sir John, Mr. Magrath, It should seem, altho' you are a very knowing man, you never read of the Knight of the Sun, or of his brother Ross Clear, or of Rogero, or any of the famous and brave men at arms, how they suffer'd for their mistresses: If you had, undoubtedly you would in some measure have consider'd me, who of myself can consider nothing in comparison to my mistress; for when I remember or call to mind that what I suffer or endure, is for her, it sweetens all my sufferings. I must confess, liberty is a very pleasing thing, especially after such hardships as have been put upon me, and what I should covet and court. Was it to be purchased either by labour, coin, or blood, I should not stick in such a case; but to relinquish my pretence to my mistress, as if I would prefer any worldly considera-tion before her, I will never do it, nor is it in the power of the whole world to make me do it. Let these fellows and you, whose prisoner I now am, inflict what punish-ment you please, it shall never be of force sufficient to divorce me from your daughter's service. This speech wrought so upon Mr. Magrath's wife, as also upon them that heard it, that it mov'd them all to pity; she never left solliciting her husband till she obtain'd Sir John's liberty; then were all the servants striving who should do him most service; one brings water, another the towel, another his hat, all waited upon him at supper, and from thence to his chamber. Next morning, having his horse and pistols deliver'd him in very good order, he takes his leave very handsomly, especially of Mr. Magrath's wife, that procur'd him his liberty out of the stocks.

Sir John being now quite out of conceit for stealing fortunes for himself, he steer'd his course for Dublin, in which metropolis of the Kingdom of Ireland he had not been above four months before he was arrested for a debt of 120 Pounds, and sent to goal. Here he was under very pressing circumstances, and having a very familiar acquaintance with the daughter of the Earl of

Twomond, who was a Roman-Catholick, he takes the liberty to signify by a letter the bad state of his condition under a hard imprisonment, without any hopes of redemption; and that being reconcil'd to the See of Rome, desir'd her ladyship, with much earnestness, to continue ſtill his friend, to whom he had also an humble request, which was, that she would be pleas'd to command her Chaplain to come to the prison to hear his confession, by reason it related to the great concern of his soul. The lady acquiesced to what he so seemingly desir'd. Her Chaplain puts on his disguise and went to the prison, where he was carry'd to a private room: The door being shut close, he begins to tell Sir John by whose command he came, and desir'd him to consider how he, and all those of his funćtion, were persecuted now K. William had juſt made a conqueſt of that nation; and that he could not ſtay long, and therefore doubted but he was prepar'd for his confession. Sir (says Sir John) I know it very well, and shall not keep you long, my confession is but short; I am sensible what you have said is very true, that you are a Prieſt, my confession is then that I want money, which you can and muſt supply me with before you leave this place, or else I'll inform againſt you. The lady's Chaplain was so ſtartled at this confession, that he knew not what defence to make, for finding all his arguments fruitless, he was at laſt forc'd to give Sir John all the money he had, which was 80 broad pieces of gold and his bond for 80 more to be pay'd at a certain day agreed on. The Chaplain goes home to his lady like a diſtraćted man, to whom he tells what befel him, imputing the blame of his misfortune to her ladyship, at whose intreaty and command he undertook that unfortunate business of going to confess one that was a rank heretick. However, the lady being much troubl'd, as conceiving herself the absolute occasion of this disaster, knew no way to repair this injury but by making her Chaplain satisfaćtion, which she did by paying him his 80 pieces of gold, with a promise of bearing him harmless from making good his bond.

With this money Sir John then did make such a composition with his creditors, that he soon obtain'd his liberty. He shortly after came to England, where being out of all business, he took to gaming, and became such a notable gamester at cards, that he got a great deal of money by playing at Putt, at which game he was so dexterous, that by flipping the cards he would give his antagonist two Treys and an Ace, which good cards tempting him to putt he would be sure to see him, because he had secur'd for himself two Treys and a Duce, which won the game. If he play'd at Whist, he would seldom fail of having all the four Honours when he dealt; or at leastwise deal them betwixt himself and his partner. And also if he play'd at Cribbage, besides securing good cards for himself, both in Hand and Crib, he would always have a great advantage in that game, by nimbly putting his Pegs more forward than he ought. People may think that if they had but a steddy eye on the person they play with when he deals it is impossible for him to palm or flip the cards upon 'em; but indeed they are much mistaken, for look upon them that are real gamesters and sharpers ever so earnestly, your eyes, can no more perceive their slight, than they can the dexterity of those juglers who shew the tricks of hocus pocus, or legerdemain; therefore it is 20 to 1 odds for a man that knows only how to play upon the square, to play with one of these bites.

But as money gotten by gaming seldom thrives with any body, so it did not with Sir John Johnson, whereupon he was obliged to hang on the charitable disposition of his countrymen; and being intimately acquainted with with one Archibald Montgomery, he conspir'd with him to be assisting in stealing one Mrs. Mary Wharton, a fortune worth 1500 per Ann. for James Campbel, Esq; who violently took her away from her guardian Madam Bierly in Queenstreet, by carrying her off in a coach and six horses, and was marry'd to the young gentlewoman at the coachman his house, by one Dr. Clewer, commonly known by the title of the Parson of Croyden. But tho' the bride, after this candeſtine marriage, writ thus to her guardian, Dear Aunt, be not troubled, nor take care for me, for I am very well with my husband Captain James Campbel, and in a short time I will bring him to wait on you ; yet her lodging being found to be at an apothecary's house in Newgate-ſtreet, she was fetch'd away from thence by an order of the Lord Chief-Juſtice Holt's. Before she left her landlord, she said to him, 'Tis true, that what I have done is by my own consent, but however, I cannot love him, and therefore will no: ｉve with him, but I will not hurt one hair of any of their heads. Never- the less, an advertisement being inserted in the London Gazette, which promised the reward of 100 Pounds for any person that should apprehend James Campbel, and 50 Pounds for taking Montgomery or Johnson, the latter of 'em being betray'd by one Angiere his Landlord, he was committed to Newgate, and being try'd at the Sessions-house in the Old-Bailey, was condemn'd for being an accessory in ſtealing the aforesaid heiress ; then being convey'd in a mourning coach to Tyburn, on Tuesday the 23d of December 1690, he was there hang'd, in the 42d year of his age.

Bully DAWSON, *a Sharper.*

THIS fellow was a noted bully about London for many years, and was also as noted a coward, for rather than venture his life on the point of a sword, when he hath met men of courage indeed, he hath often undergone the penance of being toss'd in a blanket, well kick'd, severely cuff'd, pull'd by the nose, and sometimes pump'd : However, such was his impudence, that going very well dress'd, he hath often attempted to court gentlewomen and ladies of considerable fortunes. Thus, having once a good equipage, and pretending to be a person of quality, he presum'd to woo a great lady, who was a widow in the North of England ; but his mean birth and parentage, and infamous course of life, being one day discover'd to her ladyship by one that knew Bully Dawson very well, she so highly resented his presumption, that she order'd her servants to abuse him the next time he came to her house, according to their own discretion. Not long after, this infamous rascal going to pay this rich widow a visit, before he could have a sight of her ladyship, her footmen, grooms, and others gave him such a rough entertainment, that they left him almost stark naked, without hat, without wig, without coat, without wastcoat, or any other thing in the world, excepting a pair of breeches and his shirt, which were also torn almost to pieces: Then after this disgrace Bully Dawson stealing a little horse in Yorkshire, and providing him with a bundle of straw for a saddle, a hay-band for a bridle; in this state he rid through the country to London, where he was so well known, that the people believ'd he had broke some goal, and by that means had made an escape.

Here soon recruiting himself again, among those common strumpets who paid him contribution in Dog-and-Bitch-Yard, Whetstone's-Park, Milford-Lane, or Salisbury-Court, he took another country journey to Sturbridge Fair, where meeting with other sharpers like himself, to whom saying he was upon marrying a gentlewoman in Cambridge worth 4000 Pounds, but that he only wanted so much money as would furnish him with some apparel, that he might not always appear in one dress; they, upon his faithfully promising to reward them generously for their civility, rais'd sixty pounds among 'em, and lent it him. Bully Dawson no sooner had the money *in salvo custodia*, but he bilkt his lodging, disappointed his friends of their expectation, and went strait to London. There at an ordinary happening into company with a gentleman who was talking of travelling into France, and therefore was willing to put some money into a honest man's hands, to save him the trouble of exchange, Quoth Bully Dawson, If that, Sir, will be a service to you, I am sure I can help you, for there is a noble person at Paris that has a considerable sum of money of mine in his hands, who shall pay you upon sight of my Bill : 'Tis the Duke of Tyrconnel, a nobleman very well known to be responsible and juſt. The gentleman hearing the name of Tyrconnel, deposited 150 Pounds in Dawson's hands, who drew his Bill with a very careful earneſt Letter of Credence, with which the gentleman was very well satisfy'd; and shortly after setting out for France, he no sooner arriv'd at Paris, but he deliver'd his Bill and Letter to Tyrconnel. The Duke seeing the name of Dawson subscrib'd to what was given him could hardly contain himself from laughing, wherefore he was forc'd to make an apology, by telling the gentleman, that the many former stories he had heard of that rogue, being brought fresh into his memory by this Bill and Letter, he could not forbear laughing : However, he was very sorry that any gentleman should fall into the hands of such a notorious cheat, and for his part he never had any money of Dawson's in his keeping; therefore he knew not how to advise him for the recovery of his money, any otherwise than to make what haſte he could back again to London, where probably he might find the villain before all the money was spent. These words was such a surprise to the gentleman, that he knew not what to say or do; he ſtood ſtock ſtill like an image or statue without life or motion; but upon second thoughts, and serious consideration, he resolv'd to take the Duke's advice : After a very little reſt and some small repaſt, coming from Calais to Dover, he rid poſt to London, where finding out Bully Dawson, who dream'd not in the leaſt of his so sudden return, he arreſted him, and sent him to Newgate, where he was a prisoner two years, and then clear'd by an aċt made for the relief of insolvent debtors.

Now Bully Dawson had not been many months at liberty, before he went to try his fortune in Ireland, where at Dublin running very much in debt, he was necessitated to quit the Kingdom in a short time. Accordingly he went on board a ship bound for Cheſter, but by contrary winds was driven into Beaumaris in Wales. Here he takes lodgings at the Poſt-maſter's house, where he had not been above an hour when there chanced to arrive a young lady from London that was bound for Ireland; which our Bully underſtanding by one of her servants, desir'd him to acquaint his lady that there was a conveniency very lucky come into the harbour, which undoubtedly she would be glad to make use of, for it was a ship in which he came out of Ireland; a ſtrong well-built vessel, with good accommodations, and very skilful seamen. The servant goes joyfully to his lady, and acquaints her with all that the gentleman had told him; whereupon the lady being desirous to be rid of a tedious, troublesom journey, was extreamly glad to hear of such a conveniency, was it but to save her the labour of going to Holyhead, which muſt have coſt her the toil of another day. Hereupon she sent her servant to desire that gentleman to come to her chamber, if it was not troublesom to him after his voyage; of whom she expeƈted a more exaƈt account of particulars, in order to her transportation; which the servant negleƈted not, but went forthwith to Dawson and deliver's his message. The bully, you may believe, would lose no time to obey the commands of a fair lady, as he found her to be, and no sooner comes into the room, after a kind salute, but the lady desires to know more of those conveniences, as being altogether a stranger to matters of that kind, or any thing that belong'd to sea-affairs. Bully Dawson told her, that there was no conveniency to be expeƈted in any ship upon the Irish Seas as this ship had, which he was extreamly glad of for her sake; and also, that he had the good fortune to be messenger of so good news to her. Some time was spent in discourse till they were call'd to supper, at which Dawson very diligently observ'd each motion or look of hers, and that in such a way as muſt have express'd a passion, which was impossible but she muſt take notice of him, and is probably not much dissatisfy'd therewith. Thus they continu'd some days, the wind being still cross, till at laſt he plainly told her, he had not the power any longer to conceal his affections, which he had so long smother'd to his unspeakable prejudice and disquiet. She, with a great deal of modesty, told how sorry she should be to occasion the prejudice or disquiet of any body; and that she believ'd all this to be but words of course, and that he did it but for his pastime, she being very sensible there could be no such attractiveness in her that could produce any such effect : To which Bully-hack thus reply'd, That if she doubted the truth of what he had said, he should evidence it to the hazard of his life, and turn back from his intended journey to London without regard or consideration of anything, and wait on her into Ireland, with a resolution never to quit his pretention, or decline her service. Thus Dawson lays close siege to the lady, having two friends to joyn with him in his undertaking, opportunity and importunity, which have all play'd their parts so successfully, that the tender-hearted lady was at last forced to yield, but upon the most honourable terms of marriage, which was soon consummated, to the unexpressible comfort and consolation of both, as the bride thought. This siege held about six days, to the expence of many bottles of wine, at the Bully's charge, whose whole study is how to reimburse himself by the help of his lady, whose money, with a considerable parcel of jewels, are most willingly deliver'd by her into his hands as a marriage-portion, with which he ran away : Then coming to London, he lost it soon at play, which was a just judgment befel him for that barbarity : And tho' he had ruin'd a great many attorneys clerks, and mercers and drapers prentices at dice, yet not thriving with all his ill-got money, he grew very poor in his declining days, and being a most debauch'd fellow, he was so rotten at last with the foul disease, that he was forced to seek for a cure thereof in the Lock in Southwark, where he ended his miserable life in 1699, aged 43 years.

Major PEPPER, *a Gamester.*

THIS person was born of pretty wealthy parents, at Ennis, in the County of Clare, in the Province of Connaught in Ireland : But being a younger brother, he was put an apprentice to a drugster in Dublin ; where early learning to be vicious, he addicted himself very much, through the temptations of ill company, to drunkenness and gaming : Insomuch, that losing one night 40 *l.* of his master's money at dice, he was resolved to go the next morning to France or Flanders. Having acquainted the maid with his design, (to whom he gave a Bill to give his master, for the aforesaid 40 *l.* that he might not acquaint his friends with it, protesting, that if ever he was worth it, he would pay him to a farthing) his fellow-servant having so much money by her, lent it him, saying, she would accept of his Bill, and conceal the matter from his master and friends, provided he would never play again.

Accordingly he made a promise against all manner of gaming, and was as good as his word 'till he was out of his time, when going to see his friends, they gave him wherewithal to set up his trade ; and then returning to Dublin, he married this maid, for her former civility of lending him 40 *l.* in a time of need ; but they had not been long in a state of matrimony, 'ere his wife died ; and being again seduced by his old gaming companions, he follow'd cards and dice as much ever, 'till they broke him, and then he was forc'd to seek for sanctuary in England, to avoid a gaol in his own country.

At his first arrival in London, he became a journeyman to a certain drugster, living near Kingstreet in Cheapside, who being a man in years, had married a very young, handsome woman ; to whom Mr. Pepper had a mind to pay his respects ; but, perhaps, being (like the rest of his countreymen) too hot in his amours, she had an utter aversion to his Irish officiousness, and settled her affections upon her eldest apprentice : Wherefore, having no hopes of gaining his mistress's favours, he became a more intent and diligent spy upon the actions of her and her young gallant, the apprentice ; critically marking their glances, smiles and winks, and scrutinizing the nicest symbols of love, 'till he very believ'd his master was very near, if not already, enter'd the kingdom of cuckoldom ; and laying all the gins and snares imaginable to catch his rival (as he supposed the aprentice to be) in a trap, it happened that one evening his mistress feign'd herself indisposed, and would needs go to bed sooner than ordinary, which made Pepper more sedulous in putting himself on the watch for a further discovery of what he suspected : and thereupon, sneaking up before her, as soft as if he had trod upon eggs, he was soon concealed behind the hangings. His mistress was scarcely enter'd and in a posture charming enough to receive her lover, but the apprentice came tripping up stairs, and gave a gentle rap or two at the door upon which she jumpt out of bed, and gave admittance to him that was more welcome to her arms than her husband. Having almost stifled him with kisses, and whisper'd many expressions of love into his ear, (for it seems, being one of Cupid's novices, he was somewhat bashful in encountering those enjoyments) he quickly unstript, and his lovely Venus as soon enfolded him in her arms, and so they began a citizen's galloping pace at this first setting out ; but after frequent repetitions, tired and satiated with sweet enjoyments, after some pretty murmurings and love-toyings, so long a silence ensued, that Pepper concluded them asleep ; and so intending to steal away undiscover'd, he crept from them as silent as a ghost ; but as he was going out, spying a glew-pot over a glimmering fire in the chimney, left there by the forgetfulness of a joiner, who had been cementing the disjointed frame of a great looking-glass that stood in the room, another whim came into his head ; for perceiving their opticks fast closed, he with a gentle hand stroak'd 'em over with the glutinous matter, and leaving them in that condition, he lock'd the door on the outside, and crept down ſtairs as softly as he ascended.

Shortly after, which was betwixt 12 and 1 of the clock at night, his maſter coming home from the tavern, and knocking at the door, whilſt the maid was letting him in, Pepper by the help of a bit of candle, which he had in a dark lanthorn, set an old tatter'd map of the world, hanging on the ſtair-case, on fire; and being sure, that before it could do any harm, it would be discovered by the blazing light, he crept to bed as faſt as he could; which he had no sooner done, but his ears were saluted with the noise of Fire! Fire! This dismal outcry alarm'd the watch, who came thundering at the outer door, and had the sooner admittance, because they might be a good help in case of any necessity. The Night-Governour no sooner advanced with his guard of tip-pling blades, but they soon quench'd the fire, which had done no other damage than that of burning the map; but their leaden-heel'd trampling up ſtairs, with a bounce or two at the door, making the two lovers, the miſtress and the apprentice, ſtart out of their sweet and pleasant dreams, juſt as the door was open'd by Pepper's maſter (for the key was ſtill on the outside) they leap'd out of bed in their shifts; and not being able to see, their eyes were so faſt glew'd, but hearing a great number of voices, verily supposed them thieves and murtherers, who had killed the reſt of the family, and were come to dispatch them at laſt; wherefore, running screaming about the room, as supposing themselves in the dark, though several lights were brought in, in seeking for shelter, they tumbled headlong over the chairs and stools, which Pepper had set out of rank for some such purpose, so that his miſtress's delicate white buttock turn'd up, and she produc'd her ace of trumps for higheſt, by rolling over, whilſt her young amoriſt being hindermoſt, and taking his turn at tumbling, pitch'd directly over a chair, with his head between her haunches.

Those that saw 'em at these vagaries, took them to be a couple of diſtracted persons; whilſt Pepper's maſter putting on his spectacles, perceiv'd how the game had gone, and like a good-natur'd husband, though it fretted his gall, to be privately injur'd, and publickly disgrac'd, hasted to cover his dear wife's naked beauty, which lay too temptingly expos'd to vulgar eyes, by carrying her into bed, and throwing the cloaths over her. Hearing her husband's voice, she was a little comforted, as knowing, now this was not the last hour she had to live, nor the last time she should serve him so, but with hopes of better luck than to be so basely betray'd into such disgrace, by over drowsiness ; yet she alledg'd, she knew not how his 'prentice (who was upon his knees begging mercy and forgiveness) came into her chamber, or how their eyes came to be shut up, unless it was by witchcraft ; which the old indulgent cuckold believ'd, or at leastwise feign'd so, to hide the shame, and hinder these passages as much as he could from being made publick ; nay, at that time he positively concluded they were both bewitch'd ; and then dismissing the watch with money and thanks, intreated them not to scatter any words abroad of what they had heard and seen ; but they were no Privy-Counsellors, for in a short time all the neighbourhood rung of this adventure. Warm milk was immediately brought, which, with much rubbing, struggling and pain, opened the opticks of our blinded lovers, like our first parents in Paradise, when fallen, to blush the more at what they had offended in. Pepper's master suppressing his anger, said no more of it that night, but order'd the 'prentice to his bed, and went himself to another though his wife courteously desired him to lie in her arms ; but with what sincerity you may imagine. Early in the morning he came to his spouse, having broke his rest by a thousand fancies and imaginations running all night in his head, and labour'd to get out of her the truth of the matter, in generals or particulars : But she being a cunning baggage, and having a great ascendant over his credulity, persisted still that it was done by witchcraft ; and she knew no more how it otherwise came about, than the man in the moon ;

wherefore the old man feeling there was no good to be done, he very contentedly, like a great many other citizens, put his horns in his pockets.

It was not long after Pepper's playing this exploit, that having lost 50 *l.* of his master's money at dice, he was forced to fly back to Ireland again, where receiving a legacy of 150*l.* left him by an uncle, he bought a Lieutenant's Commission in Colonel Fitz-Patrick's Regiment, and going with it into Flanders, he quickly became a Captain, and afterwards Major of the same regiment; however, when he arriv'd to that post, being try'd by a Court-Martial for committing several irregularities in his company, he was broke; and then return'd to England, where he was chiefly maintain'd by one Madam Cosens, a noted bawd, formerly living in Milford-Lane in the Strand: and became a great gamester, especially at Gleek, which is a game on the cards wherein the Ace is called *Tib*, the Knave *Tom*, the 4 of Trumps *Tiddy*. *Tib*, the Ace, is 15 in Hand, and 18 in Play, because it wins a Trick: *Tom*, the Knave, is 9; and *Tiddy* is 4; the fifth *Towser*, the sixth *Tumbler*, which if in Hand, *Towser* is 5, and *Tumbler* 6, and so double if turn'd up; and the King or Queen of Trumps is 3. Now as there can neither more nor less than three persons play at this game, who have 12 cards apiece dealt 'em at 4 at a time, you are to note, that 22 are your cards; if you win nothing but the cards that were dealt you, you lose 10; if you have neither *Tib*, *Tom*, *Tiddy*, *King*, *Queen*, *Mournival*, nor *Gleek*, you lose, because you count as many cards as you had in Tricks, which must be few, by reason of the badness of your hand; if you have *Tib*, *Tom*, *King* and *Queen* of Trumps in your hand, you have 30 by Honours, that is 8 above your own cards, besides the cards you win by them in play. If you have *Tom* only, which is 9, and the King of Trumps, which is 3, then you reckon from 12, 13, 14, 15, till you come to 22, and then every card wins so many pence, groats, or what else you play'd for; and if you are under 22, you lose as many. But though Major Pepper was a great gamester, and very expert in palming and shuffling the cards to his own advantage, insomuch that he had in his time won some thousands of pounds at 'em, especially at this game of Gleek, yet he was never rich, for as his money was ill got, it thriv'd as bad with him; for being very poor in the declining part of his life, his mean condition drove him to that despair, that he shot himself through the head with a pistol, at his lodging in Dutchy Lane, in 1696, aged 49 years; and was interr'd in the Church-yard of St. Mary le Savoy in the Strand.

Colonel PANTON, *a Gamester.*

THIS gentleman was the youngest son of 'Squire Panton, living near Ashby-de-la-Zouch in Leicestershire, who having a great many children, their portions were the lesser; whereupon the person we here talk of, coming up to London a little after the Reſtauration of the Royal Family, in the Year 1660, by the favour of some friends, he was honour'd with a Captain's Commission in a Marching Regiment. His pay, and the benefit of his company, were not sufficient to maintain him, therefore he endeavour'd to live by his wits, that is to say, by gaming; and generally having good luck with his great skill at L'Ombre, Basset, Picquet, and other games upon the cards, he won a great deal of money, with which he soon procur'd a Major's Commission; shortly he rais'd himself to a Lieutenant-Colonel's poſt, and next got a Regiment of his own.

He was very extravagant, living in the fineſt lodgings about the Court; keeping 4 or 5 footmen at once in good liveries, and eating and drinking very high, but above all, being always of an amorous disposition, he car'd not what expences he was at to carry on an intrigue of love; as it plainly appears by his amour once with a goldsmith's wife near Charing-Cross, who being young and handsome, and full of wit; seem'd to him a proper object to become his mistress. Accordingly he addrest himself to a gentlewoman who was a great crony of hers, and having engag'd her, by a piece of money, to do him all the service she could with respect to his amours, he was surpriz'd, when the old woman told him the next day, that his mistress was haughtier and wiser than Lucretia; and that, as for her own part, she had been roundly abused for him. This did not, however, baulk the Colonel's fancy, who, on the contrary, watch'd all opportunities of getting a sight of the goldsmith's wife, and never let a day pass without giving her assurances that he died for the love of her. After 2 or 3 months admirable patience under the most violent passion, chance, or caprice made him happy. The goldsmith's wife saw, with regret, that several of her neighbours were drest in finer cloaths than usual; nor had she been wanting in her repeated intreaties to her spouse to buy her new cloaths, in which she might appear shining like them; but he being a saving, industrious man, instead of granting her request, still represented o her the burthern of his numerous family, and the true circumstances of his affairs; assuring her withal, that as soon as the cloaths, of which she had enough, were worn out, she should dress herself as she pleas'd. This answer was far from giving his wife the satisfaction she expected; so she cry'd, and complain'd, and grunted, and grumbled, and would scarce look upon him; but all to no purpose: The good man persisted in his care of the main-chance (as we term it) without regarding either the tears or menaces of his wife. Colonel Panton, who was so confoundedly in love with her, was soon let into this secret by old Madam Crony; whereupon, he conjur'd that beldam, to nick the opportunity, and to improve the misunderstanding between his mistress and her spouse, into a good understanding between her and himself; promising her, in case she succeeded, the reward of 10 Pounds. The old woman assur'd him of her best endeavours; and waiting her opportunity one day, when the goldsmith's wife had been

affronted by her spouse, and was all in tears, she left
nothing unsaid of the Colonel's love and generosity. In
a word, she made so good use of her time, and so well
improv'd the critical moment, that, before they parted,
the goldsmith's wife promised to entertain Panton one
night, when her husband was asleep.

The price of that night's lodging was agreed upon
at 100 guineas. The lover would have given all he was
worth to satisfy the passion that had so long devoured
him. He promis'd to be at the rendezvouz, with all the
qualities requisite, on Saturday night at 12 of the clock;
upon a certain signal, which was agreed upon, they were
to introduce him into a back parlour, where his mistress
would be ready to receive him. In the evening the
goldsmith coming home from Hammersmith, told his
wife, that he was very weary, and would therefore go to
bed betimes. As she had pretended to be reconcil'd,
she made no scruple of obeying him; but scarce had
they been an hour in bed, but, O! Dear, she said with
a deep sigh, I am, certainly, the most unfortunate and
hare-brain'd woman living; I never once thought of a
clean band for you, though to-morrow's Sunday! What
would they say of you and me at Church? I won't
sleep 'till I have got one for you, and then I'll come to
bed to you again. All that ever the husband could say,
to save her that trouble signify'd nothing; go she would;
and he found himself under the necessity of yielding to
the importunity of his wife, who was of a notable resolution. She gets up, the gallant makes the signal, and is
introduc'd into the house; he tarried there the time agreed
upon, and came away so chagrine and melancholy for
his excessive charge of enjoying his mistress, that the very
reflection had like to have made him mad. It was about
midsummer, and consequently day-break, soon after our
lover parted from his lady; and as he was asham'd to go
home 'till he had been shav'd, and his wig adjusted,
he went into a barber's shop. The barber perceiving the
Colonel to be out of humour, endeavour'd to divert him
by all the little puns and tricks he could think of. The

Colonel scarce taking notice of his witticisms, which did not then in the least affect him, occasion'd *Tonsor* to be very importunate, to get out of him what his pain was. The senseless lover thinking to get a little hearts-ease by the bargain, makes the barber the confident of his amour, but without naming names. Cutbeard, on the other hand, endeavour'd to hearten him up, and promised to keep the secret. In the morning, when the barber's shop was full of customers, all were told of this adventure, and all laugh'd their sides sore at it. The goldsmith, who was a neighbour, and very intimate with the barber, came likewise to be shav'd, and heard the story as well as the rest, and seem'd extreamly diverted with it. But tho' he laugh'd, 'twas on the wrong side of his mouth, for having heard all the circumstances of that fatal intrigue, and, upon his return, finding the purse of 100 guineas, as had been related, he immediately ordered his wife to dress herself in her best cloaths, and conducted her home to her parents; assuring them, that he was come to deliver their daughter to 'em again; and, that he would not keep in his house a work-woman, who, in a night's time, could get 100 guineas, by starching a band. Every body admir'd at the moderation of the goldsmith, who was divorc'd from his wife; and ballads of this adventure were daily sung for some time through the streets of London.

The Colonel was (as we have said before) a very great gamester at cards, by which means he won a great deal of money from the Duke of Monmouth, Duke of Lauderdale, and the late Duke of Buckingham; but one day he was cunningly drawn in by Mrs. Davis, (a Mistress to King Charles II.) who being visited by this gamester, and entring into play with him at Basset, she pull'd 150 guineas out of a great bag of gold, saying that as she found fortune favour'd her in the first game, she would venture next what she had lying by her. The bulk of what was in the bag, seeming to be not less than 14 or 1500 guineas, the Colonel purposely lost the first game, in hopes of winning all that money before he left her; but she taking up the stakes she had won, would not play any more then, because, she said, she never took any diversion in playing above one set at a time. Panton was much vex'd to see how he was taken in by a woman for 150 guineas, but how to help himself he could not tell; he took his leave of her with an air of complacency, and went to seek out for a better adventure. Not long after he paid another visit to Mrs. Davis, with whom being engag'd at a game of Basset again, he plac'd her back towards a looking-glass, so that as she held her cards up, he could see what she had, and by this stratagem (still used by old sharpers upon young gamesters) he won above 1100 *l.* in gold and silver, and then laugh'd at her for her folly.

There was no game but what he was an absolute artist at, either upon the square or foul play; as at English Ruff and Honours, Whist, French Ruff, Gleek, L'Ombre, Lanterloo, Bankafalet, Beast, Basset, Brag, Picquet; he was very dexterous also at Verquere, Ticktack, Grand Trick-track, Irish, and Back-Gammon; which are all games play'd within tables: And he was not ignorant of Inn and Inn, Passage and Draughts, which are Games play'd without the tables. Moreover, he had great skill at Billiards and Chess; but above all, his chief game was at Hazard, at which he got the most money; for in one night, at this play, he won as many thousand pounds as purchased him an estate of above 1500 *l.* per annum, insomuch that he built a whole street near Leicester-fields, which, after his own name, he called Panton-street. After this good fortune, he had such an aversion against all manner of games, that he would never handle cards nor dice again, but liv'd very handsomly on his winnings to his dying day, which was in the year 1681.

This game of Hazard has been very fatal to many a good gentleman, of which it will not be amiss to give one example, for the better information of them who are so bewitch'd as to venture their fortunes on the turn of the dice. Suppose 7 is the Main, the caster throws 5, and that's his Chance, and so has 5 to 7; if the caster throws his Chance, he wins all the money was set him, but if he throws 7, which was the Main, he must pay as much money as is on the board: If again, 7 be the Main, and the Caster throws 11, that is a Nick, and sweeps away all the money on the table: but if he throws a Chance, he must wait which will come first; Lastly, if 7 be the Main, and the Caster throws Ames-Ace, Deuce-Ace or 12, he is out; but if he throws from 4 to 10, he has a Chance, though they two are accounted the worst Chances on the Dice, as 7 is reputed the best and easiest Main to be flung: Thus it is in 8 or 6, if either of them be the Main, and the Caster throws either 4, 5, 7, 9, or 10, this is his Chance, which if he throws first he wins, or otherwise he loses; if he throws 12 to 8, or 6 to the same Cast with the Main he wins; but if Ames-Ace or Deuce-Ace, to all he loses; or if 12 when the Main is either 5 or 9: And it is to be noted, that nothing nicks 5 but 5, nor nothing 9 but 9.

CHARLES HEATON, *a Gamester*.

THIS celebrated sharper was born at Rumsey in Hampshire, of very good parents, who put him apprentice to a chyrurgeon in London; but forfeiting his indentures by marrying his master's maid, two years before his time was expired, he in a short time became an absolute rake; and burying his wife in less than six months after Hymen had brought them to perform his ceremonies, he then had such an aversion to matrimony (as confining a man to one woman, if he would observe his nuptial contract) that he made it his *Summum bonum* in this life, to live on the reversion of many of the female sex.

But having by this unaccountable course of life been often clap'd, pox'd, flux'd and salivated, he design'd to have married again, and fixed his affections on one

Madam De-Coster, a great heiress; but he could not justify his pretensions, either by wit, or birth, or fortune. All that seem'd to favour him was, that the gentlewoman being very ugly, he supposed, she would be the more willing to bestow herself, and all she had upon a handsome man, as he thought himself; and was (I must needs say) in some few respects.

In vain had he made use of his eyes and billets-doux! and seeing she slighted the talents, by which he thought to render himself agreeable, he resolv'd to have recourse again to living upon women of the town. Accordingly, he stood bully to one Madam Crisp, who was in Newgate, for desiring a Lieutenant to kill a blackamoor, for stealing her lap-dog; and the gentleman to shew his honour, did stab the negro, as he was pissing at Temple-Bar. Charles was first invited to do this great piece of bravery, but thinking it beneath such a good Christian as he was to fight an Infidel, as he supposed him to be, because he had a collar about his neck, Madam Crisp cast him off; so being obliged to seek for fresh quarters, he then, by the good word of one Newman, got familiarly acquainted with one Madam Clerk, who ply'd at a Coffee-house near the Fleet-Prison.

He had not stood kick and cuff long for this *Bona Roba*, who danc'd incomparably well, and was shewing her activity at a Musick-Booth in Bartholomew-Fair, when it happen'd, that the late Earl of D—— passing by the booth, she beckon'd to his Lordship, who perceiving her to be a very pretty woman, he had the curiosity to go up, and speak to her, and finding her discourse to be very taking, he was easily persuaded to enter the place of iniquity. As it was almost night, his Lordship heard in a very little time, a consort of organs, violins and bas-viols, in the booth, whither his mistress conducted his honour, which was so illuminated, that he began to fancy himself in a Popish Chapel. Among abundance of damsels, who were present in that illustrious rendezvouz, his Lordship found none so charming as Madam Clerk, that had introduced him. She was, indeed, full of wit, and very engaging in her discourse, not only giving him a brief history of her genealogy, but also assuring him, that she was descended of one of the ancientest families in Ireland. She also told his Lordship, that misfortunes had reduced her to the necessity of leading the life she did; adding, that it was sore against her will, that she had pitched upon a course of life so contrary and derogatory to her birth. In a word, his Lordship found the courtezan so agreeable, that he promis'd to come and see her again the next day. I must shew you then, said she, where I live, which is hard-by; but as for this place, I am only here by chance. Thereupon his Lordship paid for what they had call'd in, which was about a guinea, and went with her, to see where she lodg'd. Nor was it far from the place where he met her, as being but in Hosier-lane in Smithfield. Being come to the door, she press'd the Earl to go in, for one moment, which he unfortunately agreed to. His Lordship found the rooms very handsomly furnish'd, and, therefore made no scruple to attend her to her chamber, where there was a good fire. As soon as he had enter'd the room, she desir'd him to sit down, and order'd the maid to bring up a bottle of wine, saying, his Lordship should tast her Champagne. Far from supposing himself in the least danger, his Honour was as easie as possible in that treacherous strumpet's company, when all of a sudden, he heard, in the next chamber to that which he and she were in, a kind of confus'd noise of mens and womens voices together. Asking what could be the matter, Madam Clerk reply'd, that it was only two gentlewomen that lodg'd with her; and that as for the men, she suppos'd they were some friends come to see them. But alas! how far was this from truth! and what a dreadful danger did incur in that execrable house! His Lordship never made a narrower escape in his life, than thence; for, soon after he had ask'd that she-devil, what men they were, Charles Eaton with 4 or 5 other ruffians, disguis'd in seamens habits, enter'd the chamber; and Charles coming first up to his Lordship,

ask'd him, but in a very surly tone, What he did there?
The Earl answer'd him, trembling, that he came thither,
only because that gentlewoman had invited him to walk
in; and turning himself towards Madam Clerk, to desire
her to witness what he said to be true, she had given him
the slip, and was gone. This convinc'd his Lordship
that he was betray'd, and that it now only remain'd for
him to recommend himself to God, and beseech him to
deliver him out of the hands of those villains: and as in
his extream confusion, he cry'd out aloud, O my God!
quoth Charles Eaton to his Lordship, with an air of
insolence, this is not a place for thee to say thy prayers
in; thou shouldst have done that before thou hadst
come hither, that he might have kept thee away; but
now that we have thee here, we shall make thee pay
sufficient Import before thou art Exported. With that
all the villains fell upon his Lordship, some taking him
by the hands, others by the feet, and began to strip his
honour. When he was stark naked as ever he was born,
bound him in a chair, and Charles making a signal to
the rest, out pulls each of them a butcherly knife. At
that horrid sight, his Lordship cry'd out as loud as he
could baul, but all to no purpose, for blindfolding,
gagging and trying his hands behind him, they carried
away his cloaths, a gold watch, and a purse, in which
was 80 guineas, and never any of 'em came to that place
again.

A little after this villanous transaction, Madam Clerk
dying of the pox in the hospital at Kingsland, this
notorious fellow listed himself in Colonel Braddock's
Company in the Second Regiment of Foot-Guards,
commanded then by the honourable Lord Cutts; but
his pay being not sufficient to maintain him, he gave it
his officer, that he might have the liberty of being duty-
free, and so going about the town with *Luck in a Bag*,
in company with Tom Flack, Ned Dalton, Joseph Johnson, Isaac Peterson, Jack Neeves, Tom Ganthem, Humphry Jackson, Jack Hawkins, Solomon Vesey, a poulterer
formerly in Clare-Market, and other sharpers upon that

cheating lay, Cups and Balls, Buckle and Thong, and Preaching the Parson, he got a great deal of money; but being also a great gamester at cards, he bit a great many people of very considerable sums, by letting them shuffle the cards as long as they please, and he would cut to a certain card pitch'd on, as the Ace of Clubs, King of Diamonds, Queen of Hearts, or Knave of Spades, of which he would never miss, because a fine nine-size needle being run into the edges of one of the cards, so that the head thereof was but just out, whenever he cut, he felt for the aforesaid needle, and then turn'd up the card which he laid on.

Besides, Charles Eaton being in his time the best dancer in England for the dance call'd Cheshire-Rounds, he did not only get a great deal of money by dancing in the most noted Musick-Houses about town, but also in the Theatres in Dorset-Garden and Drury-Lane; for which he was accounted so famous, that he was honour'd with having his name inserted in the Play-House bills, whenever he was to make any performance in that kind. However, his extravagancy exceeding the gains of any of his projects, he was very much in debt, for which he was often arrested, and many times sent to goal; insomuch that being quite reduced to a very low condition, by being often in trouble, he chose at last to go over, with a detachment drawn out of the Second Regiment of Foot-Guards, to Flanders; there he set up a Pass-Bank, and picking up some money, was disposed to leave the army by desertion. Accordingly he ran away from his colours; but being apprehended at Rotterdam, he was carried back to Ghent, where being confin'd for near four months, with no other subsistence than bread and water, unless he had wherewithal to supply himself with better diet, he was then try'd by a Court-Marshal, and being condemn'd, was shot in 1702, aged 34 years.

Monsieur SHEVALIER, *Captain of the Grenadiers in the firſt Regiment of Foot-Guards.*

THIS person was born of pretty wealthy parents, living at Roan, an inland town, situated in that part of France call'd Upper Normandy. In his younger years he was page to the Dutchess of Orleans, but growing too big for that service, he was resolv'd to seek his fortune abroad, and accordingly came to England, where his French smirks and Spanish shrugs recommended him to the favour of some persons of quality, who are too apt to prefer a foreigner before one of their own country, he became an Ensign in the firſt Regiment of Foot-Guards; but his pay being not sufficient to maintain him, he was obliged to become a gameſter, whereby, after he had learnt the sharping part of play, he got such an income as could keep an equipage much above his station.

Being one day at the Groom-Porters, he was so fortunate as to win above 2300 guineas of several noblemen, all whom I could name, but that it is not necessary. Among the bubbles, who had the misfortune to fall into his hands, was a certain person, who had loſt a larger sum of money than suited with his conveniency to pay presently. The nobleman ask'd time; in the granting of which, after a very courteous manner, Shevalier shew'd himself so obliging, that the other, about a fortnight after, to let him see that he had taken notice of his civility, and thought himself beholden to him, came one morning to Shevalier, and told him that he had a Company of Foot to dispose of; if it was worth his while, it should be at his service. Never was proffer more acceptable to Shevalier than this; With a thousand proteſtations, as we may suppose, of being his Lordship's moſt humble and devoted servant for ever, he ſtruck the iron whilſt it was hot; and with gratitude in his countenance, laying hold of the opportunity, he had his commission sign'd the next day.

One might wonder, since Shevalier had found out so beneficial a calling as gaming, he should be so over-joy'd at this preferment, for fear that one day or other it would draw him from court, where his pleasure as well as his livelihood lay; but it seems his captainship fell to him in time of peace, and when officers did what they pleas'd: Besides, it was an admirable cloak to shelter under. Shevalier understood the world entirely well; he knew that a man of no employ, or any visible income, that appears and lives like a gentleman, and makes gaming his constant business, is always suspected of not playing for diversion only; and, in short, of knowing and practising more than he should do. He likewise foresaw, that his gains would not be always the same; it was possible he might be found out; or, if not, by fleecing great numbers, every body would shun him in time.

Shevalier was very glad of having this certainty to trust to; and truly he forgot nothing of what by false musters, or robbing his men, could be squeez'd out of his Company; and now, being perpetually us'd to noise and great company, he thought it death to be in a place where there should be no gaming, which brought the most grist to his mill. But one time he won 20 guineas of mad Ogle the Life-guard man; who understanding this French officer had bit him, call'd him to an account, demanding either his money back, or satisfaction in the field: Shevalier having always courage enough to main-tain what he did, chose the latter; however, tho' Ogle fought him in Hyde-Park in his jack-boots, yet was he so successful as to wound his antagonist through the sword-arm, and obtain his money again. After this they were always good friends, and very great cronies to-gether; playing (as being both arch sparks) several comical tricks, one of which being very remarkable, take an account thereof as follows.

Shevalier and Ogle meeting one day in Fleetstreet, they justled for the wall, which they strove to take of each other; whereupon words arising between 'em, they drew their swords, and push'd very hard at one another; but being prevented by the great croud which was gather'd about 'em from doing any mischief, Ogle seeming still to resent the affront, he cry'd to Shevalier, If you are a gentleman, pray follow me. The French hero accepted the challenge, so going together up Bell-yard and through Lincolns-Inn, with some hundreds of the mob at their heels, as soon as the two seeming adversaries were got into Lincolns-Inn-Fields, they both fall a running as fast as they could, with their swords drawn, up towards the Lord Powis's house, which was then building, and leapt into a saw-pit. The rabble presently ran after them, to part 'em again, and fear'd mischief would be done before they should get up to 'em; but when they were arriv'd at the saw-pit, they saw Shavalier go to one end of it, and Ogle to the other, with their breeches both down a s———ing together as lovingly as if they had never fell out at all. But the mob was so incensed at this trick upon 'em, that had not some gentlemen accidentally come by, who knew Shevalier and Ogle, they (but by their entreaty) had knock'd 'em both on the head with brick-bats.

Shevalier has an excellent knack at cogging a die, and such a command in the throwing, that chalking a circle on a table, with its circumference no bigger than a shilling, he would at above the distance of 3 foot throw a dice exactly into it, which should be either Ace, Deuce, Trey, or what he pleas'd. Although the right honourable Aubre de Vere, the late Earl of Oxford was a great gamester, and often in a morning standing an hour or two in his shirt, throwing a Main for a supposed friend, and a Chance for himself, he would, according to the success of this way of experiencing his sole pleasure and delight, go presently to the Groom-Porters with hopes of good luck on his side, yet would Monsieur Shevalier by his dexterity at dice convince his Lordship, that no certainty relies on the good success which may accrue to a person that plays in jest by himself: for he always beat the Earl, from whom he had at times won several hundreds of pounds; and that Peer, who lost most of his estate at gaming before he died, ought to be a warning to all other noblemen how they impoverish themselves and their families to enrich sharpers.

Indeed Monsieur Shevalier could tell how to load dye with quicksilver, as well as a fuzee with powder and ball; but having been sometimes detected in his sharping tricks, he hath been obliged to look on the point of the sword, with which being often wounded, latterly he would decline fighting if there was any way; for once having chous'd Mr. Levingstone, Page of Honour to King James the Second, out of 50 guineas, at Locket's Ordinary, he gave our French Captain a challenge to fight him next day, behind Mountague-House. He seemingly accepted it, and next morning Mr. Levingston going to Shevalier's lodging, whom he found in bed, put him in mind of what he was come about; in the mean while, Shevalier with the greatest air of courage imaginable, arose, and having drest himself, said to Levingstone, Me must beg de favour of you to stay a few minutes, Sir, whilst I step into my closet dere, for as me be going about one desperate piece of work, it is very requisite for me to say a small prayer or two. Accordingly, Mr. Levingstone acquiescing to his desire, he was willing to stay, whilst Shevalier went into his closet; but hearing the conclusion of his prayer to end with these, or the like words, Me verily believe spilling man's blood is one ver' great sin, wherefore I hope all de Saints will interceed vid de Virgin for my once killing Monsieur Des Blotieres at Rochel; my killing Chevalier de Cominge at Brest; killing Major de Tierceville at Lions; killing Lieutenant de Macche Falliere at Paris; with half a dozen other men in France; so being also sure of killing him I'm now going to fight, me hope his forcing me to shed his blood will not be laid to my charge. Quoth Levingstone to himself, And are you then so sure of me? But I'll engage you shan't, for if you are such a devil at killing of men, you shall go and fight by your self, and be d——nd.

Whereupon, making what haste he could away, shortly after, Monsieur Shevalier, coming out of his closet, and finding Levingstone not in the room, he was very glad of his absence.

A little after this being call'd to account by another gentleman, for affronting him at the Groom-Porters, they met at the appointed hour in Chelsea-Fields, where the challenger demanding satisfaction for the abuse offer'd him over night; quoth Monsieur Chevalier, Pray Sir, for vat do we fight? The gentleman reply'd, For Honour and Fame. Whereupon Shevalier pulling a halter out of his pocket, and throwing it betwixt him and his antagonist, Begar, (quoth he again) we only fight for dis one piece of rope, so e'en win it and wear it. Which jest prevailing much over the gentleman's passion, they put up their swords, and went home together very good friends.

Monsieur Shevalier continuing his sharping courses for about fourteen years, he ran that wicked race, sometimes with much, sometimes with little money, but always as lavish in spending, as he was covetous in getting it: till at last, King James ascending the British throne, the Duke of Monmouth, a little after his wearing the Crown, raised a rebellion in the West of England; where, in a skirmish between the Royallists and the Rebels, Monsieur Shevalier was shot in the back, and the wound thought to be given by one of his own men, to whom he had been always a most cruel harsh Officer, whilst a Captain of the Grenadiers in the first Regiment of Foot-Guards. He was sensible himself, how he came by this misfortune, for when he was carried to his tent mortally wounded, and the Duke of Albemarl came to visit him, quoth he to his Grace, Dis was none of my foe dat shot me in de back. By G—d, (reply'd the Duke) he was none of your friend that shot you. So dying within few hours after, he was interr'd in a field near Philips-Norton-Lane, much unlamented by all that knew him.

Count CONINGSMARK.

CHARLES JOHN, Count Coningsmark, was born at Dresden, the antient seat of the Dukes of Saxony, standing in the country of Misnia, and contains in compass about the walls, the circuit of two English miles. Of six sons, he was the youngest brother; but it being the custom of that country to call all the sons, though ever so many, by the title enjoy'd by the father, he assum'd the dignity of a Count wherever he went; but oftentimes wanting money to support that character, he gam'd very much to maintain his grandeur, and won a great many thousand pounds beyond sea, especially of the Duke of Monmouth, when he was General of the English forces at the Siege of Maestricht.

From him he got 2500 guineas and pistoles in one night, at the play of Hazard or Dice; moreover, he was an excellent gamester at cards, as too many persons of the highest rank found to their cost, when he came into England; where, for his being a very handsome man, of a good shape and mien, he found a favourable acceptance among some ladies at Court; though his acquired parts were not extraordinary, yet his natural ones were none of the least, and which were much improv'd by his travels through Holland, France, Spain and Italy, in which last country he arriv'd to the greatness of a general in the Venetian army. After his arrival in the metropolis of this island, he was a constant visiter of the Dutchess of Mazarine, at whose lodgings there being perpetual gaming, this foreign Count pick'd up a good livelihood; for having been among sharpers abroad, he had learnt the sharping part of play himself, by which means he kept a very handsome equipage, and liv'd in splendor upon other men's losses, whose covetous disposition will not let them see their folly, which many times proves their utter ruin. I think the incomparable Ben. Johnson, in his excellent comedy, call'd *The Alchymist*, hath truly touch'd on such unhappy miserable persons; where, in the fourth act, introducing all the cheated people, opposing the man that would open their eyes, he shews covetousness the motive of the actions of the puritan, the epicure, the gamester, and the trader, whose endeavours, how differently soever they seem to tend, center only in that one point of gain. It is the greatest madness in the world, for a nobleman to stake his honour and riches, against dishonour and poverty; however, he's so intoxicated with the vain recreation of dice and cards, as to venture distinction against infamy, and abundance against want; in a word, all that's desirable, against all that's to be avoided. Moreover, how often does it fall out, to see a common sharper in competition with a gentleman of the first rank; though all mankind is convinced, that a fighting gamester is only a pickpocket, with the courage of a highway-man. Thus one cannot with any patience reflect on the unaccountable jumble of persons and things in this town and nation, which occasions very frequently, that a brave man falls by a hand below that of the common hangman, and yet his executioner escapes the clutches of the other.

Now Count Coningsmark, by his good fortune generally at play and a maintenance from several women of quality, making a very considerable figure in his own person and retinue, his arrogance prompted him to court the Lady Ogle, the daughter of the Earl of Northumberland, who being a great heiress, wanted not many suitors; among whom was Thomas Thynn, Esq: worth ten thousand pounds per annum, and who, by her friends consent, obtain'd her Ladiship for his wife; and our Count being this frustrated in his aim, it may be reasonably suppos'd to revenge the loss of this great fortune, he contriv'd the murder of that unfortunate gentleman, the manner whereof take as follows.

On Sunday, the 12th of February, 1681, about a quarter after eight at night, the aforesaid Thomas Thynn, Esq; coming up St. James's-Street, from the Countess of Northumberland's house, at the lower end of St. Alban's-street, Captain Christopher Uratz, a German; Lieutenant John Stern, another German; and Charles George Boroski, a Polander, stopping his coach, they fired a blunderbuss therein, and shot in four bullets, which entring his body, tore his guts, wounded his liver, and stomach, and gall, broke one of his ribs, and wounded the great bone below, of which wounds he died the next day; when the three assassines being apprehended, and committed to Newgate, as also Count Coningsmark, they came on their trial before the Lord Chief-Justice Pemberton, at the Old-Bailey, on Tuesday, the 28th of February following. Boroski own'd that he fired the blunderbuss, but did not know how many bullets there were, because he did not charge it, but he could tell who did: However, the Lord Chief-Justice said, that would not be material, because his evidence could charge no body but himself. Captain Uratz confess'd, that he came into England with a design to fight Squire Thynn, having sent him challenges by post from Holland, for speaking ill of Count Coningsmark, (who was his friend) and of himself, at Richmond, and that he could never receive satisfaction, and therefore he came to force him to fight, and took the other two with him, as his servants, Squire Thynn being a gentleman that had always a great many servants about him to carry him off, in case he should be knock'd on the head, or be hindred from escaping, resolving to make a rencounter of it, because duels, he understood, were forbid in this kingdom. He farther own'd that he did stop the coach, but that the Polonian fired by mistake, he not bidding him fire, unless he should be hindred from fighting, or making his escape. And Lieutenant Stern confessed, that Captain Uratz told him he had a quarrel with an English gentleman, and that if he would assist him in it, he would make his fortune, and gave him money to buy the blunderbuss; and he went out with the Captain, and Polander, on horseback, about five or six a clock on Sunday, and when they were got into the Pall-mall, he heard the Captain say to

the coachman, stop, and turning immediately, being then
nine or ten yards before the coach, he saw the shot go
off, and they riding away, he follow'd them : And he
farther said that before the Polander came over, the
Captain desired him to get an Italian to stab a man.

These were the confessions they made on their examination before Mr. Bridgman, and Sir John Reresby, as
their Worships depos'd in open Court. Then Count
Coningsmark, by his interpreter, Sir Nathaniel Johnson,
told the Judges in his defence, that he came into England
with a design to have got a Regiment, and serv'd England
against France, hearing of an Alliance to be between
England, Holland, and Swedeland, against that nation.
That he lay incognito, because he was broke out in spots
on his arms and breast, and design'd to take physick,
and avoid drinking of wine, and his equipage was not
come to him. That he remov'd his lodgings, the first,
because it was too cold for him ; and the second, because
of a smoaking chimney. That he sent for the Polander
over to dress his horses after the German way, which he
came to buy, and had return'd one thousand pistoles for
that end, and had bought one horse, which the Count's
brother testified. That had it not been for the stormy
weather, the Polander had arriv'd sooner, he having writ
for him four months ago. That he had no quarrel with
Squire Thynn ; nor, to the best of his knowledge, ever
saw him. That it was strange he should ask a scullion-
boy whether people might ride on Sundays, when he
himself, over and over, has rid upon Sundays to Hyde-
Park, which was testified by Major Oglethorp, and divers
other gentlemen. That Captain Uratz visited him on
Sunday, only because he was sick. That he gave the
Polander to the Captain, because he should have no use
for him himself; bought him cloaths and a sword,
because he wanted them. That he absconded because
one Markham, his taylor, told him he heard him nam'd,
as concern'd in the murder, and that if the common
people should catch him, they would tear him to pieces,
and so his friends did counsel him to withdraw. That he

heard the people say, the murderers follow'd Squire Thynn's coach, but would not shoot till the Duke of Monmouth was gone out. Then he spoke of his apprehension and imprisonment, as being a stain to his blood; mentioning something of the repute of his own family, and his zeal for the Protestant religion, and love for the English. After which Sir Francis Winnington, and Mr. Williams, summ'd up the evidence; and then the Lord Chief-Justice withdrew, and the Court adjourn'd for half an hour, and then sent for the jury, who brought in Uratz, Stern, and Borosky, Guilty, and the Count Not-guilty. Who being dismiss'd, Mr. Recorder sentenc'd the other three to be hang'd, who were accordingly executed in the Pall-Mall, on Friday, the 10th of March following; and Borosky was afterwards hung up in chains, a little beyond Mile-End, by the command of King Charles the Second.

Count Coningsmark departed this kingdom a little before the execution of his friends; and going to France, there made some unmannerly reflections on the Duke of Devonshire, and the Duke of Monmouth; which coming to their ears, they sent him a challenge to fight on Calice Sands, single, or with a second, which he accepted; but when those noblemen went to the place appointed, he never had the bravery to meet 'em; and afterwards travelling into Hungary, and playing with some gentlemen, who found they had been impos'd on by his cheating, it created a quarrel, in which the Count was killed, Anno 1686, aged thirty-one years.

PATRICK HURLEY.

THIS unaccountable sharper was born at the City of Cork, in the Province of Munster, in Ireland. As for the parentage that own'd him, his father was a wild Irishman, betrothed to a chamber-maid of the same country, who lived very lovingly together, for about five months, when being in bed, all on a sudden she was taken with a violent pain, the true cause of which, she could no longer dissemble; but taking him about the neck, and almost stifling him with kisses, and bedewing his cheeks with tears, intreated him to rise, and call a midwife. At this Patrick's reputed father started, and mutter'd his resentment and discontent betwixt his teeth; but finding that it was but too true, and that there was now no other remedy, out he jumps and as secretly as he could, fetch'd a midwife, who in a short space brought this, our Patrick Hurley, into the world.

Now Teague being much jeer'd in the neighbourhood, with his wife's forward breeding this hopeful babe of grace, he left Cork, and went to dwell at Athlone, where he kept an alehouse; and no sooner was their son Patrick so fledg'd, that he could run about without a rowler, leading-strings, or a goe-cart, but the Countess of Galway, passing by his father's door in her coach, and eying him narrowly, was mightily taken with his physiogmony, and pretty manner of tatling, to his diminutive play-fellows; whereupon she demanded whose pretty boy he was; and having got out of him who his father and mother were, and understood, by his pointing to the house, the place of their abode, she order'd her coach to drive nearer to the door; his father and mother happening to be at home, wonder'd what great visitant this might be; but more, when they saw her hugging their hopeful issue in her arms. They accosted her with what complements, on a sudden, bolted into their heads; and she return'd them suitable civilities; But when she came to start the question, of parting with him, and what great things she would do for him, his mother, whose darling he was, (though by this time she had another son) seem'd very averse to it: But Patrick's father, who seldom look'd on him with pleasing eyes, (it still running in his mind, that he was none of his begetting,) was more attentive to her discourse, and prevail'd with his mother, that within a week he should be sent to her ladiship.

This Countess, by reason of her great quality, not

being unknown to either of them, at the time appointed, young Patrick was sent to her, where he was splendidly cloathed, entertained, and attended; and by his pretty discourse, and little apish tricks, diverted his lady in her fits of melancholy, more than her buffoon or monkey; and for his better accomplishment, being arriv'd at his tenth year, that no qualifications might be wanting in him, worthy acquiring, and for the improvement of education, he was put under the tuition of a famous pedagogue, or school-master, who spar'd no correction for the benefit or furtherance of instruction. He learnt to read and write French pretty tolerably the first year; and by conversing with an Italian youth, he pretty well understood that language; But the next year, being put to the hard grammatical methods and rules of scholastical learning, it grew tiresome to him; yet having with great difficulty, in another perambulation of the sun through the twelve signs of the Zodiack, crouded himself into the company of adverbs, prepositions, interjections, and the like, with which he did so kick, cuff, and scuffle, that notwithstanding his master gave all possible assistance to his disciple, yet he found the opponents too crabbed to be overcome; which unhappy contests, frequently ended in most cruel flagellations, that made him but the more stubborn and regardless, though he plow'd and furrow'd his buttocks, till they carried the marks and characters of all languages on 'em.

Our young scholar, to divert the trouble his master's severity put him into, bent his study upon all manner of boyish recreations, and became very expert therein, beyond the rest of his companions; as tipcat, cricket, skittles, span-farthing, trap-ball, and the like; by which, over and above the allowance he had from his lady, whom rarely he went to visit, but she clapt a crown into his hand at parting, he gain'd considerably in money and experience; and finding his old pedagogue covetous, he fell into a dextrous way to buy off his faults with presents of curious fruits, and choice wines, which he pretended his mother, or his lady, had sent him; and some-

times, he being none of the richest, or best husbands,
with money he suggested to have found in the streets;
which so charm'd him, that much of his usual punishment
was abated, though his learning made no better progress.

This trade continued till he was about fifteen years of
age, when the Countess dying, his Lord went beyond-
sea, and took Patrick along with him through France,
Spain, Italy, Germany, and so over all Europe; and so
well had this sharper improv'd himself in his travels with
his master, that in seven years he could very fluently
speak most European languages; when his Lord returning into Ireland, died soon after. Now Patrick being
out of employment, and being very expert in all manner
of games, either on the cards or dice, he one night won
two hundred and fifty pounds at Dublin; then embarking
for England, he landed at Bristol, in the habit of a Quaker;
to some of which sect addressing himself, he not only held
forth in their meetings, but also pretended that he was
inspired, and could speak all the languages in Christen-
dom; the noise whereof, brought several gentlemen,
for many miles round the country, to discourse with him,
in Spanish, Dutch, Swedish, Portugueze, and other
tongues, whereof he was an absolute master. In the
learned languages he pretended to no knowledge;
alledging, Latin was the language of the beast; Greek,
the tongue wherein the heathen poets wrote their fictions;
Hebrew, the speech of the unbelieving Jews; and
Arabick, the tongue wherein the blasphemous Alcoran
of Mahomet is written! He only alledged he was inspired with an understanding in all Christian tongues,
for a conversion of them to be all Quakers; but one
gentleman bringing him a Welsh Bible to translate,
Patrick knowing nothing of that guttural tongue, his
inspiration was confuted; which making Patrick asham'd,
he pack'd up his awls and went away with three thousand
eight hundred pounds, which the Quakers had gather'd
to present this supposed Prophet.

Coming next to London, he there became acquainted
with the most celebrated sharpers, and haunted all the

raffling-shops about town; where in a short time, by
his great dexterity, of making all Rugg at Dice, as the
cant is for securing a die between two fingers, he won
above one thousand five hundred pounds; and afterwards at the Bath, he, in one night, won six hundred
and odd guineas, by putting wax on his fore-finger,
which held a die in the box at his devotion. He was very
acute in all manner of sharping; for he, and two more of
his comrades, being one time at cards at a rich widow's,
who kept an alehouse in Southwark, they call'd the woman
up, and delivering one hundred pounds into her hands,
they gave orders that she should not re-deliver it to any
one or two of them, but keep it till they all came together.
Accordingly she took the money, and about two months
after, Patrick Hurley coming to this widow's house
again, with a formal ſtory, that the gentlemen who were
laſt there with him, were both dead, he demanded the
one hundred pounds deposited in her hands, which she
very innocently gave him; but about a month after, the
other two sharpers coming to demand the money, she
told them what had happen'd, and that she had paid it
already, and therefore would not pay it over again.
They thereupon sued her, and the cause went so hard
againſt her at the Queen's-Bench-Bar, that she had like
to have been caſt, had not one of her council said, My
Lord, we don't deny but that one hundred pounds were
deposited in my client's hands, by three gentlemen, upon
condition that she should not deliver it to any one or
two of them, but to them all together: And now here
being but two of these gentlemen which sue for this
one hundred pounds, we humbly hope they will (or at
leaſt muſt be oblig'd) to bring the third man, and there's
the money ready in Court to pay 'em. Which third
man, Patrick Hurley, not appearing, the two other
sharpers loſt the day.

Patrick had not been in England above a year and a
half, before he had got five thousand pounds by gaming;
(for here that scandalous practice of gameſters, and common sharpers, playing with person of quality of both

sexes, is as much us'd as in any country in Europe.)
He never went without a fine coat, and a gaudy equipage,
which has got him admittance into the best of company,
by whom he hath been caress'd to a very high degree.
After which, he made a tour to the Court of France,
and appear'd at Versails in a very rich attire, attended
with an equipage of half a dozen servants; where he
personated the Earl of Donnegal and acted quality in
disguise with such an air, and graceful decorum, that all
who had any conversation with him took him for no other
than a nobleman. Here he kept no less company than
Dukes, Marquisses, and Earls, and had the honour to
be introduced by the Duke of Berwick, into the presence
of the French King, whose hand he had the honour to
kiss. Now becoming intimately acquainted with the
chief of the French nobility of both sexes, who knew not
that sharping and cheating was his trade, by which he
liv'd in great splendour and luxury; he often play'd
with them at Piquet, L'Ombre, or Basset; at which being
very dextrous in palming, slipping, or bending the cards,
he won in less than six months above six thousand
pistoles; besides one thousand one hundred pistoles
from the Pretender, more from the Duke of Berwick,
the Duke of Vendome, the Mareschal Villeroy, and
Mareschal Villars. In such repute was he among the
nobility, that having the honour once of playing with his
Most Christian Majesty, he won of him in one night,
fourteen thousand pistoles. Thus we may see, that this
vice of excessive gaming, is as frequent in that nation,
as in England; where a foot-man shall play with a
Marquis, or an Earl; a black-guard-boy with a Dutchess; barbers, pedlars, tinkers, taylors, and ostlers,
with Generals, Brigadiers, and Colonels of the Army.
A wise man would scarce believe there should be in this
kingdom of Great-Britain, such a fool in nature, as a
person of quality that puts himself upon the level with
one, that he knows makes gaming his livelihood, as he
must do, if he condescends to play with him for money;
yet this is matter of fact, and every day produces a

thousand inſtances of it; for new-invented games at this time, notwithſtanding the law that was lately made to prevent 'em, are grown more numerous, and barefac'd than ever.

After this success, not holding it convenient to ſtay longer at the Court of France, he went incognito into Italy, where passing for the Viscount Dillon of Coſtello, he soon ingratiated himself among persons of diſtinction, with whom he often play'd, and won a great deal of money at Billiards, a game which had its firſt original in Italy; and for the excellency of the recreation, is of late years much approv'd of, and play'd by moſt nations in Europe, especially in England, there being few towns of note in this kingdom, which hath not a publick Billiard-table. In one night he won fifteen thousand pounds at L'Ombre of the Duke of Venice; but miſtruſting his being a conſtant winner, might bring him into suspicion amongſt the cautious Venetians, he declin'd playing in their territories for the present, unless it was for such a small sum, that he car'd not whether he loſt or won. From thence therefore he went to Naples, where lighting in company with a rich Jew, that was a great banker; he attack'd him at Bankafalet, (a game on the cards, which muſt be cut into as many heaps as there are players, or more, if you please, and every man lays as much money on his card as he thinks fit, or on the supernumerary heaps) at which he won in less than four hours, above three thousand nine hundred ducatoons, by his dexterity on the cards; for at this game the cheat lies in securing an Ace in the sleeve, or bosom, or on the hat, or any other sure winning card; or if you mark the cards aforehand, so as to know them by the backside, you know accordingly how to make your advantage.

He was also very expert at Beaſt, or the game on the cards, call'd La Bêt by the French; and at that other French game, call'd Basset, which in its nature is not much unlike our late Royal-Oak-Lottery; for as that, by the Lottery-man's having five figures in two and thirty for himself, muſt be a considerable profit to him in length of time; so here the dealer, that keeps the bank, having the firſt and laſt card at his own disposal, and other considerable priviledges in the dealing the cards, has (without doubt) a greater prospeét of gaming, than those that play. This was a truth so acknowledg'd in France, that the King made a publick ediét, that the priviledge of a Talliere, or one that keeps the bank at Basset, should only be allow'd to principal Cadets, or sons of great families; supposing, that whoever was so befriended, as to be admitted to keep the bank, muſt naturally, in a very short time, become possessor of a considerable eſtate. But ſtill Patrick Hurley aéting the part of a nobleman, he travell'd with his retinue into Holland, where passing for an Irish person of quality at the Hague, by his cunning insinuations of generosity, and outward splendor among the Dutch, he obtain'd so much favour among them, as to borrow ten thousand pounds of the Bank of Amſterdam, which he carried clear off the ground, without ever coming to an account for their unusual civility to ſtrangers.

Notwithſtanding these several vaſt sums, his way of living being very extravagant, in fine coaches, chariots, and calashes, rich liveries, and extraordinary wages to his pretended footmen, high eating and drinking, very chargeable lodgings, and rich apparel for his own use, he could scarce keep buckle and thong together; besides, being a great cully to the fair sex, he hath often thrown a thousand or two of pounds on a woman, for no other conversation than a month or six weeks. Thus being sometimes reduced to great ſtraits, he had no other way of raising his fortune, but by resorting to common gaming-houses, where, if money was short with him, he would often get half a crown, and a dinner, for ſtanding the Sweetning-Lay, which is decoying young gentlemen to be bit, or cheated by old sharpers; But sometimes, when his necessities were very great, he hath ventur'd to come the Levant over gentlemen; that is, to play without any money at all in his pocket, at Hazard, whereby, if he had luck on his side, he got their money for nothing ; and in case he loſt, 'twas but a good kicking, unless he had the courage to vindicate his villany by his sword.

He plays very well at Brag, which game being the main thing by which the second ſtake is to be won by the ingenuity of its management, it takes from thence its name ; for you are to endeavour to impose upon the judgment of the reſt that play, and particularly on the person that chiefly offers to oppose you, by boaſting of cards in your hand, that are better than his or hers that plays against you. Thus it is to be observ'd, that the witty ordering of this Brag is the moſt pleasant part of this game ; for those, that by fashioning their looks and geſtures, can give a proper air to their actions, as will so deceive an unskilful antagoniſt, that sometimes a pair of Treys or Deuces, in such a hand, with the advantage of his compos'd countenance, and subtle manner of over-owing the other, shall out-brag a much greater pair, and win the ſtakes. It is not to be doubted, that Hurley wanted any qualifications that might be any ways advantageous to him, in playing the laſt-mention'd game ; though he play'd very clean at any thing, yet would he always use foul means to beat his adversary. Thus when he hath play'd at Whiſt, a game so called from the silence that is to be observ'd at it, he hath us'd siniſter practices, in discovering to his partner what honours he hath in his hand ; by winking, or using some other motion, as, the wink of one eye, or putting one finger on the nose, or table, signifies one honour ; shutting both the eyes, two ; placing three fingers, or four, on the table, three or four honours.

These gameſters have also several ways of securing an honour or more, in the bottom when they deal, either to their partners or selves ; if to their partners, they place in the second list next to the top, one, two, three, or four Aces, or court cards all of a suit, according as they get them together in the former deal, and place a card of the same suit in the bottom, when the cards are cut, they muſt use their hand so dexterously, as not to put the top in the bottom, but nimbly place it where it was before. If they would secure honours to themselves when dealing they then place so many as they can get upon their lap, or other place undiscerned; and after the cards are cut, then clap them very neatly under. But the cleanest rooking way is by the Breef; that is, take a pack of cards, and open them, then take out all the honours, that is to say, the four Aces, Kings, Queens and Knaves, then take the rest, and cut a little from the edges of them all alike, by which means the honours will be broader than the rest; so that when your adversary cuts to you, you are certain of an honour; when you cut to your adversary, cut at the ends, and then it is a chance if you cut him an honour, because the cards at the ends are all of a length; thus you may make Breefs end-ways, as well as sideways. All your cunning sharpers in the City of London, and Court-end of the town, before they go to play, will plant half a dozen of these packs, (nay, sometimes half a score) in the hands of a drawer, and, to avoid being suspected, will call to their confederate-drawer, for a fresh pack of cards, who brings 'em as from a shop new; and some of these packs shall be so finely mark'd, whereby the gamester shall plainly and certainly know every card therein contain'd, by the outside, although the best of eyes shall not discern whether any mark was made at all; and this is done with that variety, that every card of every suit, shall have a different distinguishing mark. Some have a way to slick with a slick-stone, all the honours very smooth, by which means he will be sure to cut his partner an honour, and so his partner to him again; and that is done by laying a fore-finger on the top of the pack indifferent hard, and giving a slurring jerk to the rest, which will slip off from the slick'd card.

Though no man was ever better qualified by a gamester than Hurley, and though by his luck and skill, he has won above one hundred thousand pounds at cards and dice, yet did his great winnings thrive so little with him, that he hath often been forced to have recourse to cheating in other ways, in which he has been no less famous than the other, as may appear by what follows:

The firſt session of the laſt Parliament, Anno 1710, he (being then a Faggot in Colonel Charter's Company, in the Foot-Guards,) had recourse to one Mr. Joseph Billers, (who was order'd to attend the committee, appointed to enquire into the false muſters, and other abuses committed by the officers of the said Guards) to whom he made such discoveries, and afterwards managed his part so well before the House of Commons, that he got the applause of all those that knew that affair, and even a Vote in his behalf, (with four or five more) for their discharge from the service, and an Address to the Queen that they should not be impreſt, &c. Upon this management, and other fine ſtories, he was made very welcome by Mr. Billers, and his friends, amongſt whom he got acquainted with one Mr. Thomas Cotchet, who had then left trade, and had money to dispose of; and Hurley finding by his discourse, that Mr. Cotchet aim'd at a genteel poſt, pretended to have found out one for him, which, as he said, was a Receiver of the Cuſtoms of the Port of Briſtol; and that he (viz. Hurley,) had a considerable intereſt with the Lady Masham, and would feel her pulse on that subjeƈt. Mr. Cotchet found the ſtory so agreeable to his inclinations, that he readily equipt Mr. Hurley with contingent money, and for a few weeks after with treats, till he had brought the matter to bear, in the following manner. The Lady Masham was to have a present of three hundred and fifty guineas for her good services, in procuring the Privy-Seal for the Lord-Keeper to pass a Patent, under the Great-Seal, to eſtablish Mr. Cotchet at Briſtol, and this to be aƈted with all the secrecy imaginable. Mr. Cotchet having got his three hundred and fifty guineas ready, in bank and goldsmith's notes, Hurley appointed the day that the Lady Masham would deliver to Mr. Cotchett's agent, (Mr. Jos. Holding, then a servant to Mr. Billers,) a full power to the Lord Keeper for passing the Patent; and that, pursuant to what had been agreed upon, she would, on such a day, take the air in Kensington-Gardens, and then he would be there, to usher her out of the coach; after which, Mr. Holding should, at a distance, follow her, and when she had walk'd such a walk, steal close behind her, and put a paper under her fur-below-scarf. These matters being adjusted, and a house at Kensington being appointed for a good dinner, &c. after dinner, Hurley asked Mr. Cochett whether every thing was ready on his part? Cotchett answer'd Yes. Soon after which, a gentleman came in a coach, and ask'd for Mr. Hurley, who went down to him, and after having talk'd a little time, return'd to his company, and ask'd Mr. Cotchett in what nature he was ready? for that a gentleman had been that minute with him from the Lady Masham. Cotchet answer'd, he had the sum in bank-notes. Says Hurley, so I told him, (i. e. the gentleman in the coach) but he huff'd me, and said, Sure, Mr. Hurley had not made my Lady so mean, as to trade with cits with their paultry notes. Upon the debate, it was order'd that Mr. Holding should immediately take the notes, and away by coach to St. James's-Park, from thence to White-Hall, and so by water, in a four oar boat, and bring gold to the same value; with a caution to buy a handsome large green purse, to put it in; all which Mr. Holding effected with all the expedition imaginable; and when he came into the room, and shew'd the gold in the purse, Mr. Hurley said, that it must be made up firm in a sheet of white paper, which was done; and so all was ready on that side, and waited only for the Lady's coming and acceptance. About an hour after came by a fine charriot, with a lady in it; whereupon Hurley started up, and said, there's my Lady come; Mr. Holding, mind your cue; accordingly they left the company, and Mr. Hurley ushering the lady out of the coach, she drop'd him a nod, and walk'd on; Mr. Holding following, till she came to the appointed walk; when turning about to him, she said, Sir, I suppose you are Mr. Cotchet's agent, there is orders for his place; I hope he is well-affected to her Majesty, that I may not come under any blame upon his deportment. Go away to the Lord-Keeper's immediately, and he'll pass the Patent. Mr. Holding, with a very low bow, took the packet and went off, but Mr. Hurley waited till the pretended Lady Masham's return, which she did in a little time, and he handed her into the coach, bow'd, and then turn'd to Mr. Holding, and congratulated him upon the success of his friend; after which, full of joy, they went to their company, paid the reckoning, and posted away to the Lord Keeper's. When they came to the door, Hurley step'd out of the coach, and spoke to a gentleman very well drest; and then returning into the coach, he told Mr. Cotchet that my Lord was busie, but in about two hours he would be at leasure; whereupon they went to a tavern hard by, and staid: after the two hours were expired, a messenger was sent to know whether my Lord's company was gone; answer was brought no. The same message and answer was repeated three times, and then Mr. Hurley said, it would be to no purpose to wait any longer, it being then past 11 at night; but the morrow morning would be better. Cotchet upon this began to be somewhat uneasy, and ask'd, whether if they should open the packet, it would be any damage? Sir, says Hurley, I dare not presume any such thing, knowing the consequence of breaking a Privy Seal, it's as much as our lives are worth; (for it was seal'd with two seals as big as half-crowns.) Upon the whole they agreed to meet at a coffee-house the next morning, at such an hour, in order to wait the Lord-keeper's Levee. Mr. Cotchet kept his time, but no Hurley came. At length 12 clock being come, and no Hurley, Mr. Cotchet was very uneasy, and sent for Mr. Billers, to whom he unravels the whole story, who immediately suspecting the trick, said you are cheated; and breaking open the packet, found it contain'd an old ballad or two, and a bantering letter, and that was all the honest gentleman had for his 350 guineas, and expences.

Another time he went pretending to buy a quantity

of lace for some persons of note of his acquaintance, that were to be speedily married; the lace-woman having not so much by her as he seem'd to want, she told him she would be provided for him against next day. At the hour appointed Pat. came again, when the woman having what he had bespoken, which came to above 100 and odd pounds, they went to the old Palace-yard at Westminster, where having entrance into a very handsome house, and next introduced into a richly furnish'd room, pretty well filled with a great many people of both sexes, who by their dress and mien seem'd to be no less than persons of quality, the lace was view'd and approv'd of by the seeming gentry; then Hurley pulling a bank note out of his pocket, which came to more than the lace-woman's goods, he desired her to give him the overplus; but having not so much money about her, quoth Hurley to her, Madam, I am going home to my lodgings in Hatton-Garden, and if you please to go along with me thither, I will pay you in ready specie for the lace, which you must leave here. Accordingly the lace-woman leaving her lace behind her, they took coach, which Hurley ordering to stop at Symonds-Inn Coffee-house in Chancery-lane, quoth he, Madam, I'll but just step in here to speak my lawyer about some earnest business, and I'll wait on you again in an instant: So stepping out of the coach into the coffee-room, and coming not out in above half an hour, the lace-woman sent in the coachman to enquire for him, but no such person being there (for he had slipt out at the back door) she rid presently back to Palace-yard, from whence the birds were all flown: However, accidently meeting Patrick Hurley in the Meuse about a week after, she had him apprehended, and committed to Newgate; then being convicted for a cheat at Justice-Hall in the Old Bailey, he was sent down to old Bridewell by Fleet-Ditch, there to receive the correction of the house, and be kept at hard labour for a year: But from thence he found means to escape, and has not since been heard of.

Captain H——, *a Gamester.*

CAPTAIN H—— was the only son of a parson, who had a benefice at Newark upon Trent in Nottinghamshire, where he was born, and having some small matter of education bestow'd upon him, his inclination tending more towards the sword than the book, he became a Cadet in the Second Regiment of Foot-Guards, otherwise call'd the Coldstream Regiment, from being first raised at a place of that name in Scotland. In this station he continued without any higher preferment for the term of 6 years, which his father dying, and leaving him an estate of 60 *l.* per Annum, he converted it into mony, and with some of it bought a Captain's Commission, in that Regiment which was raised in the reign of King James the Second, for the pretended Prince of Wales, and then commanded by Colonel Hales, next by Colonel Goodwin, and next by Colonel Colt, who was killed by one Captain Swift in a duel in Hide-Park.

In the time of the Revolution, Captain H—— refusing to take the Oaths of Allegiance to the late King William and Queen Mary, he lost his Commission; and by his extravagancy having nothing left to subsist on, he took to gaming, in which he became such a proficient, for the sharping part, that he liv'd meerly by it, and had been in a short time the utter ruin of several lawyers clerks, and mercers and drapers apprentices, in and about the cities of London and Westminster; who being his chief bubble at first, lost some of 'em sums too considerable for such youngsters to come fairly by. Bullying and gaming, were the chief supports of his life, which made him a mighty man with the constables, beadles and bailiffs; for he had so effectually brib'd himself into their acquaintance, that he had the insolence to imagine, he had establish'd himself and his partners, above the reach of the law: So making cheating and sharping his sole business, he stuck at nothing to promote that interest:

for it daily appears, that rooks are grown of late so intolerably rude and insolent, and commit so many open violences and outrages, that a ſtranger that ventures among 'em, runs the risque of being robb'd or murder'd. But whether this growing mischief be moſt owing to the defect of our laws ; the negligence of the magiſtrate, or the knavery of some of those they employ, I won't take upon me to determine ; but be that as it will, I'm confident the thing in itself is so highly scandalous and pernicious in all respects, and reflects so much upon the wisdom and honour of our country, that the Chriſtian world laughs at us for the unaccountable folly.

As for cards, he play'd incomparably well at French Ruff, but was much addicted herein to revoke, or not follow suit. He was a very acute player at Gleek and Lanterloo, in which laſt game, he who hath 5 cards of a suit in his hand, Loo's all the gameſters ; but if Captain H—— had but 4 of a suit, and he wanted a fifth, being skill'd in the cleanly art of conveyance, he would for that fifth make an exchange out of his pocket ; or else make use of one of his sharping companions, who never fails to do him that kind office and favour. This broken Captain was not unskilful at Picquet, and the Spanish game call'd Primero : But his chiefeſt delight was in those games which requir'd dice ; so that none of those sort came amiss to him, especially Verquere, which is the only noted game within the tables, practis'd in Holland, and at which that people are so good, that it is common amongſt 'em, to learn it in their childhood, that by early beginning, they may become greater proficients at their maturity, and be the better able, when they are divertively engaged, and their business will allow leisure, to excel and over-reach one another. He play'd excellently at Tick-Tack, which is so call'd from touch and take ; for if you touch a man, you muſt play him, though to your loss. He was not ignorant of Grand-Trick-track, a French game, moſt commonly us'd by persons of the firſt quality ; from whom he won one night 1450 *l.* at Pawlet's Ordinary at the Blue-Poſts in the Haymarket.

He also play'd often at Irish and Back-gammon, at both which games he us'd the false dice for the benefit of entering; wherefore such as play muſt have a special care that they have not Cinque-Deuces and Quarter-Treys, put upon them, which may be quickly perceived by the running of the dice. The sharper that is cunning at play, has great advantage of a novice or ignorant man, which is commonly by topping or knapping, which by its often practice, may be suspected by his adversary; to prevent which, he has recourse to dice which run particular chances to his purpose; which the other being ignorant of, is almoſt an equal advantage with the former: For example, he provides dice that run 6, 5, 4, 'tis his business to secure those points; so that if he happens to surprize any of your men coming home, as 'tis two to one but he does, he does without a kind of miracle win the sett. 'Tis possible sometimes they make use of 3 and 2, which are the low chances; but that they seldom do, for this reason; The high and forward points being supply'd, he muſt enter, if at all, upon the low points, which keeps him backwards, and gives you advantage; which in this game is to be forward, if possible upon safe terms; and to point your men at that rate, that it shall not be possible for your adversary to pass, though he hath entred his men, till you give liberty, having two to one the advantage of the game.

Both day and night Captain H—— spent his time in all the moſt noted gaming-houses about town; where at one table you shall find a sharper affectedly behaving himself, and with great formality acting the part of a gentleman, when, take him out of his cheating business, and you shan't have a word of good sense from him in twenty four hours, nor of one good action in his whole life. At another table perhaps you shall see a broken tradesman, who had good business till he fell into game-ſters hands; so firſt losing his money, and then his character, is since turn'd sharper too, and one of the vileſt in that hellish society. Thus these fellows are forc'd to shift and shirk about from one gaming-house to

another, and to commit abundance of little pitiful
actions to support themselves from starving. Our
Captain was also a mighty gamester at Chess, which
Royal Game is more difficult to be understood than any
other whatever, and will take up often in the playing so
long a time, that two persons may play a month at times,
before the game is ended ; and though some are of opinion
that Chess, as well as Draughts, may be play'd by a
certain rule ; I cannot incline to believe it, because the
first remove is diverse, according to the judgment of
either of the gamesters.

This sharper had great skill at Inn and Inn, a game
very much us'd in Ordinaries, and may be play'd by
two or three, each having a box in his hand. It is play'd
by four dice ; but if a gamester would win without
hazarding much money, dice that will run very seldom
otherwise than Sixes, Cinques, Quaters, and other
chances, are very necessary : If those instruments are
not to be had, a taper box will not be amiss, that as the
dice are thrown in, they may stick by the way, and be so
thrown to advantage. He also play'd much at Passage,
a game at dice to be play'd at but by two, and is perform'd
with 3 dice. The caster throws continually, till he has
thrown doublets under 10, and then he is out, and loses ;
or doublets above 10, and then he passes and wins :
high runners are most requisite for this game, such as
will rarely run any other chance than 4, 5, or 6, by which
means, if the caster throws doublets, he scarcely can
throw out. There is the same advantage of the smooth
taper-box aforesaid, in this game, as at Inn and Inn ;
with the like benefit of the dice, whether by palming,
topping, slurring, or knapping.

In fine, there was no manner of game, whether English
or foreign, on the cards or dice, but Captain H——— was
a master of it, who in his gaming was also very covetous
and passionate ; insomuch, that being once at play with
one Bisset, another sharper, and falling out but for the
small matter of half a crown, they went late at night into
Lincolns-Inn-Fields to decide the quarrel in the dark.

When they came there they both drew, and after a short engagement Bisset was run through the body by Captain H——; which wound being mortal, he died on the spot; but not without some suspicion of foul play on the survivor's side, who having a scratch thwart the palm of the hand with which he did not use his sword, 'tis suppos'd that he had palm'd the deceased's rapier. For this murder H—— was apprehended, and committed to Newgate, and being try'd for the same at Justice-Hall in the Old Bailey, and found guilty of Man-slaughter, was burnt in the hand! Afterwards remaining almost a year under confinement, before he obtain'd his liberty, he was reduced to a very miserable condition; insomuch that when he procur'd his enlargement, being very poor, and slighted by his old sharping comrades, he was arrested in an action of 120 pounds, and for want of bail was carried a prisoner to the Gatehouse at Westminster; from whence, after three months imprisonment, he remov'd himself by a Writ of Habeas Corpus to the Queen's Bench Prison in Southwark. Here by cards and dice he rifled most of the prisoners on the Masters-side of their money, which coming to the Marshal's ears, he turn'd H—— into the Common-side; but finding not such good bubbles in those quarters, he soon died with grief, and was interr'd at his sister's sole cost and charge, though he had been unkind to her, in St. George's Church-yard in Southwark, being 51 years of age when he departed this mortal life, Anno 1705.

JOE HAYNES, *a Sharper.*

THE parentage of this fellow being very mean, he was brought up to be a sharper from his very infancy; and being naturally of a licentious inclination, he left his friends at about 17 or 18 years of age, to have a greater swing in his vicious temper. Roving about London, he soon became acquainted with persons as wickedly inclin'd as himself, and one day being got into loose company at a bawdy-house in Whetstone's-Park, a hot imprest being then about town, as being at war with the Dutch, a gang of tarpaulins took him along with them, and put him aboard a smack, lying at St. Catherines; but proving himself to be no seaman, he was discharg'd by the Regulating Captains, and put on shoar again: However, his delivery was but leaping out of the frying-pan into the fire; for just as he landed, an officer imprest him for the land-service, and clapt him into the Tower, till an opportunity serv'd to send him to the English forces, then under the command of the Duke of Monmouth in the Low-Countries; and being shortly after appointed to go with other recruits to Dover, in order to be sent over sea, the following dialogue pass'd betwixt him and his Captain, who was a Frenchman.

Joe. Have you got a horse for me, Sir?

Capt. Far vat do you vant one horse?

Joe. To ride upon, Sir.

Capt. Begar, you must go on foot; you be one foot-soldier.

Joe. Indeed I cannot, for I have got the French-Pox upon me.

Capt. De French-Pox, Sirrah! vere did you get it?

Joe. In Dog and Bitch Yard, Sir.

Capt. In Dog and Bitch Yard, vere is dat place?

Joe. In that part of Great-Britain call'd England.

Capt. Begar den you be one lying dog, for dat be one English-Pox.

Joe. Well, Sir, let it be what pox it will, as I am not fit for marching, I will ride.

Capt. Begar you be de sad rogue as e're me met; but if you must ride, me tell you vat, you shall have one horse, and you shall throw de dice vid him; and if you vin, de horse shall ha' no vitels, but if de horse vin, you shall go vidout pay for dat day.

Joe. I never, Sir, yet play'd at dice with horses, but nevertheless I don't much care if I throw a main or two with a horse for once, and not use it.

Accordingly a horse being got ready, and the bargain made that the higheſt was to win, a pair of dice was put betwixt the horse's lips, which falling from thence 6, Joe Haynes takes 'em up and throws 8; whereupon the Captain crying out, Begar you sheat de horse, for dat vas no fair caſt; Joe reply'd, I vow it was very fair, ask the horse else: So the horse saying nothing, he went that day and night without any provinder. Next morning setting out from Dartford for Rocheſter, the French Captain oblig'd Joe Haynes and the horse to throw dice again for that day's allowance; but Joe being now the winner too, the Captain swore he should fling no more with the horse, for at that rate it would be ſtarv'd, and he should have a horse to pay for. The third day Joe rid to Canterbury, whilſt the reſt of the recruits went a foot; and the day after arriving safe at Dover, he there gave his officer the slip, and came ſtrait up to London.

Now raking up and down town, he became a true Bacchanalian, always drinking as ſtoutly as if he meant to carry liquor enough with him in his belly to quench the flames of hell; or rather as if he meant to drink himself so far into a beaſt, as he might thereby become incapable of damnation. When he had drank his fill, he ſtudied how to make the next young heir pay his reckoning; or else if he chanced to meet with some poor innocent young woman, whom a sweet word or two might make his miserable prey, he would make a shift to screw a ring or two off her finger, with which he would pay both the shot and his common-she for his next nights lodging. But to support him in his extravagancies, he was a sharper at cards, and play'd very well at Primero; in which game it is to be observ'd, that whoever of the players has in his hand Cinquo Primero, which is a sequence of 5 of the beſt cards, assiſted with Spadillo, which is the Ace of Spades, and counted the beſt card, or any other valuable trump, he is sure to be successful over his adversary.

He could likewise play very well at Picquet, in which game you muſt observe these rules: If the dealer gives more cards than his due, whether through mistake or otherwise, it lies in the choice of the elder hand, whether he shall deal again or no, or whether it shall be play'd out. He that forgets to reckon his Blank, Ruff, Sequences, Aces, Kings, or the like, and has begun to play his cards, cannot recall them; so it is with him that shews not his Ruff before he plays his first card, losing absolutely all the advantage thereof. He that misreckons any thing, and has play'd one of his cards, and his adversary finds at the beginning, middle, or end of the game, that he had not what he reckon'd, for his punishment he shall be debarr'd from reckoning any thing he really has, and his adversary shall reckon all he has; yet the other shall make all he can in play. He that takes in more cards than he discards, is liable to the same penalty. He that throws up his cards, imagining he hath lost the game, mingling them with other cards on the table, though afterwards he perceives his mistake, yet he is not allow'd to take up his cards, and play them out. No man is permitted to discard twice in one dealing. He that has a Blank, shall hinder the other Picy and Repicy, although he hath nothing to shew but his Blank. He that has 4 Aces, Kings, Queens or others dealt him, and after he has discarded one of the 4, reckons the other 3, and the other says to him, *it is good*, he is bound to tell the other, if he asks him, what Ace, King, Queen, or other card he wants. If after the cards are cleanly cut, either of the gamesters know the upper card by the backside, notwithstanding this, the cards must not be shuffled again. In like manner, if the dealer perceives the other has cut himself an Ace, and would therefore shuffle again, this is not permitted; and if a card be found faced, it shall be no argument to deal again, but must deal on; but if two be found faced, then may he shuffle again. Lastly, whosoever is found changing, or taking back again any of his cards, he shall lose the game, and be accounted a foul player, as has been already noted.

He was a very facetious and pleasant man in his humour, a scholar, one who wrote many witty pieces,

and on the stage play'd the comedian with as great applause as any of the most famous players of comedy, in the
laſt or present age. In the reign of the late King James
he travell'd in my Lord Caſtlemain's retinue, when he
went Ambassador to Rome, where he profess'd himself
a member of that Church (which was the firſt time he
ever pretended to any religion) and there he made use
of his skill in gaming, by which he got considerable sums
from the cautious Italians; and being for some mis-
behaviour left behind at my Lord Caſtlemain's return,
he was obliged to make use of all his wit and sharping
to support himself there, and in his passage home to
England; where being arriv'd, he was again admitted
on the stage; but age and infirmities had render'd him
uncapable of those excellent performances he was
formerly maſter of: Yet, a recantation-prologue (written
as well as spoken by himself) brought vaſt audiences to
the house, and kept his playing in some reputation. But
his allowance from the house abating with his merit,
he apply'd himself to base means to procure money; such
as, a Newgate Sollicitor, a Retainer to Clippers and
Coyners, a Sham-Bail, Evidence, Setter, or any thing
that was villainous; so that he became scandalous to all
men of any reputation; and was besides so very nauseous
and ſtinking, by reason of diſtempers contraćted by his
irregular living, that none who had the sense of smelling
would come within some yards of him if they could avoid
it. In this state of body and reputation he continued for
a few years, and then taking his bed for some time, dy'd
about the beginning of this century, aged 53 years. He
had (as is said before) written a great many witty things,
which if he had liv'd a little longer, he would have
printed; but, by what mischance we cannot learn,
moſt of them are loſt.

Lives of the Gamesters

RICHARD BOUCHIER, *Esq; a Gamester.*

ALL those persons who are addicted to the most covetous recreation of gaming, esteem it a thing so innocent
in itself, for wasting their precious time, that they seem
to apprehend a goodness in it, great enough to make them
a pretence for all their other vices, and sinful employments, shrouding them all under the generally approved
names of necessary pastimes and diversions. Of these
sort of sparks call'd gamesters, or rather sharpers, was
Mr. Bourchier, a plaisterer's son, born in Harts-horn-lane,
near Charing-Cross; but being not above 16 years old
when his parents died, and then an orphan, altogether
friendless, he was forced to shift for himself as well as
he could, and did, but with some difficulty, swim through
a vast ocean of hardship, 'till he was about 20 years of
age; when hankering about the Court, which was then
very debauch'd, he quickly became as bad as those he
conversed with. Now having his fortune to seek in the
wide world, from his very first launching into it, he never
had an inclination for any company but what liv'd above
him; and seeing, that at the rate he began his expences,
a good purse was requir'd, he took to gaming, especially
at Tennis; and being no bad player, won a pretty deal
of money at it, not so much by his skill, as his dexterity
in hiding it, and covering his play. From this pastime he
was brought to exercise other games; and being fortunate, in a little time he saw himself master of 800 *l.*
Thus puft up with success, he rais'd his hopes very high,
and with them his expences: For as gaming occasions
the keeping of ill hours, and that an abundance of vices,
so being flusht in the pocket, he soon fell in with whoring
and drinking, and began to be what the bright sparks
call a good companion.

The beginning of Bourchier's time was an age in which
nothing went down but pastime and pleasure; and few
virtues were then allow'd of at Whitehall, but pimping

and lying; but fortune not favouring Mr. Bourchier always alike, he was reduced to such a very low ebb, that before he was four and twenty, he was obliged to be a footman to the Right Honourable the Earl of Mulgrave, now Duke of Buckingham; in this nobleman's service, he wore a livery above a year and half, when, by his genteel carriage and mien, marrying one Mrs. Elizabeth Gossnam, a lace-woman's grand-daughter in Exeter-Change in the Strand, whom he had about 150 pounds, it being then the solemn festival of Christmas, in the twelve days whereof, great raffling was then wont to be kept in the Temple, he carried his wife's portion thither to improve it, but was so unsuccessful as to lose every farthing. This ill luck made Mr. Bourchier stark mad, but borrowing 20 pounds of a friend, he went to the Temple again, but had first bought a two-penny cord to hang himself in case he lost that too; but the dice turning on his side, and having won his own money back again, and as much more to it, of one particular gentleman, who was now fretting and fuming in as bad manner as Bourchier was before, he very courteously pull'd the cord out of his pocket, and giving it to the loser, said, Having now, Sir, no occasion for this implement my self, it is at your service with all my heart: Which bantering expression made the gentleman look very sour upon the winner, who carried off his booty whilst he was well.

However, Mr. Bourchier being very extravagant, he soon ran out what he had won at the Temple; and truly, if he could have liv'd upon two or three hundred a year, the Tennis-Court might have maintain'd him; but not being able to be without horses, and two or three servants, and being expensive in his pleasures, when all his substance was gone, he was forc'd to betake himself to several shifts; he ran in every body's debt, he borrow'd money of all he knew, and never went without any thing, that was to be had for asking. Notwithstanding all this, he was generally bare; till considering at last that his inclination to gaming was the chief cause of his misfortunes, and more than suspecting that (as cunning as he took himself to be) he had not always lost upon the square, he resolv'd to try if luck could not be forc'd, and began with great application to study the cunning part of the play; that is, to be more plain, turn sharper. This prov'd a very profitable trade the first year, and brought him a good revenue. To keep up his credit, as money came in, he paid off most of his debts, always keeping to the same rule which I have been told they follow at the Navy; the small ships first. Mr. Bourchier was very industrious, and pick'd up new bubbles every day, insomuch that he was in short time worth between two and three thousand pounds.

Besides, this notable sharper was a great lover of women, and as he was resolv'd to leave nothing unattempted, that might turn to profit, knowing himself to be a handsome clean fellow, fell to intriguing, and by this means often made a penny of the pleasures which he before us'd to pay for. In his amours, rather than stick out, he would joyn in matrimony with any woman, whom his fair promises could not intice to his embraces before the performance of Hymen's ceremonies; for, while his first wife was living, he married one Mrs. Morris, a taylor's daughter living in Covent-Garden. A little after this marriage, being at the Groom-Porters, he flung one main with the Earl of Mulgrave for 500 pounds, which he won; and his honour looking swiftly at him, quoth he, I believe I shou'd know you. Yes, (reply'd the winner) your Lordship must have some knowledge of me, for my name is Dick Bourchier, who was once your footman. Whereupon his Lordship supposing he was not in a capacity of paying 500 pounds in case he had lost, cry'd out, A bite, a bite. But the Groom-Porter assuring his Honour that Mr. Bourchier was able to have paid 1000 pounds provided his Lordship had won such a summ, he paid him what he plaid for, without any farther scruple.

But yet, to give Bourchier his due, we must needs say, that when he came to have a great deal of money by him, he was very generous to such of his friends as were in necessity, as not letting them want any thing in what he could serve them; and his generosity was as often extended towards meer ſtrangers, whom he knew to be really indigent. Now going to the Court of France, and having before heard what a humour of gaming reign'd there, he had caused a great number of false dice to be made, of which himself only knew, the high and low fullums, and hired men to carry 'em into that kingdom; where, after they had bought up and convey'd away all the dice they could meet with in Paris, they supply'd the shops with these false ones; by which means Bourchier having as it were bound fortune to be on his side, he insinuated himself into the acquaintance of the nobility, and by the favour of some of his own nation, he was soon admitted to the presence of Lewis-le-grand, as a gameſter; he not only won 15000 piſtoles of the King, but the nobility also taſted of the same fortune; for he won 10000 piſtoles of the Duke of Orleans; almoſt as much of the Duke D'Espernon, besides many of his jewels, and a prodigious large piece of ambergreese, valued at 20000 crowns, as being the greateſt piece that was ever seen in Europe, and which was afterwards laid up by the Republick of Venice in their Treasury, to whom it was sold for a great rarity: But we need not wonder at persons of quality playing so extravagantly in these days, since it was as cuſtomary in former ages; for the Emperor Nero was so addiⅽted to gaming, that he ventur'd 400000 seſterces upon every spot of the dice, which is above 3300 pounds sterling; and the same thing is also said of Caligula, that second monster of men. And one Sir Miles Partridge plaid at dice with King Henry the Eighth, for four of the largeſt bells in London; but though he won, and brought the bells to ring in his pocket, yet the ropes catch'd him by the neck; for in the reign of King Edward the Sixth he was hang'd for High Treason. But to return to Bourchier, being once a little while at Madrid, he play'd there with one John de Domingo, a rich Spaniard, of whom he won above

1000 double moiaders; and the Don's son shewing some dislike as he stood by, quoth our English gamester to the young man's father, Pray, Sir, what makes your son look so much out of humour? The old man reply'd, Alexander the Great hearing of a victory which his father Philip had won, is reported to have been sad at the news, as fearing there would be nothing left for him to gain; but my son, Sir, is afflicted at my loss, as fearing there will be nothing left for him to lose when I die.

Besides, Mr. Bouchier was not without his decoys abroad, to bring bubbles into his clutches, as appears by one Mr. Thomas Charlton, a young gentleman, who having by the death of his father an estate of 600 pounds per annum left him, thought himself wise enough for the management thereof, without the advice of his friends; by which means it was his misfortune to manage it all away in less than two years; upon which he became very needy, and so a fit subject, Bourchier thought, to be moulded into any shape that had an appearance of profit. One day Bourchier meeting him in the Strand, he ask'd him to accept of a pint or two of wine; the young gentleman, after some excuses, agreed to go; when they were at the tavern, Bourchier began to lament his case, and withal told him, that his condition was not irretrievable, for if he would be rul'd by him, he would engage he might live as well as ever he did, and be worth 1000 or 2000 pounds at the year's end. The young gentleman hereupon enquiring by what means this must be done? the other says, come along with me, and I'll let you know. The hopes of recovering himself out of his mean states made him soon yield. Bourchier then call'd for a coach, and conducted him to his lodgings, not inferior to the best in London. Here, after some discourse, telling him that he had heard of his misfortunes, for which he was very sorry, and would out of kindness propose something to his future advantage. I know (quoth Bourchier) you have liv'd very well, and are yet acquainted with many gentlemen; now, I'll give you a note of 200 pounds, which you may go and receive presently, and get into company with them, and by some means or other help me to get into their acquaintance, and when we are together, propose to play a game at something or other for diversion. Now when we are at play, be sure you always lay wagers on their side, that you losing your money, you may continue to be unsuspected by them; and as for what you lose, I'll return it again, with your share of what I win of them: And by this means you need not doubt but that you may soon bid adieu to poverty and meanness, and may live in more grandeur than ever. A proposal of such consequence put our young gentleman to a sort of nonplus at present; but at last breaking silence, he told Bourchier, he thank'd him for his extream civility to him, but he desir'd a day's time to consider of this matter; which being granted, he took his leave and departed. When he came home, he was extreamly pensive; but at last reflecting on the ill consequences of striking in with the proposal, he resolv'd with himself to refuse it; for, thought he, should I agree, I may perhaps get money; but then I shall be the ruin of many young gentlemen of my acquaintance, who having lost all, and thereby disobliged their friends, they will perhaps take refuge on the highway, and there commit such crimes, as may bring 'em to an untimely end: And shall I (quoth he to himself) build my fortune on the ruin of my friends lives and estates? Heaven forbid that I should be ever guilty of so inhumane a crime. By such honest considerations he strengthen'd his mind to resist this temptation, and in a short time overcame it, by returning answer the next day, that he would not comply with such dishonest desires. But nevertheless, Bourchier plainly perceiving the good principles of this unfortunate gentleman, he was so compassionate to his misfortunes, as to allow him 100 pounds per annum to support him in his distress.

By such tricks as these, profess'd gamesters make it their sole practise and employment to noose unwary woodcocks, and deprive them of their plumes, when they meet with 'em, which sometimes makes the losers desperate, as appears in the relation of one Adam Steckman of Alsace, a vine-dresser; who having receiv'd his wages once, loſt it all at dice; and then wanting wherewithal to maintain his family, he grew so diſtemper'd in mind, that in his wife's absence, he cut the throats of his three children, and would have hang'd himself; but not effecting it before his wife's return, she seeing so dismal a spectacle gave a fearful shriek, and fell down dead; upon which the neighbourhood being rais'd, they came in and apprehended the man, who was according to his demerit adjudg'd to be broke on the wheel, which moſt tormenting death he accordingly suffer'd. But for a farther unqueſtionable teſtimony of the mischiefs that often arise from gaming, this is a very remarkable, but dreadful passage, which I'm now going to recite: Near Bellizona in Switzerland, three men were playing at dice on the Sabbath-Day; and one of 'em call'd Ulrick Schræteus having loſt his money, and at laſt expecting a good caſt, broke out into a moſt blasphemous speech, threatning, That if fortune deceiv'd him then, he would thruſt his dagger into the very body of God, as far as he could. The caſt miscarrying, the villain drew his dagger, and threw it againſt heaven with all his ſtrength; when behold the dagger vanish'd, and several drops of blood fell upon the table in the midſt of 'em; and the Devil immediately came and carry'd away the blasphemous wretch, with such a noise and ſtink, that the whole city was amaz'd at it. The others, half diſtracted with fear, ſtrove to wipe out the drops of blood that were upon the table, but the more they rubb'd 'em, the more plainly they appear'd. The rumour hereof flying to the city, multitudes of people flock'd to the place, where they found the gameſters washing the board, whom they bound in chains, and carried towards the prison; but as they were upon the way, one of 'em was suddenly ſtruck dead, with such a number of lice crawling out of him, as was wonderful and loathsome to behold: And the third was immediately put to death by the citizens, to avert the divine indignation and vengeance, which seem'd to hang over their heads. The table was preserv'd in the place, and kept as a monument of the judgments of God on blasphemers and Sabbath-breakers; and to shew the mischiefs and inconveniences that often attend gaming.

Now as Mr. Bourchier always appeared very well dreſt, he would sometimes act the part of those rooks, whose outside speaks them gentlemen of the firſt rank, yet they seldom play in an ordinary, but will sit there a whole evening to observe who wins; if it be considerable, and the winner seems pliable and generous, why then Mr. Bourchier would endeavour to insinuate himself into his acquaintance, by congratulating his success, and applauding his happy hand; then he'll prompt him to a glass of wine, to drink to the continuance of his good fortune. Having gotten him to a tavern, the next ſtep he would wheedle him in to play, and it being perhaps late at night, and the gentleman's eyes dim with looking earneſtly and watching, he would be sure to put the false dice upon him, or otherwise cheat him by palming, slurring or topping; by which means he was always sure to win a good part of the gentleman's money, if not all. And that he might not be suspected, he would play sometimes upon the square, and lose considerably; but then he would soon recover it again, when he thought he was gone down hill far enough: Though it sometimes so happen, that the cheat may be serv'd in his kind, but only the bubble perhaps has not wit enough to leave off while he's on the winning hand, or at leaſt upon the turn of his fortune.

Once Mr. Bourchier, going over to Flanders, with a great train of servants, set off in such a fine equipage, that they drew the eyes of all upon them wherever they went, to admire the splendor and gaiety of their maſter, whom they took for no less than a nobleman of the firſt rank. In this pomp making his tour at K. William's tent, he happen'd into play with that great monarch, and won of him above 2500 *l*. The Duke of Bavaria being also there, he then took up the cudgels, and losing 15000 *l*. the loss put him into a great chafe, and doubting some foul play was put upon him, because luck went so much againſt him, quoth Mr. Bourchier, Sir, if you have any suspicion of the leaſt siniſter trick put upon your Highness, if you pleaſe I'll give you a chance for all your money at once, tossing up at Cross and Pile, and you shall have the advantage too of throwing up the guinea your-self. The Electorfor admir'd at his bold challenge, which nevertheless accepting, he toſt up for 15000 *l.* and loſt the money upon reputation, with which Bourchier was very well satisfied, as not doubting in the leaſt ; and so taking his leave of the King, and those noblemen that were with him, he departed. Then the Electorfor of Bavaria enquiring of his Majeſty, who that person was, that could run the hazard of playing for so much money at a time, he told him it was a subject of his in England, that though he had no real eſtate of his own, yet was he able to play with any Sovereign Prince in Germany. Shortly after Bourchier returning into England, he bought a moſt rich coach and curious sett of six horses to it, which coſt him above 300 *l.* for a present to the Electorfor of Bavaria, who had not as yet paid him any thing of the 30000 *l.* which he had won of him. Notice hereof being sent to his Highness, the generous action incited him to send over his Gentlemen of Horse into England, to take care of this present, which he receiv'd kindly at Bourchier's hands, to whom he return'd Bills of Exchange also, drawn upon several eminent merchants in London, for paying what money he had loſt with him at play.

Some people may talk what they please of deciding cases relating to the proportions of hazards in gaming ; but such calculations, I am sure, are above the beſt mathematicians to perform. For it is very well known, that Bourchier would never venture 4 or 500 guineas purely on fortune, or meer event of chance, nor hazard his money on misfortune, when it daily appears, that ordinary matters run in the channel of second causes. Indeed, he had an art of preventing the dice from falling on such a determined side as chance should direct ; and therefore, where is the probability for an unexperienced gamester to gain any thing by a calculation of chances? Whenever Bourchier play'd, his judgment had such a command over fortune, that his chance was 10 to 2, against any one that unluckily attempted to be his antagonist, either at cards or dice; or else he could never have been master, as he was, of so many thousands pounds, with the small stock of setting up first of all for a gamester, with less than 50 guineas. His Leger-de-main tricks, and slight of hand with cards and false dice, was security enough against chance; and by his dexterity in gaming, he became worth above 100000 *l.* in a few years.

Not but that he was also very expert at the Royal Game of Chess; in which, the first and highest piece is a King, the next in height is a Queen, the cloven heads are Bishops, they who have heads cut aslaunt, like a feather in a helmet, are call'd Knights, the last are call'd Rooks, with a round button'd cap on their heads, which signifie the country and peasantry; the Pawns are all alike, and each nobleman hath one of them to wait upon him. Now he that would be an artist in this noble game, must be so careful to second his pieces, that if any man advanced be taken, the enemy may be likewise taken by that piece that guards or seconds it; so shall he not clearly lose any man, which should it fall out contrarily, might lose the game: He must also make his passage free for retreat, as occasion shall serve, lest he be worsted. In defending, you must also be very careful, that you are able to assault as well as your enemy; for you must not only answer your adversaries assault, by foreseeing his design by his play, and preventing it, but you must likewise devise plots, to pester and grieve your assailant, and chiefly how to entrap such pieces as are advanced by him, preventing their retreat; among which a Pawn is soonest ensnared, because he cannot go back for succour or relief; but Bishops and Rooks are harder to be surprized, because they can march from one side of the field to the other, to avoid the ensuing danger; but the Knights and Queens, of all, are with most difficulty betray'd, because they have

so many places of refuge, and the Queen more especially :
Where note, as a great piece of policy, that, if possible,
you constantly have as many guards upon any one piece
of yours, as you see your enemy has when he advances
to take it; and be sure withal, that your guards be of
less value than the pieces he encountereth you with;
for then if he falls to taking, you will reap advantage
thereby; but if you see you cannot guard yours, but must
of necessity lose it, then be very circumspect, and see
whether you can take a far better piece of his, in case
he takes yours, by advancing some other piece of yours
in guard; for so, as it often falls out, that yours which
you had given over for lost may be saved, whereas no
other way could have done it. When an adverse piece
comes in your way, so that by it all may be taken, consider
with yourself, first, whether it be equal in worth to yours,
next, whether it can do you any damage in the next
draught; if so, let it alone; for as it is best to play
first, so it is to take last; unless you might take the piece
clear, or get a better than that you lose to take it, or at
least disorder him one Pawn in his taking your man that
took his; but when you have the advantage, be it but
of one good piece for a worse, or of a Pawn clear, then it
is your best way to take man for man, as often as you can;
besides, you are to note, that whatsoever piece your
adversary plays most, or best withal, be sure, if it lies
in your power, to deprive him thereof, though it be done
with loss of the like, or of one somewhat better, as a
Bishop for a Knight; for by this means you may frustrate
your adversaries design, and become as cunning as himself. Now the chief aim of chess, is to give the check,
which is when you so check the King of the adverse
party, that he can neither take the checking piece, because it is guarded, nor yet remove out of it. Your care
ought to be in the interim, how to deprive him of some of
the best pieces, as his Queen or Rook; and the way to
entrap a Queen is twofold, first by confining her to her
King, so that she may not remove from him, for leaving
him in check of an adverse piece; secondly, by bringing

her to, or espying her in such a place, as a knight of yours may check her King, and the next draught take her: In the same manner you may serve a Bishop, if the adverse Queen covers her sloap-wise, but if she ſtands not in such a poſture, she may be brought to it; entice her thither with some unguarded man, which she out of eagerness of taking for nothing, may indiscreetly bring herself into trouble. But if you intend to catch a Queen with a Knight, imagine that the adverse King ſtands in his own place unremoved, and that the Queen has brought her self to ſtand in that place, where the King's Rook's Pawn ſtood; firſt, the ſtanding in this poſture, bring, if you can, one of your Knights to check her King, in the third house before his own Bishop; and if there be no man ready to take up your Knight immediately, he will take up the Queen at the next draught. The Rooks are also to be surprized two ways; firſt, by playing your Bishop into your Knight's Pawn's firſt place of ſtanding, which Bishop shall march asloap towards the adverse Rook of the opposite corner, which if you can make uncover'd of the Knight's Pawn, your Bishop will then undoubtedly take clear for nothing; the other way is like that of surprizing the Queen, with a Bishop or a Knight; where you muſt take notice, that your adversary's Queen Rook, is so much the easier to be taken with your Queen's Knight, that that Knight at his third draught may check the King, and take the same Rook at his fourth draught. There are several other ways to take a Rook, which practice muſt inform you. There is an ingenious way of taking a great man for a Pawn; when you espy two great men of your adversary's ſtanding in one and the same rank, and but one house between them, then prepare a guard, if you have it not ready to your hand, for a Pawn, which bring up to the rank to them, in the middle or front of both of them; and without doubt, if he save the one, your Pawn will take the other; and this way of taking is called a fork or dilemma.

But to conclude, Mr. Bourchier having got a great deal of money by gaming, he purchased a very pretty estate near Pershore in Worcestershire, on which he liv'd very handsomly and genteely till he was afflicted with an asthma, of which he died at his lodgings in Tothill-street in Westminster, in 1702. Aged 45 years, and was decently interr'd near his seat in the country.

Miles Corbet, *a Cheat.*

This notorious cheat was born but of very poor parents at Bromley, in the County of Kent, who not having wherewithal to send him to school, want of literature brought him, as he grew up, to be very impudent; and as soon as he could begin to think himself a man, he came up to London, where he found acquaintance suitable to his own inclination, and quickly became acquainted with all the growing vices of the town, and a most celebrated gamester at Back-Gammon, at which game he won in one night 2500 pounds of Beau Seymour, who was kill'd in St. James's Park, by one Kirk, a Captain in the Earl of Oxford's troop.

Having this success, he was so much buoy'd up therewith, that he thought fortune had resolv'd ever to be on his side; but shortly after losing 1400 *l.* of his former booty, he was resolv'd, because he could neither read nor write, to turn Doctor of Physick. Accordingly he went to the drugsters, bought the sweepings of their shops, and made medicines, like other quacks, for the destruction of mankind. Next putting out printed bills, with such specious titles as Tetrachymagogon, or any other nonsensical words; he was sent for to visit a sick lady, whose name the messenger told him was the Lady Wilmot. It was hard by Leicester-fields. They conducted him into a chamber very well furnish'd, where he was received by a young lady, who could not be above one or two and twenty at the most; she told him, that the lady who was desirous of consulting upon an extraordinary malady, did not live there, but that she would come in a minute, for that she had sent her footman to inform her he was there. Physicians visits are not generally tedious; so that to tarry too long in a place would be to derogate from that genteel character: But Miles dispensed with this punctilio for once, because the person with whom he had to do, appear'd to be extremely beautiful and so witty, as to pick his pocket of 66 guineas, and 18 half guineas, which he never had again, by reason he did not miss 'em till he went home, and before he got back to his sham lady, she had shifted her lodgings.

Now Miles Corbet, being ruin'd by this loss, he lifted himself in Lieutenant Bradock's Company, in the second regiment of Foot-Guards, and then learnt the art of playing at cups and balls, at which most notorious way of cheating fools, he became as dexterous as one Phil. Lipscomb, who is now reckon'd for that ingenious manner of bubbling, the best sharper in England. By these cups and balls Corbet got a great deal of mony, and spent it as fast; but at last Death serving upon him a Writ of *Diem clausit extremum*, he died as rotten as a pear of the pox, in the year 1712, aged 46, and was buried in the Churchyard of St. Giles's in the Fields.

Justice HIGDEN, *a Gamester*.

THIS gentleman descended of a very good family in the West of England, was in his juvenile years admitted a Member of the Honourable Society of the Middle-Temple, but his inclination being in a little time averse to a close study of the law, he quitted the Inns of Court and went into the army, and by his good behaviour and courage beyond sea, he obtain'd, after his coming over into his native country again, not only a commission in the first Regiment of Foot-Guards, but also a Commission of the Peace for the County of Middlesex; in which he continu'd for three or four years; When one time being on the guard at the Tower, a man being apprehended for clipping money, and being brought before him his Worship began to threaten him with hanging, and taking about an hundred-pound-bag full of clippings from the conſtable. Quoth he, I'll see if I can make this fellow an evidence to discover his accomplices. So taking him by himself into another room, Truly (said he) you are a fine rogue indeed to cut money to pieces, when so scarce as it is; come, come, let's see what money you have about you, and if it is possible, I will do what I can to save you for this once. The prisoner gave his Worship 50 guineas; then bringing him out again, quoth he to the conſtable, you may go about your business, I'll detain you no longer; for as soon as I have made his mittimus, I'll send a file of musqueteers with him to Newgate, for fear he should make an escape. The conſtable went home, and the Juſtice provided a file of musqueteers to convey the prisoner to goal, to whom he had given private orders what to do when they were at the Poultry-Compter, where happen'd to be a croud of people, occasion'd thro' a ſtop of coaches, carts, etc., he gave a sudden spring from his guard, and running as faſt as he could, also crying out an arreſt, he got clear away. The soldiers carrying this news back to Juſtice Higden, he fell a swearing and ſtamping like a mad man, asking why they did not shoot him; They reply'd, they durſt not presume to fire after him, for fear of killing other people. Whereupon he committed them to the Marshalsea, where they liv'd very well upon his coſt for two or three days, and then were set at liverty. But this escape of the prisoner coming to the conſtable's ears, he demanded a share of the clippings; which his Worship not allowing him, he made such a complaint againſt him, which turn'd him out from ever being a Juſtice of the Peace for the future.   .   .   .   .   .

One day Captain Higden meeting with Mr. Watson, in Fleetſtreet, they went to dinner at the black Spread-Eagle in Chancery-lane, and being both notable trenchermen, and eating with all the eagerness they could, for fear one should eat more than the other, Higden being very dry, he declin'd drinking, lest he should lose any time ; at last drought compelling him to wet his whistle, he takes up a tankard of beer, and holding his comrade by the knife-hand, quoth he, Honest Watson, here's to you with all my heart. And so prevented his eating till he had took a hearty draught.

Mr. Higden was a great customer among the brokers in Harp-Alley by the ditch-side, for buying old keys of 'em, which he generally turn'd to a good account ; as particularly one day, when taking a hackney-coach early in the morning at Charing-cross, he carry'd him to Westminster, from thence to the Royal-Exchange, from thence to the Tower, from thence to Bloomsbury-Square, so that what with making the coachman wait at each place, it was grown quite night ; then ordering the coachman to drive to the Middle-Temple-Gate, he takes an old key out of his pocket, and giving it to the coachman, quoth he, Go to my Chambers at such a number in Pump-Court, and if my clerk is not at home, do you open the door yourself, and bring my cloak, which you'll find hanging behind the door, but be sure take care you shut it fast after you again. The coachman goes, as he was order'd, to his chamber, where finding no body within, he began to make use of his old key, which not fitting the wards, it would not open the door ; but whilst he was tampering with the lock, the gentleman himself came up stairs, and finding the coachman endeavouring to open his chamber, which had been lately robb'd, he cry'd out thieves, and had him presently secur'd. The coachman alledging his own innocency, told the person who seiz'd him, he was sent thither by a gentleman he had in his coach to fetch him a cloak ; but going to the coach, and finding no body in it, the coachman was carry'd before a Magistrate, where the gentleman deposing, that his chamber had been but very lately robb'd, and that he found the prisoner attempting to open his chamber with an old key, which he did not deny, he was committed to Newgate. Afterwards taking his tryal at the Sessions-house in the Old-baily, the matter went so hard againſt him, that he had been certainly caſt for his life, if Higden had not appear'd in Court, to juſtify that the coachman had the key of him, and also brought half a dozen other coachmen to prove that they had been bilk'd so by him in the like manner before.

This comical spark was also a great gameſter, especially at dice; and one night he and another of his fraternity going to a gaming-house, Higden draws a chair and sits down, but as often as the box came to him, he paſt it, and sat only as a ſpeĉtator; till at laſt one of those who were at play said to him in a pet, Sir, if you won't play, what do you sit there for? Upon which he snatch'd up the box, and said, Set me what you will, and I'll throw at it. One of the gentlemen set him 2 guineas, which he won, and then he set him 4, which he nick'd also; the reſt of the gentlemen who were at the table took his part who had loſt, and set to Higden, who by some art, and some luck, won 120 guineas; and presently after throwing out, he rose up from the table and went to his companion by the fire-side, who ask'd him how he durſt be so audacious as to venture at firſt to play, knowing he had not a shilling in his pocket. One of the losers over-hearing what was said, How's that, quoth he, had you no money when you began to play? That's no matter, reply'd Higden, I have enough now; and if you had won of me, you muſt have been contented to have kick'd, buffeted, or pump'd me, and you should have done it so long till you said you was satisfy'd. Besides, Sir, I am a soldier, and have often faced the mouths of thundring canons for 8 shillings a day, and do you think I would not hazard the tossing in a blanket for the money I have won to night. All that were concern'd wonder'd at his confidence; but he laugh'd heartily at their folly, and his own good fortune; and so march'd off with a light heart, and a heavy purse. Afterwards, to make himself as miserable as he could, he turn'd poet, when going into Ireland, he writ there a play or two, and shortly after dy'd there very poor, in 1703, aged 44.

Monsieur GERMAIN, *a Gamester.*

MONSIEUR GERMAIN came but of mean extraction, for his parents kept an ordinary at Delft in Holland, where he was born, and coming over into England at the time of the happy Revolution in 1688, he quickly advanced his fortune by being a great gamester; but the chief promotion of him was occasion'd by his being a stallion to the Lady Mary Mordaunt, Consort to his Grace the late Duke of Norfolk, who proving her in parliament to be guilty of adultery, he was divorced from his Dutchess, who then liv'd publickly with Germain; who was the first man that ever brought up the game of Spanish Whist, which is a meer bite, perform'd after this manner:

Having a pack of cards, the 4 Treys are privately laid on the top of 'em, under them an Ace, and next to that a Deuce; then letting your adversary cut the cards, you do not pack 'em, but deal all them that are cut off one at a time betwixt you; then taking up the other parcel of cards, you deal 6 more cards, giving yourself 2 Treys and a Deuce, and to the other person 2 Treys and an Ace, when laying the remainder of the cards down, wherein are allow'd no trumps, but only the highest cards win, so they are but of the same suit, whilst you are playing, giving your antagonist all you can, tho' 'tis in your power not to let him, you seem to fret, and cry you have good Putt-Cards, he having 2 Treys and a Ace, will be apt to lay a wager with you, that you cannot have better than him; then you binding the wager, he soon sees his mistake. But in this trick you must observe to put the other three Deuces under yours when you deal.

Mons. Germain, who died a little after the Lady Mary Mordaunt, in the country, in 1712, aged 46 years, was very expert at L'Ombre, the manner of which game is thus incomparably describ'd by Mr. Pope in his Hero-comical Poem, intitul'd

THE RAPE OF THE LOCK.

Belinda now, whom Thirst of Fame invites,
Burns to encounter Two advent'rous Knights,
At *Ombre* singly to decide their Doom ;
And swells her Breast with Conquests yet to come.
Strait the three Bands prepare in Arms to join,
Each Band the Number of the Sacred Nine.
Soon as she spreads her Hand, th' Aerial Guard
Descend, and sit on each important Card :
First *Ariel* perch'd upon a *Matadore*,
Then each, according to the Rank they bore ;
For *Sylphs*, yet mindful of their ancient Race,
Are, as when Women, wond'rous fond of Place.

Behold four *Kings* in Majesty rever'd,
With hoary Whiskers, and a forky Beard ;
And four fair *Queens* whose Hands sustain a Flow'r,
Th' expressive Emblem of their softer Pow'r ;
Four *Knaves* in Garbs succinct, a trusty Band,
Caps on their Heads, and Halberds in their Hand ;
And parti-colour'd Troops, a shining Train,
Draw forth to combat on the Velvet Plain.

The skilful Nymph reviews her Force with Care :
Let Spades be Trumps ! she said, and Trumps they were

Now move to War her Sable *Matadores*,
In Shew like Leaders of the swarthy *Moors*.
Spadillio first, unconquerable Lord !
Led off two captive Trumps, and swept the Board.
As many more *Manillio* forc'd to yield,
And march'd a Victor from the verdant Field.
Him *Basto* follow'd but his Fate more hard
Gain'd but one Trump, & one *Plebeian* Card.
With his broad Sabre next, a Chief in years,
The hoary Majesty of *Spades* appears,
Puts forth one manly Leg, to sight reveal'd ;
The rest his many-colour'd Robe conceal'd.

The Rebel-*Knave*, that dares his Prince engage,
Proves the juſt Victim of his Royal Rage.
Ev'n mighty *Pam*, that Kings and Queens o'erthrew,
And mow'd down Armies in the Fights of *Lu*,
Sad Chance of War! now, deſtitute of Aid,
Falls undiſtinguiſh'd by the Victor *Spade!*

Thus far both Armies to *Belinda* yield;
Now to the *Baron* Fate inclines the Field.
His warlike *Amazon* her Hoſt invades,
Th' imperial Consort of the Crown of *Spades*.
The *Club's* black Tyrant firſt her Victim dy'd,
Spite of his haughty Mien, and barb'rous Pride:
What boots the Regal Circle on his Head,
His Giant Limbs, in State unwieldy spread;
That long behind he trails his pompous Robe,
And, of all Monarchs, only grasps the Globe?

The *Baron*, now his *Diamonds* pours apace;
Th' embroider'd *King* who shows but half his Face,
And his refulgent *Queen*, with Pow'rs combin'd,
Of broken Troops an easy Conqueſt find.
Clubs, Diamonds, Hearts, in wild disorder seen,
With Throngs promiscuous ſtrow the level Green.
Thus when dispers'd a routed Army runs,
Of *Asia's* Troops, and *Afric's* sable Sons,
With like Confusion-different Nations fly,
In various Habit, and of various Dye,
The pierc'd Battalions disunited fall,
In heaps on heaps; one Fate o'erwhelm's them all.

The *Knave* of *Diamonds* now exerts his Arts,
And wins (O shameful Chance!) the Queen of *Hearts*.
At this, the Blood the Virgin's Cheek forsook,
A livid Paleness spread o'er all her Look;
She sees, and trembles at th' approaching Ill,
Juſt in the Jaws of Ruin and *Codille*.
And now (as oft in some diſtemper'd State)
On one nice *Trick* depends the gen'ral Fate,

An *Ace* of *Hearts* steps forth: The *King* unseen
Lurk'd in her Hand, and mourn'd his captive *Queen*:
He springs to Vengeance with an eager Pace,
And falls like Thunder on the prostrate *Ace*.
The Nymph exulting fills with Shouts the Sky;
The walls, the Woods, and long Canals reply.

JACK OGLE, *otherwise called Mad* OGLE, *a Gamester*.

JACK OGLE was a man well born, and well bred; and tho' his parents always liv'd in the country, at a place call'd Ashburton in Devonshire, yet had he been chiefly brought up in Exeter: He had a gentleman-like skill in most exercises, of which his masterpiece was riding the Great-Horse. When he was young, his father dy'd worth 250 pounds a year, of which 50 were his wife's joynture. He never had more than two children, John Ogle, and his sister; and that his son's estate might not be incumber'd, by his frugality he saved 500 pounds, as a portion for his daughter. On his death-bed he left every thing under the tuition of this wife, with a great charge that his son should have all the education bestow'd upon him that he should be capable of receiving; which was not overmuch, by reason Jack was too unlucky to be too great a scholar.

About half a year after he came to age, and was possessed of his estate, he came to London: He was generous and bold, more cunning than witty, and set out with very few faults, and of them a little conceit, and an itch to romancing, were the worst, though not very conspicuous. Here he had not been long, but his extravagancy compel'd him to mortgage part of his estate: However, he was endu'd under his misfortunes with great valour and good humour, which in a short time he found an opportunity to let the world see; for happening to meet with two quarrels, the first with one that was famous for fighting, namely, young Talbot, the Duke of

Shrewsbury's brother, kill'd by the present Duke of Grafton's father; the second with a man of a great estate, but a noted coward; he behaved himself with as much bravery and evenness of temper in the one, as he shew'd knowledge in point of honour and good breeding in the other: And as there is not any thing that makes a man more known than a duel, especially if it be with one of distinction, and procures him greater applause than the managing of it with discretion as well as courage; so these two rencounters falling out not long from one-another, gain'd him no small reputation, and in less than a twelvemonth Jack Ogle had a general acquaintance at Whitehall, where, in the reign of King Charles the Second, men of spirit were much esteem'd, and very well receiv'd.

Not long after Ogle's being in London, his sister also came up to town, qualify'd to wait on a lady by a boarding-school education; where, give me leave to tell you, I have often observ'd that young gentlewomen may be taught to sing and dance, to work and dress, and, if they will, receive good instructions for a genteel carriage, and how to be mannerly; but these things chiefly concern the body, the mind remains uninstructed: They lead easie and lazy lives, and have abundance of time upon their hands, especially those whose relations are rich and foolish enough to furnish them with as much money as may enable them to bribe their teachers to neglect their duty, and wink at their faults, and by cramming them-selves with custards and cheesecakes all day long, oblige their mistress with having no stomach to their dinner. I have often taken notice now they have run together in shoals whispering and hugging one-another, and standing still between whiles, all at once set up a laughter with so much loudness, and so many grimaces, as if they were tickled to death; and all this occasion'd by some silly naughty word they have got by the end; perhaps a baudy monosyllable, such as boys write upon walls, which they have seen in coming from Church, and is often all they bring home. It is incredible to unthinking

people, how the tender fancies of those young chits are
wounded, and really debauch'd, where there is such a
parcel of them together: All the week long they are
barr'd from the sight of man, Sundays excepted. Some
of 'em are arch, moſt of 'em wanton, and when they
grow up, all fill one-another's heads with so much
rubbish of courtship and love, that it is a wonder they
don't run away with the firſt man they see. But to proceed with this digression, we shall return again to Madam
Ogle, who being gentlewoman to the Countess of Inchiquien, her extraordinary beauty, genteel carriage, and
graceful mien, soon recommended her to be the Duke of
York's miſtress; after which preferment to the embraces
of a King's brother, she was much tormented by Jack
Ogle, whom she was continually oblig'd to supply with
money, or else he would soon let the neighbours know his
siſter's character, by calling her in the open street all the
whores, and other moſt odious names, he could think on.

But the better to support his extravagancy, the Duke
of York put him into the firſt Troop of Guards, commanded then by the Duke of Monmouth; soon after
which he was call'd Mad Ogle, from the many mad
pranks he often play'd. For being a great gameſter,
and moſt an end on the losing side, by playing with those
who were sharper than himself, he could never afford to
keep a horse out of his pay; and being to be muſter'd
one day in Hide-Park, he took a hackney-coach, which
had a good pair of horses, and alighting there at the
gate, quoth he to the coachman, Honest Friend, I muſt
make bold to borrow one of your horses for a little while,
you shall have it safe again as soon as the muſter is over.
'Twas in vain for Mr. Switch to deny him, unless he
was dispos'd to be shot through the head; so Jack
taking his accoutrements out of the coach, and mounting
the coach-horse, away he rid up to his troop, where the
Duke of Monmouth observing not only then, but also
oftentimes before, his having a new horse, quoth he,
Mr. Ogle, I think you keep more horses than I can.
I can't tell (reply'd Ogle) whether or not I keep more

horses than you do ; but however, if your grace pleases, I can shew you the fellow to this too. And accordingly, when they were going out of the Park, Ogle riding up to the coach, which stood all the while at the muster but with one horse, he cry'd to the Duke, Here, an't please your Grace, here's the fellow to my gelding : At which the Duke smil'd, without any farther chiding him.

Another time having lost his cloak at play, and being to muster next morning, he borrow'd his landlady's scarlet petticoat ; which bundling up behind him, as he stood in his rank, either his right or left hand man perceiving it to be a petticoat by the border of it, which he had not carefully hid in the folding, he privately acquainted the Duke of Monmouth therewith. His Grace presently order'd the whole troop to cloak, which word of command was perform'd in the twinkling of an eye by all the gentlemen, excepting Ogle ; who was swearing and staring, and crying out, Cloak ! Cloak ! what a pox must we cloak now for ? It neither rains, hails, or snows as I see ; the weather's very fine. Thus whilst he was expostulating to himself, without making any offer to cloak, quoth the Duke, Mr. Ogle, Why don't you obey the word of command ? Pray, Sir, cloak. Yes (reply'd Ogle) if I must cloak, I will cloak ; but since the sun shines, I think 'tis hot enough without cloaking : So hastily putting the petticoat over his shoulders, thro' the top whereof his head was peeping like an owl out of an ivy-bush ; the spectacle caus'd a great fit of laughter thro' the whole troop, and among all others that saw the comical sight.

A little after this transaction Mad Ogle having lost a great sum of money at Billiards (tho' that game was his masterpiece) he went next morning to his sister to recruit his pockets. Being admitted into her chamber, with whom the Duke of York was then in bed fast asleep, she softly told him, she would answer his expectation as soon as she was up ; so drawing the curtain, order'd him to come about noon. Jack seem'd to be satisfy'd with her promise, but having not patience till the appointed time, he softly ſtep'd to the table, and took away all the Duke's cloaths, Star and Garter, and all that came to hand, and went clear off with great content, as finding in his breeches a fine gold-watch, and a great quantity of guineas. When the Duke came to rise, and the cloaths were missing, there was a great confusion in the house, but the servants making it appear that none but Mr. Ogle could have them, his Highness was obliged to send for other apparel; and being dress'd, departed from Madam Ogle in a great passion for the affront put upon him. In a short while after, the Duke being walking in the Mall in St. James's Park, he espy'd Ogle at some diſtance walking there also, with his cloaths on his back, which he got alter'd and made fit for himself; whereupon his Highness having left his nobles, and made what haſte he could up to Ogle in a great rage, Ogle perceiving him, made also up towards his Highness, and then unbuttoning and offering to ſtrip himself as faſt as he could, quoth he, I know your Highness wants your cloaths; here, take them, Sir, for I would not wear your caſt-off things another day if any man would give me 40 pounds. The Duke seeing Jack in this angry poſture, and very loth that the matter shou'd be publickly known, quoth his Highness, Hold, hold, pray Mr. Ogle, don't ſtrip yourself, I don't want my cloaths again, nor any thing else; but all that I desire of you is, that you never serve me so again: So they parted very good friends.

Another time Mad Ogle being at Locket's Ordinary among several persons of quality, they fell into gaming, at which Ogle having great luck, he order'd the servants to go and fetch all the poor they could find betwixt Whitehall and Charing-Cross, and give them as much victuals and drink as came to 12 pence apiece, man, woman and child; accordingly about 50 beggars of both sexes were brought together into the yard, old and young, blind and lame, deaf and dumb, all, excepting them that could not speak or hear, praying heartily for Mr. Ogle's long life, health, and prosperity, and also wishing him good luck. At laſt, having broke all the gameſters, he departed with his pockets full of gold and silver; and being met in the Spring-Garden by the Duke of Monmouth, quoth his Grace, So, Mr. Ogle, where have you been this way? Been (reply'd Ogle) why an't please your Grace, I have been fulfilling the scripture. That's very well, said the Duke, I'm very glad thou'rt turn'd so godly; but what part of the scripture haſt thou been fulfilling? Indeed, reply'd Ogle, a very good part, I have been filling the hungry with good things, and the rich I have sent empty away: For by Heavens, of above 20 noblemen, I have not left one of 'em a farthing in his pocket to bless himself withal. At which the Duke fell a laughing, and was very glad for his good fortune.

At laſt Mad Ogle had got so much of the sharping part at play, that those who knew his person would not play with him; thus finding him no more bubbles at ordinaries, the Groom-Porters, or other places of gaming; he haunted then Cock-pits, at which paſtime, being a novice, he loſt in less than a year's time at cocking above 900 pounds; then being reduc'd to a very low ebb, hard drinking and the pox kill'd him; aged 39 years.

Marquis DE GUISCARD, *a Gameſter.*

THIS person was born of more rich than noble parents at Orleans, a large, pleasant and beautiful City, seated on the river Loyre, 98 miles S.W. from Paris. Being the youngest son, he was sent to school, and having a liberal education beſtow'd on him at the university of Bourdeaux, became a monk; but committing a rape on a nun, he was oblig'd to fly his country, and seek his fortune in foreign parts, where poverty often pinching him, he was oblig'd to beg from Convent to Convent, to prevent his dying with hunger. Afterwards, his good ſtars smiling on him, he made his address to a Marchioness in Naples, who being of an inordinate desire in luſtful pleasures, and a widow, kept him as her ſtallion, though at the same time she kept company with an officer in the army; which being known by Guiscard, he was mightily enrag'd, and meditated revenge againſt his rival; which he soon effeſted, by conveying a letter to the officer in the lady's name, who was the same day gone into the country, wherein she desir'd him to come as late as he could to her apartment, by reason she was gone a visiting, and should not come back till after supper. The gentleman following the direſtions in the letter, went about 10 of the clock at night, and he was conduſted to bed; where he had not lain long, but, in-ſtead of the lady, he had for his bedfellow an old negro slave, whom Guiscard had hired for that purpose, with orders not to speak a word all night. Mean time he had loosen'd a board of the partition between the chamber and a closet, and by that means ſtole all the officer's cloaths, except his shirt, and faſten'd the board again so dex-trously, that no body could perceive it. The next morning about 8 of the clock, it being broad day-light, the Officer perceiv'd his miſtake, and thought he had lain with the devil, when he beheld so black and frightful figure a-bed, as the hagged-fac'd old African was. Immediately he fell to invoking all the he and she Saints, and begg'd of 'em to come to his assiſtance; and the more the slave bade him hold his tongue for fear of being heard, the more noise he made. At laſt, out of bed he jump'd in a dreadful fright, and looking for his cloaths, with design to make haſte out of the house, he was perfeſtly amaz'd, when he found they were gone. By this time the people of the house were alarm'd, and running to see what had made such a buſtle, the officer made no more ado, but wrapt himself up in one of the sheets, that he might not be expos'd to the peoples raillery. The poor negro, on the other hand, was as much asham'd to be known as the officer; and for that reason took the other sheet and wound it about her. Thus, like two figures in the niches of some pieces of architeſture, they ſtood guarding the chamber-door; and you might as well speak to a mute, as to either of them; shame had padlock'd their lips and confusion

metamorphos'd 'em into ſtone. The noise, occasion'd
by this disorder, made the Marchioness's son run himself
to see what was the matter; who, knowing nothing of the
intrigue, nor the officer, would needs make him dance
thro' the ſtreets in the equipage he was in. His dome-
ſticks follow'd him, hooting and hollowing all the way,
as far as the firſt Church he came at, where he put in to
hide himself from the mob. How the officer got home
afterwards, Guiscard could not tell, but he was never seen
in Naples again. The Marchioness, upon her return,
was puzzled how to manage the affair so as to salve her
reputation. But the negro was immediately clap'd into
a dungeon, and threaten'd hard, if she would not tell
who brought her into the lady's chamber, insomuch,
that at laſt she named Guiscard, and then the matter was
hush'd all on a sudden.

But nevertheless, revenge running in the thoughts of
the Marchioness, which now transported her beyond the
pleasure she had ever taken in the love of Guiscard, she
order'd one of her confidants to give him a mess, which
would soon send him out of the world. However,
Guicard having been familiar with this messenger of
death, ſhe discover'd the plot to him; after which he
withdrew himself from Naples, and going to Leghorn,
went on board an English vessel, which brought him into
England; where assuming the title of a Marquiss, and
pretending to be a French refugee, who was oblig'd to
abscond from his native country for professing the re-
form'd religion. He found so much favour at Court as
to have 400 pounds per annum settl'd on him for a pension, besides a Regiment given him; with which going
into Spain, he had not been long there before he was recall'd, and loſt his Commission, for some siniſter practices
acted at the fight of Almanza, which gave great suspicion
that he was in the French King's intereſt.

He now had nothing to subſiſt on but pension, which
being not sufficient to support his extravagancy in keeping
several misses, he became a profess'd gameſter at Billiards,
at which paſtime a table exactly level'd is highly valuable

by a good player; for at a false table it is impossible for him to shew the excellency of this art and skill, whereby bunglers many times, by knowing the windings and tricks of the table, have shamefully beat very good gamesters, who at a true table would have given them odds. Moreover, since recreation is a thing lawful in it self, I cannot but commend this as the most genteel and innocent of any I know, if rightly us'd; there being none of those cheats to be play'd at this, as at several other games. There is nothing here to be us'd but pure art, and therefore I shall only caution you, when you go to play, that you suffer not your self to be overmatch'd; and do not when you meet with a better gamester than your self condemn the table, and swear as Sir Robert Atkins did once at playing at nine-pins with the Lord Haversham, That his Lordship had put false pins upon him. However, this game is not so much us'd as late as formerly, by reason of those spunging caterpillars, which swarm where any Billiard-Tables are set up, who make that single room their shop, kitchen, and bed-chamber: Their shop, for this is the place where they wait for ignorant cullies to be their customers; their kitchen, for from hence comes the major part of their provision, drink and tobacco, being their common sustenance; and when they can persuade no more persons to play at the table, they make it their dormitory, and sleep under it; the floor is their feather-bed, the legs of the table their bed-posts, and the table the tester; here they dream of nothing but Hazards, being never out of them; of Passing and Repassing, which may be fitly apply'd to their lewd lives, which makes them continually pass from one prison to another till their lives are ended, and then there's a full end of the game.

The Marquis de Guiscard was an incomparable player at this pastime, and got a great deal of money at it; but being not satisfy'd with his gains, he must traiterously hold a correspondence with our common enemy, for which being apprehended by a messenger, and brought to an examination before several persons of note and distinction, for that purpose appointed, at the Cock-pit in Whitehall, such was his impudence and insolence as to stab the Earl of Oxford, Lord High-Treasurer of Great Britain, with a penknife under the short ribs, in the presence of their Graces the Dukes of Buckingham and Ormond, the Viscount Bolingbroke, and other great personages ; among whom he deservedly receiv'd several wounds, and was sent under a strong guard to Newgate, on Thursday the 8th of March, 17$\frac{10}{11}$, being the anniversary of Her Majesty's happy accession to the throne.

When he was in the Press-yard, he was of such an obstinate temper, that the surgeons were oblig'd to dress his wounds by meer force ; and several persons of quality went to examine him under his confinement about his treasonable practices, but could extort no confession out of him. He had one wound in his back, which not discovering to those appointed to cure him, it fester'd and gangreen'd to that degree before they found it out, that when they launc'd it, above a pint of corruption issued from thence, which was the cause of his death, about 3 of the clock in the morning, on Saturday the 17th of March following ; which violent end he attempted to have brought upon himself sooner, by pulling the tents out of his wounds, which was prevented for the future by tying down his hands. He was most ignominiously bury'd late at night in the Church-yard of Christ-Church in Newgate-street in London, unlamented by all, but such who were of as base principles as himself.

JONATHAN LAUD, *a Sharper and Gamester.*

THIS celebrated sharper was born of reputable parents in the City of Lincoln ; who bestowing a little education on him, he was put out an apprentice to an apothecary in Burleigh-street in the Strand ; but his father dying a little after he was out of his time, and leaving him about

1500 pounds, he was so intoxicated with the pleasures of the town, that instead of setting up his trade, he put on a sword, and set up for a gentleman; by which means, having in a short time spent the major part of his patrimony, at length he began to consider how he should live hereafter; and finding but small encouragement at home, and less abroad, he began to haunt gaming-houses for a livelihood, where at first he turn'd a sort of a Sweetner, to draw in young bubbles, by enticing 'em in this manner: Gentlemen, If you are for trying your fortune at Picquet, which is one of the fairest and finest games in the world, you cannot find any place in town, where you may venture on better prospects. This is the largest bank, and the gentlemen that deal are all men of worth and honour, and above anything that looks like trick or art. If ye are for sporting, I'll put in a couple of pieces with you, and we'll go make a push at the whole cargo; they have been broken two or three times this week already, and I have a strong fancy by the run of the cards, they can't win to night.

Thus would he catch several gudgeons for his brethren in iniquity, from whom he had also a pension, for being always in the gaming-room ready to fight, or rather bully for 'em, if there should be occasion. At length he became an excellent player at Draughts, at which he had ruin'd several tradesmen in and about London; and won many hundreds of pounds by a decoy of giving such as play'd with him 4 Kings to only 1 King and 3 Men; which were so plac'd, that 2 of the men must be lost move how he would, but nevertheless he won the game, by reason his 1 King at last takes the other's 4 Kings all at one moving. He was such a great artist at this game, that he would give any man a guinea that would bring a person to play with him for three guineas, till at last he was so noted for his ingenuity at Draughts, that none would play with him.

Nevertheless he resorted to all the most eminent gaming-houses about the town, and play'd much at Hazard, which is a very proper name for this game, for it speedily makes a man, or undoes him; in the twinkling of an eye is verify'd this saying, *Aut Cæsar aut nullus*, either a man or a mouse. This game is play'd with but two dice; but there may play at it as many as can ſtand or sit round the largeſt table. Four and five to seven is judg'd to have the worſt on't, because four (call'd by the nickers and sharpers, little Dick-Fisher) and five have but two chances, Trey-Ace, and two Deuces, or Trey-Duce and Quater-Ace; whereas seven hath three chances, Cinque-Deuce, Size-Ace, and Quater-Trey; in like condition is nine and ten, having but two chances, Size-Trey, Cinque-Quater, or Size-Quater and two Cinques.

Now six and eight, one would think, should admit of no difference in advantage with seven; but if you will rightly consider the case, and be so vain to make trial thereof, you will find a great advantage in seven over six and eight, although six, seven, and eight have equal chances; for in six is Quater-Deuce, Cinque-Ace, and two Treys; in eight Size-Deuce, Cinque-Trey and two Quaters; but then the disadvantage muſt be consider'd in the Doublets, 2 Treys or 2 Quaters; for you will find that Size-Deuce is sooner thrown than two Quaters; and so consequently Cinque-Ace or Quater-Deuce sooner than two Treys. This was prov'd by Jonathan Laud himself, who once play'd with a young Barriſter, at the Fountain-Tavern in the Strand, upon this very score: The bargain was made, that Laud should have seven always, and the Barriſter six, and throw continually; and when they went to play, Laud got the firſt day 20 pounds; the next day the like sum; and so for six days together, winning in all 120 pounds, notwithſtanding the Barriſter had square dice, and threw them always himself. And farther, to confirm what I alledge, not only this rook, but many more have told me, that they desir'd no greater advantage than to have seven always, and the caſter to have six.

Certainly Hazard is the moſt bewitching game that's play'd on the dice; for when a man begins to play, he

knows not when to leave off; and having once accus-
tom'd himself to play at Hazard, he hardly ever after
minds any thing else. Thus Sir John Jacob, a Knight
in Cambridgeshire, about 70 years of age, would play
at an ordinary when his eyes were so defective, that he
was forced to help them with a pair of spectacles; and
a friend of his having one day an opportunity to say to
him, I admire how a man of your years can be so vain
and boyish as to mind play still; insisting withal upon
the folly of that action to hazard his money, when he had
not sight enough remaining to discern whether he had
won or lost: Besides, Sir, said he, you cannot but hear
how you are derided every time you come to the ordinary;
one says, Here comes he that cannot rest in quiet, but will
cry without the rattle of the dice; another cries, such an
one plays by the ear, for he cannot see to play. Let them
talk what they will, reply'd Sir John, I cannot help it,
I have been for above 40 years so us'd to play, that should
I leave it off now, I had as good stop those issues about
me, which have been instrumental in the preservation
of my life to this length of time.

Indeed Jonathan Laud had been a great winner at
Draughts; but when he took to play at dice, having
been as great a loser, he resolv'd, if he could contrive
a way to win a considerable sum, it should be the basis
of his future settlement; and after various consultations
within himself, he at length contriv'd this stratagem:
He caus'd a box to be made, not as they are usual,
screw'd within, but smooth, and procur'd it to be so
well painted and shadow'd within, that it look'd like
a screw'd box; now this box was but half-board wide at
top, and narrow at bottom, that the dice might stick,
and the box being smooth, would come out without
tumbling. With this box he went and play'd at Inn and
Inn, by vertue whereof, and his art of taking up and
throwing his dice into the box, he got the first night
1900 guineas, and the next night 350 pounds a year,
with a coach and six horses, which coach and horses being
very valuable, he sold, but the estate he liv'd on to his

dying day, with great improvements, and never would handle a dye since, well knowing how many worthy families it has ruin'd : Wherefore, I may say, happy is he that having been much inclin'd to any of those time-spending, money-wasting games on the dice, hath took up in time, and resolv'd for the future never to be concern'd with them more ; but more happy is he that has never heard the name thereof. Thus Jonathan Laud having timely left off this destroying vice, he marry'd a young woman, with whom he had a portion of 2000 pounds, and liv'd very happily with her at his country-seat near Henly upon Thames in Oxfordshire, till he dy'd, which was in June, in the year 1704.

Major-General FIELDING, *a Gamester*.

MR. FIELDING was descended of a very good family near Coventry in Warwickshire; his parents bestowing a liberal education upon him, he was sent to the Inns of Court to study the law ; but his father soon after dying, whereby he obtain'd the possession of about 600 *l.* per ann. his inclination to vanity incited him not to follow the profession of revolving ancient Records, reading old Statues, searching worm-eaten Charters, and poring on dull Reports.

Now his vain imaginations roving after the fair sex, he distinguish'd himself always by his extraordinary dress, and fanastick habit of his footmen, who generally wore yellow coats and black feathers in their hats, and black sashes, or else some other characteristick of foppishness, to signalize himself for the greatest fop which ever appear'd in England ; as may plainly be perceiv'd by the following character of him.

This spark put up for a Beau, which word in the sober man's dictionary signifies a coxcomb, whose heterogeneous soul is such, that no less than a combination of all the vices in the world must be summon'd in to make up a partial description of him. When Fielding was in the land of the living, one might properly have call'd him a volume of methodical errata, bound up in a gilt cover; or rather, he was a man's skin full of prophaneness, a paradise full of weeds, and a heaven full of devils. His very name's enough to blaſt the gentility of all that went before him, and to breath a perpetual disgrace upon the sleeping ashes of his progenitors. His chief employment was to scorn all business, but the ſtudy of the modes and vices of the times; and when he firſt came to town, he soon learnt how to make a choice of his boon companions, by their moſt profound wickedness. As for his habit and garb, he daily endeavour'd that all should appear new about him, except his vices and his religion; he is too much in love with the firſt to change them, and the latter he could not change because he never had any. He was generally trick'd up in gauderies, as if he had resolv'd to make the whole female sex his conqueſt; and by his variety of fashions his very creditors durſt never swear him to be the man they had truſted. His draper was afraid of losing him in a labyrinth of his own cloth, it was so cover'd with the finery of the laceman. He took as much care and pains to new-mould his body at the dancing-school, as if the only shame he fear'd was the retaining of that form which God and Nature gave him: Every ſtep he took presented you with a perfeɛt puppet-play; and Rome it self could not in an age have shew'd you more anticks than this notorious fop was able to imitate in half an hour. He was a very bungler at paying his debts, about which he never troubl'd himself; for a certain honeſt gentleman once saying to him, considering how much money you owe, Sir, to trades-men, I wonder how you can sleep a nights for thinking on't. He reply'd, I can take my reſt very well, Sir; I wonder more how they can sleep to whom I owe any thing.

When he first launched abroad into the world, he appear'd often at court; where King Charles being pleas'd to call him Handsom Fielding, this royal notice, which that monarch was pleas'd to take of him, made him in great vogue among several of the female sex, by whom, after he had resign'd up his Commission of the Peace, which he bore for the City and Liberty of Westminster, he was maintain'd as a stallion; but the income which this unlawful practice brought him in, being not answerable to his extravagant way of living, he was obliged to support his ambitious grandeur by horse-racing at New-Market-Heath, and other places, and herein was often successful, by bribing jockeys to ride foul matches: And likewise by dawbing in the fist those fellows who fed game-cocks, he hath won many hundreds of guineas at the Cock-pit at Westminster, and other places to which people resort to venture their money on that destructive diversion of cock-fighting.

He much frequented the Royal-Oak-Lottery; in which sort of gaming is neither truth nor profit, because the master thereof runs away with all the gains; here Fielding could obtain but very little to uphold his old extravagancy, and therefore was still obliged to live upon the reversion of the females; being so much debauch'd, that he could never be without women, for whom he often pretended to expose his person, where he was sure there was no danger.

He happen'd to be once mistaken in the exercise of his prowess, when he encounter'd Mr. Price, a Welsh gentleman, who can'd and wounded him at the Theatre in Lincolns-Inn-Fields; tho' he was afterwards more successful in attacking and running a linkboy thro' the body in St. Martin's-lane. And tho' he had the ayre of a hector, and look'd big, yet his want of true courage being known, made him the object of every young beau that wou'd shew his valour at a rapier. Not to mention his being kick'd and pull'd by the nose by several noblemen, when they have discover'd the clandestine methods he us'd to bite them in horse-matches at New-Market; which, besides giving the losers leave to speak, he bore without the least resentment.

He sometimes descended so low as to visit the ducking-pond, where he often found a great many bubbles, and chouced them out of a deal of money by the goodness of his spaniels. But his talent lay much in Chess and Backgammon, which two games have often lin'd his pockets with large sums of gold, got from persons of quality who were meer novices at all manner of plays. And tho' noblemen ought to be above knowing what biting or sharping is, yet ought they so far to learn it, and know the tricks of all games, to be secure against the cheats of others. However, the best way not to be cheated, is not to play at all; and indeed there's nothing more miserable than a gamester, in whom is no one ordinary trace of thinking to be found, but strong passion, violent desires, and a continued series of different changes are continually tearing it to pieces. There appears no middle condition; the triumph of a Prince, or the misery of a beggar, are his alternate states. He that is worth 4 or 5000 pounds at noon, shall not be worth a farthing by night; and what can be a greater scandal for noblemen, than to play with fellows who have no other visible livelihood than that of shaking the elbow? who are so very poor, that if ill luck strips 'em of all their money, they must borrow half a crown of the maid that cleans their shoes, with which gaming in Lincolns-Inn-Fields, among the boys for farthings and oranges, till they have made up three pieces, they then return to the Rose-Coffeehouse, or some other place for raffling, with hopes of retrieving their late losses.

Mr. Fielding, tho' he had two strings to his bow, namely, dice and women, yet living too profusely, what accru'd to him by gaming and whoring could not maintain him an extraordinary equipage; therefore, intending to better his fortune by marriage, interest directed him to one Madam Delaune, a gentlewoman of about 20000 pounds portion, living near Tunbridge in the County of Kent; with which sum he was extreamly in love, tho' he had never seen the lady; and getting acquainted with an old bawd who pretended to have a more than ordinary acquaintance with Madam Delaune, she had not a little parcel of money to carry on the intrigue, which she managed with such subtilty, that in a very little time she had impos'd a wrong person on Fielding, by bringing him into the company of one Mary Wadsworth, a jilt of the town, who cunningly personated Madame Delaune, and was marry'd to him after the rites and ceremonies of the Church of Rome.

Not long after they were joyn'd in matrimony, the bride leaving Fielding in London, under pretence of going down to her country-seat, to settle some matters with her uncle, who was her guardian, before the news of the match reach'd his ears, and not coming up according to her appointed time, which he thought an age of divorce betwixt him and her portion, he went down to Tunbridge in a coach and six horses, where boldly entering Madam Delaune's house, he ask'd the servants whether the Lady Fielding was at home : They told him, Madam Delaune was at home ; but they knew no Lady Fielding. Quoth he again, Why, Madam Delaune is now the Lady Fielding, and my wife. This saying put the servants all into a great consternation, and Madam Delaune was as much surpriz'd to hear of her being demanded for a wife, before she was betroth'd to any body ; but Fielding seeing the lady, found he had been impos'd on, and returned to London no richer, tho' something wiser, than he went.

Notwithstanding this mortifying disappointment, he still bore up with his wonted assurance, and being resolv'd to venture all rather than not support his vanity and grandeur, he made his addresses to Barbara Dutchess of Cleveland, to whom, after a short courtship, he was marry'd ; whom he treated with so much insolence and barbarity, that she was oblig'd (for security of her life) to swear the peace against him before the late Lord Chief-Justice Holt, who, for want of sufficient bail, committed him to Newgate.

His barbarous usage of the Dutchess, and her persecution of him making a great noise in the world, brought about a discovery of his former marriage with Mrs.

Wadsworth; whereupon her Grace prosecuting him at the Sessions in the Old-bailey, he was found guilty of bigamy, but escap'd burning in the hand by Her Majesty's gracious pardon. After which, her Grace proceeding in the Spiritual Court, obtain'd a divorce, and so got quite rid of her tyrant. Being thus reduc'd to his state of want again, he was imprison'd for debt, and oblig'd to cohabit with his first spouse, Mrs. Wadsworth; who having compounded with his creditors, they liv'd together a small time in Scotland-yard, when he. was seiz'd with a violent fever, which in eleven days carry'd him out of this world, at the age of 61.

Major-General MACARTNEY, *a Gamester.*

THIS Irish spark was born but of very mean parents at Belfast, a seaport town in the north of Ireland, but having a little education bestow'd upon him at a Free-School at Galway in the same kingdom, he became qualified, by that time he was about 15 years of age, for a Colonel's *Valet de Chambre*, with whom coming in England, and learning to pimp extempore for his master, he became so much his favourite, that he bestow'd an Ensign's Commission upon him in his own Company. Still being belov'd by his Colonel, in a little time he came to be a Captain, and the Regiment to which he belong'd being commanded to Flanders, he there committed several insolent actions, in ravishing women, which was no admiration in him, when his lewdness incited his libidinous temper to force his own sister before he first left Ireland.

Afterwards returning to his native country again, to raise recruits, in his passage thither, a parson's wife, who at the same time was a passenger in the same ship with Maccartney, being fast asleep in her cabbin, this Irish Satyr undrest himself, and going into the gentlewoman, offer'd that abuse to her, which modesty obliges me here to conceal. Such was his intollerable lust, that he hath often sworn that he would debauch his own mother rather than go without a whore, for being a thorough-pac'd Papist, he imputed incest but a venial sin, or rather no sin at all. At the Battle of Hochflet he, by favour of some general Officers, got a Regiment of his own ; next was made a Brigadier at the fight of Ramellies ; and afterwards was prefer'd to a Major General's post, but for no other reason than to verefie this proverb, *Non cuivis homini contingit adire Corinthum,* that is to say, Kissing goes by favour.

The more he ascended the hill of honour, the more lewd he grew, and car'd not what money it cost him to accomplish his lustful desires. Thus lodging once at Brussels, he set his eyes on a young milk-maid, who came to the house every morning and evening, to serve the family with whom he lodg'd with milk, and seem'd to him so charming and agreeable, that maugre all his efforts, he was forc'd to submit to the superior power of love. He consider'd her attentively every time he saw her and found her beauty so incomparably perfect, that he gaz'd on her, the more he admir'd her, and his passion grew really uncontroulable. But one day as he was making some reflections on her extraordinary beauty, he heard the voice of that lovely girl cry, D'ye want any milk? At that Macartney went down, and resolv'd to follow her to know where she liv'd ; and being got a little distance from his lodging, he waited for the milk-maid's coming away, designing to dodge her home. She went through one of the city gates, and hous'd at a little cottage, about musquet-shot from thence. He made no question, but that was the place where she liv'd ; to make sure work on't, went by the door and found he had guess'd right. This intrigue commenc'd in the charming month of June ; a season in which the inhabitants of Brussels use to go in great numbers, and eat cream, or drink a sillabub in the villages ; and serv'd for a fit opportunity for him to introduce himself into the milk-maids company, and take the necessary measures to gratifie a

passion which began to consume him. One Sunday in
the afternoon, therefore, he went to the milk-maids
mud-house, which he had no sooner enter'd, but he
found all things concurring to render him happy, the
beauty being all alone, and her mother gone to Church.
The charming peasant was so neatly dreſt, and set off
with so many pretty ornaments, that they made a
wonderful addition to her beauty. Now being alone
he attempted to ravish her, but she making a vigorous
resiſtance, he could not succeed in his enterprize,
though to tempt her he gave her 110 piſtoles, which
she accepted, with a promise of obliging him, if he
would take her from her mother to live with him in
private lodgings.

Hereupon Maccartney return'd home, very well
satisfied, and full of hopes; expeċting, with the utmoſt
impatience, the hour appointed for their rendevous
the next day; when taking convenient lodgings for her
in the city, he brought all his effeċts thither to live with
this beloved milk-maid; but whilſt he went out to buy
his dear peasant new cloaths and scarfs *Alamode*, she
bundled up all Teague's baggage, and march'd clear off.
Being return'd home with a great deal of fine rigging for
his miſtress, whom he design'd to have enjoy'd at night
with as great a guſt as Jove did Leda, he was inform'd
by his landlady what had happen'd; so taking the key
and opening her chamber-door, he went in, where he
found the neſt, but his bird was flown away with above
the value of 600 *l.* in money, plate and apparel. Now
whilſt he was agitated with a thousand dismal apprehen-
sions for his loss, and revolv'd in his mind, the moſt
tragical thoughts to assuage his vexation, he heard some-
body knock at the door, and did not, in the leaſt, doubt
but his cruel miſtress, touch'd with remorse, was come
to beg his pardon for the injury she had done him;
he flew therefore to the window; but he was far out of
his conjeċture, for 'twas only his man come to bring him
news that he could not find the milk-maid high or low;
and in rummaging a few old cloaths which she had left

behind her, he found the following letter in a petticoat pocket.

How long, Dear Angel! will you make me languish, for the sake of poor trifling reflexions, that you force upon your own mind? What can you apprehend dangerous, while with me? Everything is ready for our voyage, and your consent given, we set out to-morrow after dinner. I'll be with you by and by, at the appointed hour. Don't fail to let the party we order'd to be at the door, to give me notice if your Irish lover be there. In the name of Jove, my Dear, let us not delay the execution of our project for one moment; for I can no longer subsist under the intolerable grief of con-sidering my self only as a partner of a good which composes all my happiness! Think of me, therefore, my Dear Angel! who, in expectation of the pleasure of embracing you without uneasiness, remains wholly yours!

Adieu.

This letter most sadly netled Macartney, and rais'd him to a very high pitch of madness when he plainly perceiv'd the milk-maid had left him for the sake of another gallant: But since it was impossible for him to retrieve the disaster of her running away from him to pursue some new conquest, he went forthwith to the camp, where recovering his former tranquility, he betook himself to gaming, especially at cards, wherein being a great artist for packing, shuffling and cutting the cards to his own advantage, he won a great deal of money from the officers of the army; and one time he won above 1590 pistoles of Prince Eugene, and some other foreign generals, which made him some amends for the trick which had been put upon him by the Belgick milk-maid. He play'd extraordinarily well at Beast, otherwise called La Bet by the French; also at Bankafalet; and Lanterloo, in which game you must note, that he who hath 5 cards of a suit in his hand, *Loos* all the gamesters then playing, be they never so many, and sweeps the board; if there be two Loos, he that is the eldest hand hath the advantage; but if there be a Loo of trumps, that takes the advantage from all, except any one hath *Pamm*, that is the Knave of Clubs, who saves his Loo, and is paid for one trick out of his stock. Moreover, when you play at this game, at every deal rub off a score, and for every trick you win set up a score by you, till the first scores are out, which are 5 in all, to remember you how many tricks you have won in the several deals in the game.

But at last Major General Maccartney being in England when a quarrel happen'd betwixt the late Duke of Hamilton and the Lord Mohun, he was not only a second for the last mentioned Peer, but also carried the challenge to the aforesaid Duke; which being accepted by his Grace, he chose one Colonel Hamilton for his second; and meeting on Saturday the 15th of November 1712 in Hyde-Park, the two Peers and the two seconds engaged one another in a most bloody duel, wherein the Duke and Lord, after receiving several desperate wounds, were both kill'd. Colonel Hamilton was wounded in the foot; but Maccartney had no wound, and after he had seen the two Peers fall, he got off, and though a proclamation was issued out by the Queen, wherein was promised the reward of 500 *l*, for any person that should apprehend him, and the Dutchess of Hamilton also promis'd by an advertisement of the "London Gazette" the sum of 300 *l*. more to any that should take him, yet did he make his escape out of her Majesty's Dominions, into Germany, where he endeavour'd to get a considerable post in the Emperor's army; but meeting with no encouragement from his Imperial Majesty, he retired from his territories into Denmark, where, it is said, he is entertain'd in that King's service: However, justice perhaps may overtake him in the end, and bring him to condign punishment, if it be true, as is deposed by some people, that he should, when the two Peers were engaged, interpose betwixt them, and assist the Lord Mohun in giving his Grace one of those wounds, which unfortunately prov'd mortal, to the great trouble and affliction of that most noble family which was ever loyal to the Crown.

Bob Weedon, *a Sharper and Gamester.*

This gentleman, if I may so call him, as being descended of a very good family, in his minority was a page to James, Duke of Monmouth (who was beheaded on Tower-Hill, for the rebellion in the West of England, in the Reign of King James the Second) in whose service he was brought up to dancing, fencing, musick, and drawing in dry colours to the life; but when his more mature years made him unqualified for being a page any longer, he had other places in that family whereby he might have rais'd his fortune, if he had not too much addicted himself to follow the humours of the town, and too early learnt the way of being a rake indeed.

Nevertheless, in the height of his extravagances, he had a great assistance from his Grace, to the very time of his unfortunate exit; after which he was forced to depend on the charitable benevolence of his elder brother a very worthy gentleman of Lincolns-Inn, and to whom he had been many years very chargeable. He was a very great drinker, insomuch that his voice was always as hoarse as any boatswains; and being of the Sadduces opinion, in holding no resurrection, he would not believe there were any ghosts or spirits appear after this life was ended on earth; whereupon a controversy arising once at a tavern in Kingstreet in Westminster betwixt him and some gentlemen on that account, a wager of a guinea was laid by one of them with him, that he durst not go to the Charnel-House in St. Margaret's Church-yard at 1 of the clock at night, and fetch from thence a scull. In the mean time one of the company going to the Sexton to let Bob have the liberty of going into the said receptacle of dead mens bones, he gave him a crown to frighten him, by being there himself when he came in the dark. The hour being come Bob went into the Charnel-House, where finding the door open, he went down stairs by a rope which guided him to the bottom, and groping amongst the bones, he found a scull, with which coming up, quoth the Sexton, who was planted there in a corner, Pray lay down that scull, because it is my grandfather's. This voice utter'd in a very dismal sort of a tone put Bob into some consternation, and laying it down, he grop'd for another, and finding one, was coming away with that, but the Sexton saying again, Lay down that scull, because it is my father's, he in a greater consternation laid down that too ; and finding a third scull, as he was bringing that away, quoth the supposed ghost, You must lay down that scull, because it is mine. These words put Bob into more fear than ever, but nevertheless replying, Let it be the D——l's scull, I will have this, away he came to the tavern in a great agony, and entering the room where his companions were waiting the event of his attempt, he threw the scull on the table, saying at the same time, I have won my wager, here it is ; but by G—d the man's coming hither that owns the scull. No sooner was this said, but the whole company, being about half a score, ran in a fright down stairs, tumbling one over another in such haste, as if they meant the Devil should have the hindermost ; to secure themselves from the owner of the scull some of them hid themselves in the cellar, others in the bar, and some ran into the kitchin for shelter ; but after an hour or two when they found Bob's words not true, their fear abating, they gather'd together again, and drank the wager of a guinea out, before they parted.

Wherever Bob lodg'd, he was a very good lodger, for he would be sure never to pay for his lodging, and having never any more suits of cloaths than backs, his landlord cou'd never seize on any thing, except his little carcass, which was not worth prison-room. Having nothing to live on, he was forced to follow gaming for a livelihood, and after supply'd his wants at some tennis-court, or the bowling-green at Mary-Bone where by betting and playing he won a great deal of money. He also play'd very well at Basset, in which game these terms are to be observ'd. *Talliere*, which is he that keeps the bank, who lays down a sum of money before all those that play, to answer every winning card that shall appear in his course of dealing, *Croupere*, who is one that is assistant to the Talliere, and stands by to supervise the losing cards ; that when there is a considerable company at play, he may not lose by over-looking any thing that might turn to his profit. *Punter*, a term for every one of the gamesters that play. *Fasse*, the first card that is turn'd up by the Talliere, belonging to the whole pack, by which he gains half the value of the money that is laid down upon every card of that sort by the Punters. *Couch* is a term for the first money that every Punter puts upon each card, every one that plays having a book of 13 several cards before him, upon which he may lay his money, more or less, according to his fancy. *Paroli* is, when having won the Couch or first stake, and having a mind to go on to get a *Sept-et-le-va*, you crook the corner of your card, letting your money lie without being paid the value of it by the Talliere. *Masse* is when you have won the Couch, or first stake, and will venture more money upon the same card, which is only pursuant to the discretion of the Punter, who knows or ought to know the great advantages the Talliere has, and therefore should be subtle enough to make the best of his own game. *Pay* is when the Punter has won the Couch or first stake, whether a shilling, crown, guinea, or whatever he lays down upon his card ; and being fearful to make the Paroli, leaves off ; for by going the Pay, if the card turns up wrong he loses nothing, having won the Couch before, but if by this adventure fortune favours him, he wins double the money that he stakes. *Alpiew* is much the same thing as the Paroli, and like that term us'd when a Couch is won, by turning up or crooking the corner of the winning card. *Sept-et-le-va* is the first great chance that shews the advantages of this game ; as for example, if the Punter has won the Couch, and then makes a Paroli, by crooking the corner of his card, and going on to a second chance, his winning card turns up again, it comes to *Sept-et-le-va*, which is 7 times as much as he laid down upon his card. *Quinze-et-le-va* as next in it's turn, is attending the Punter's humour who perhaps is resolv'd to follow his fancy, and ſtill lay his money upon the same card, which is done by crooking the third corner of his card, which coming up by the dealing of the Talliere, makes him win 15 times as much money as he Suk'd. *Trent-et-le-va* succeeds Quinze-et-le-va, and is markt by the lucky Punter, by crooking or bending the end of the fourth corner of his winning card, which coming up, makes him purchase of 33 times as much money as he laid down. *Soissant-et-le-va* is the higheſt and greateſt chance that can happen in this game, for it pays 67 times as much money, as is ſtak'd, and is seldom won but by some lucky Punter, who resolves to push the extream of his good fortune to the height; besides, it cannot be won but by the Talliere's dealing the cards over again, which if his winning card turns up, pays him with such a prodigious advantage.

Bob was also very expert at the Dutch game of Ver-quere, and the Italian game of Chess; and one day having won at Back-Gammon 20 guineas at the house of one Pike, a victualler, formerly living at the end of Curl-Court in the Strand, as he was next day viewing the luna-ticks in Bedlam for his recreation, he there pickt up, as he thought, a Quaker, because the ſtrumpet for a decoying disguise was dreſt up in the habit of those precise Heathens; and with a great deal of entreaty, for she seem'd very shy; prevailing with her to go to an adjacent tavern, they drank Canary very plentiful: But still all Bob's rhetorick having not force enough to win her to his unlawful embraces, he began to promote some healths, all which the seeming saint refused, nor would she drink any but a health of her own proposing, which was, *To the Month of March*; which being an odd sort of a health to him, he desired to know the meaning of it, and was told by her, that she generally drank a health to that month, because it usually comes in like a lion, but goes out like a lamb. At length Bob, without any farther enjoyment of his miſtress than kissing her, fell faſt a sleep; Then the pretended Yea and Nay laying close siege to his pockets, took out all the 20 guineas, which he had won the day before, and about 30 shillings in silver, and went away without any opposition by the drawers. About an hour afterwards our bubble, who had bubled many in his life-time, awoke, and finding the sham Light not in the room, he began to knock and thunder like a fury, when drawer going up to him, he asked what was become of the person who was along with him, and being told she was gone, he began to swear and curse like a mad man, and damn the month of March, for quoth he, The quaking bitch is march'd off with all my money. Then enquiring what the reckoning was, and being told it came to 15 shillings, he desired to be truſted for the same, and would certainly pay them the next day; but the people of the house, not knowing their cuſtomer, they sent for a conſtable, and having him before a Magiſtrate, he was committed to the Poultry-Compter, where it coſt him above 3 pounds before he got his liberty.

Bob was also very dextrious in playing at Bragg, at which game some very nice gameſters do make the 9 of Diamonds a second favourite card, with the Knave of Clubs, which is the principal favourite, to make a Pair-Royal of Aces, so that those two joyn'd with one natural Ace shall win from any Pair-Royal of Kings, Queens, Knaves, or any other cards, but a Pair-Royal of natural Aces. But Bob never playing upon the square at any game he was reckon'd such a sharper at laſt, that those who knew him would not play with him for crooked pins; whereupon being deprived of the principal part of his livelihood, and being so much in debt, that if he ſtay'd in London, he muſt have ended his days in a gaol, he resolved to go beyond sea; and getting to be steward to a Captain of a Man of War, his brother fitted him out accordingly; which he did not enjoy long, for the ship to which he belong'd being appointed among others to carry over Colonel Liliſton's Regiment from Plymouth to the West-Indies in 1694, he died in his voyage thither, aged 51 years, and was thrown over board to make a small banquet for the fish.

Monsieur St. EVREMONT, *a Gamester.*

THE descent of this noble Norman, born in the year 1613, we must acknowledge to be noble, and his education equivalent to his birth; for whilst a child, a learned clergyman went twice a day to his father's house, to instruct him in his studies. By this means, he so far master'd the Latin tongue, in less than 18 months time, that at 13 years of age he could explain any author, though never so intricate. In a word, his genius was seconded by the indefatigable pains of his ingenious tutor; who exercis'd him in speaking, and to give him the boldness necessary for an oration, would often make him declaim in publick. Living just by a Church of the Cordeliers, he generally made his declamations therein; and thither people flockt from all parts to see him once from the pulpit present the auditory with a piece of eloquence which he did not well understand; but by the cleanness of his expression, and the excellency of his voice, he came off so well, that all the principal noblemen in the city, where he dwelt, sent their coaches to bring him home to their palaces, to declaim before their ladies.

Afterwards his parents sent him to Rome, in order to his being brought up there like a child of difinition; for which end they put him into the Romish Seminary. That place is reckon'd one of the finest nurseries for youth in Europe; and most of the Princes of Germany, and almost all the Cardinals and eminent Prelates of the Church of Rome are indebted for their education, to that famous College. The Jesuites have the sole direction thereof; and there is not (as some say) a seminary in the world, wherein so many students are maintain'd, and observe such an excellent order, both in regard to their behaviours, and for their manner of instruction. Monsieur St. Evremont was about 15 years of age, when he was admitted among them, and the Duke of Florence, being then at Rome (with whom his father had been formerly very intimately acquainted in his travels) to see his son, who was there a student, he gave him all possible demonstrations of his good will, and commanded his son in that seminary, to strike a close friendship with him. The young Prince readily obey'd, and would do any thing to oblige him. As Monsieur St. Evremont had made a greater progress in his studies than he, he did him the honour to confide in him, and made him give him his sentiments concerning his duty. The young Prince was so modest and had so great a desire to learn, that in all their conversations, he askt Monsieur St. Evremont several questions, which, at his age, he could not resolve him; and this being observ'd by their tutor, he took so much pains with these two, that they were envied by the whole College; explaining to them all the difficulties of Logick, which was then their study. Monsieur St. Evremont was not full 18 years old, when he had gone through all the theological theses; and it was upon this occasion, that he gave such a proof by his prodigious memory, by answering to all the passages they could ask him, relating to the holy scriptures; when most of the auditory fancy'd that it was impossible to be done, without some super-natural assistance. This affairs coming to the Pope's ear, his Holiness sent for him, and having read about half a page out of the first Book of Samuel to him, he repeated it, word for word, to the Pontiff, without the least hesitation, just as if he had before-hand got it by heart. Thereupon his Holiness earnestly exhorted him to dedicate himself to God's service, assur'd him, the Church was a good mother, who had treasures and crowns for such of her children, as made it their business to honour and serve her; and concluded, That he wisht he might live to see what use he should make of the precious talents, which it had pleas'd God to bestow upon him, to end he might say to him, like the householder in the Gospel, *Euge, serve bone, & fidelis* ; Well done, good and faithful servant.

But Monsieur St. Evremont's inclination not tending towards holy orders, he left Rome, and returning into France, went into the army, where his extraordinary courage rais'd him to several considerable posts, in which behaving himself with a great deal of fidelity and candour, he obtain'd the love of the supreme officers, who so much recommended him to his Sovereign, Lewis the Fourteenth the present French King, that he soon became a favourite at Court. Now, by the way, we are to take notice that his being in the army had brought him to be a gamester as well as a soldier, insomuch that he was very expert at most games in which dice were us'd ; as at Verquere, Trick-track, Grand-Tricktrack, Back-Gammon, and Irish, invented in the Kingdom of Ireland ; and which aforesaid games are play'd within the tables.

But before I proceed any farther, it will be proper to take notice, that in the game at Irish, the player in his play, must have a care of being too forwards, and ought not to be too rash in hitting every Blot, but with discretion and consideration must move slowly but securely ; by which means, though your adversary hath fill'd his tables, but withal Blots, and you by hitting him enter, you may win the game ; nay, sometimes though he hath born his men all to a very few.

This gentleman was also very expert at all games without the tables, as Inn and Inn, Passage, and Hazard ; and by his continual gaming with persons of all ranks, having learnt the tricking part of most games, as well as playing upon the square, he was generally the winner, play with who he would. Thus one time playing with the King of France at Grand-Tricktrack, he won from him above 4000 pistoles in one night ; and it being afterwards declared to his most Christian Majesty, that Monsieur St. Evremont, had put false dice upon him, the King so resented the matter, that he intended to punish him severely ; but he having notice of it, fled into Holland, where he resided till the restauration of King

Charles II after the settlement of which exil'd monarch on his throne, it was his Royal pleasure to invite Monsieur St. Evremont into this Kingdom, where he was in favour not only with that Prince, but also with King James II. and King William III. He lived also some little time in the Reign of Her present Majesty Queen Anne; and being much in years, he died of old age; and was interr'd in that part of Westminster-Abby where Chaucer, Cowley, Drayton, Spencer, Shadwel, and other English poets are buried; having a very handsome white marble stone erected over his grave, with the following inscription inserted on it.

Carolus de St. Denis, *dom de St.* Evremond,
Nobili genere in Normanniæ ortus,
A prima juventute
Militiæ nomen dedit ;
Et per varia munera,
Ad castrorum Mareschalli gradum evectus
Condeo Turennio
Aliisque claris belli ducibus,
Fidem suam & fortitudinem
Non semel probavit.
Relicta Patria Hollandiam
Deinde a Carolo II. accitus Angliam
Venit.
Philosophiam & humaniores literas
Feliciter excoluit ;
Gallicam linguam
Cum solutatam numeris astricta oratione,
Expolivit, adornavit, locupletavit.
Apud poten : Angliæ reges benevolentiam
et favorem,
Apud regne proceres gratiam & familiari-
tatem
Apud omnes laudem & applausum
Meruit.
Nonaginta annis major.
Obiit IX *Septembris* MDCCIII.

Thus Englished,

Charles de St. Dennis, Lord of St. *Evremond*, descended of a noble family in Normandy, applied himself to military affairs when very young; and after several employments in the army being advanced to the considerable poſt of a Quarter-Maſter-General, by Conde, Turenne, and other officers famous for war, he signaliz'd his fidelity and courage more than once. Leaving his country he came to Holland; after which he was invited into England by Charles II. He polisht philosophy and politer learning with good success; and improv'd, adorn'd, and enrich'd the French tongue both in prose and verse. He merited good will and favour with the moſt potent Kings of England; love and familiarity with the Peers of the Realm; and praise and applause among all men; and being above 90 years of age, he died on the 9th of September, 1703.

The Dutchess of MAZARINE, *a Gameſter.*

THE life of this eniment person having been incomparably written by Monsieur St. Evremont, we shall only take notice of such passages as were omitted by that ingenious author. This lady having often seen at the Court of France, in the time of his exile, King Charles II, whose eyes were great and black, eye-brows thick, and met together, complexion brown, visage long, hair black and curl'd, being also tall and finely shap'd, and had an auſtere presence, but yet lofty and civil, she took such a fancy to him, that when he was reſtored to his Kingdoms, she came to the Court of England to pay his Majeſty a visit, who seem'd always to look very graciously upon her beyond sea.

But before we proceed to the great respeƈt which Madam Mazarine bore that Prince, we muſt take notice that she was a daughter of one of the principal families of Picardy. Her relations for many years bore the highest places both in Church and State, she was brought up with her youngest brother for whose education nothing was spar'd, and in which nothing was wanting. It was so great a pleasure to her, to hear the instructions the masters gave him, that her mother, perceiving her inclinations was pleas'd to order her the same lessons. She was 13 years of age when she began her studies, her brother was 14; and the desire she had to learn, made her forget, that her sex was different from his, she would needs be a sharer of all his pleasures and diversions; and hunting, as laborious as it is, came not amiss to her, provided it was in company with her brother and their tutor. She learnt all the sciences with great facility; and in three or four years spoke 6 languages perfectly well; Nor was there a poet, or antient author, which she could not explain upon sight, and understand his meaning. Her genius, which inspir'd all that ever heard her, with admiration, enflam'd the master, who taught her, with love. He never vented his passion to her any otherwise than by riddle; but she apprehended his meaning by the tender and passionate manner in which he related to her one day, the fable of the vine and the elm. This private declaration of Cupid's power, incited her often to say to her self, How dangerous is it, to hear a master, whose mind and body are so well framed and match'd. Greatness of birth, and goods of fortune, are too weak fences, to confine a heart that is bent upon love and gallantry.

After these motives to the delights of Venus, she abandoned her self intirely to a passion, that wit and merit raised in her soul. Soon did that passion become so strong, that she could not master it; and Monsieur de Ruel, who had already stolen her heart, did not however, keep the sole possession thereof. For some few years, their pleasures were uninterrupted; and the liberty they had of entertaining themselves once or twice a day, was not capable of taking the least from her felicity. But at laſt, the season of repentance overtaking her, she communicated her uneasiness to her lover, who being desirous to enjoy her wholly, and without conſtraint, put her upon the resolution of leaving her father's house. And indeed, that was the only method she could take, to extricate her self out of the moſt imminent danger; that is to say, out of the fury of an angry father, in case he had found out her incontinency, young and unexperienced as she was, she relied altogether on the love and care of the moſt sincere and tender man in the world. Under pretence of going to pass a few days time at an aunt's of hers, who liv'd near Caen in Normandy, she set out from her father's and desir'd them to come and fetch her home, in about a fortnight. Her lover and she had agreed, that about 10 days after their departure, he should pretend a journey into his own country, which was Le Mans. He knew the avenues of the caſtle to which she was retir'd; and as they had appointed a time for their rendezvous, on the day agreed upon, she went into a little coppice behind the caſtle, and there found her lover, with horses and every thing ready to carry her to Paris, where they arriv'd in 3 days. They chose to retire to this great city, to be more out of the way of her friends searches and enquiries.

Three days after their arrival, her lover being gone from their lodgings, which were in the suburbs of St. Germains, she ſtay'd up for him, till one of the clock at night, with incredible fears; and so many dismal thoughts came into her head, that that night seem'd the longeſt she had ever known. An old maid, whom she had taken into her service, did all she could to divert her melancholly, but to no manner of purpose. As soon as it was light, she sent her out to enquire for her maſter, at the likelieſt places she could go to; the firſt visit she made, was to the little Chatelet, where seeing a crowd got together, before the Meurtriere, or little chamber, into which they throw the dead bodies of the unfortunate wretches whom they find murder'd, she got in, and quickly perceiv'd her maſter in his gore. Without speaking a word, home she comes, and having prepar'd her by a simple, but well-meant, discourse to receive with resignation, that ſtroke of providence, she told her the dismal fate of her lover. Thereupon, she disguis'd her self like a servant, and would needs go her self to be an eye-witness of her unhappiness, as she then thought it. Finding her maids ſtory was but too true; she fled immediately from that deteſted place; and, with much ado, got back to her chamber. There having utter'd a thousand exclamations, and pour'd forth rivers of tears, she return'd home to her friends again; where being kindly receiv'd, she in a short time came to the honour of being a Dutchess.

When she was arriv'd to this dignity, and had not only jilted her husband, but also a great many other persons of quality, (which was the heart breaking of her noble consort) she came over to England; where being mightily in favour with King Charles II. she lived to the height of voluptuousness in all degrees; and for gaming, her lodgings were more frequented than the Groom-Porters, in which she was as great a proficient as any at that time; witness her winning at Basset of Nell Gwin 1400 guineas in one night, and of the Dutchess of Portsmouth above 8000 *l.* in doing of which she exerted her utmoſt cunning, and had the greateſt satisfaction, because they were her rivals in the Royal favour. The Monarch himself contributed also to her advantage, being often taken in by her when he play'd. She would play as fair as any person, when she found her gameſter play only upon the square, for she play'd so well that scarce any one could match her; but when she had a sharp gameſter to deal with, she would play altogether upon the sharp at any game upon the cards; and generally came off a winner. Afterwards the jollity of the Court being finished by the death of King Charles the Second, she went shortly after to France, where she died in the last year of the Reign of King James the Second, in the 42nd year of her age, and was nobly interr'd at Abbeville.

Captain NEWEY, *a Sharper and Gamester.*

THIS most unaccountable fellow was born in a little village near the Forest of Dean in Gloucestershire; and his father being a farmer of pretty good repute, put him to school, which being 4 miles from the place where his parents dwelt, he boarded there all the week, so that he only came home on Saturdays, and went again on Mondays: But so unlucky was he, that the many complaints daily made on him, obliged his master to be so very harsh and severe, that his buttocks continually wore the bloody marks of the rod. This severity cast in Newey's mind various ways how to be revenged on his pedagogue; so one evening going to his study door (where sometimes he was wont to sit up late) to listen if he was there; he saw no light, nor heard that snoring he usually made, if he fell asleep and suffer'd his candle to burn out; whereupon concluding he was not there; he went into the kitchin, where he heard the maid say, she must go lay the key for her master, who was at the alehouse among his old gang, and would not come home till his usual hour of twelve. Hearing this, he also pretending to go to bed, as the rest did; but afterwards crept down again, to prepare for his master's reception, when he should enter. In the first place he drew up a trap-door in an entry he was to pass, made for the conveniency of cleansing, or emptying the sink and bog-house, which ran under it; then planting himself behind the outward door, with a frightful sort of vizard tied over his face, a cap, to which a pair of ram's horns were fixed, and an old cast off crape peticoat thrown over his shoulders, he stood there with a dozen of squibs ty'd up in one bundle, to make their fiery execution the greater, and having a tinder-box in his pocket, he struck fire and lighted a match.

Being thus accoutred, his master came somewhat sooner

than he expected; and by his grunting, and fumbling for the key under the door, he perceived he was somewhat sulky, or addle-pated; but at length he open'd it, yet advanced but a few steps e'er he blundered over Newey, who had laid himself as a stumbling-block in his way, and miserably broke his face against the pavement; but before he had time to make any noise, he had got up and fired his squibs; by the light of which unexpected Fuzes, lifting up his batter'd forehead, and seeing Newey's dreadful form, concluded him to be no other than the first begotten of Beelzebub, come to punish him for the sins of his youth; upon which, bolting up at a leap, fear adding wings to his feet, he fled, crying out, The Devil! The Devil! Help! Help! He has me! He has me! Whilst Newey pursu'd with another fire-drake at his tail, crying with a hollow and hoarse voice, through a keck, Thou art mine, thou art mine; and with me you shall go to the shades below.

Scarce had he ended these words, but the trap-door took the poor old man, and down he plung'd into the filth, over head and ears, when Newey throwing a couple of squibs more after him, he shut down the door, and was got to his chamber just as they bounced; which being just above the place, he could hear him bellow out hideously, I'm in Hell! I'm in Hell! Oh, Mercy! Mercy! Mercy! This doleful noise alarming the servants, they rouz'd; and, to be brief, being directed where he was by the noise he continually made, they lifted up the pit-fall, and drew him out, in a miserable stinking condition, almost senceless through fear and stench, wondring how possibly, he could come there, the door being shut so close down; but as soon as they had given him some spirits to revive him, he frightfully looked about with abrupt stammerings and hesitations, assured them, that a monstruous stump-footed devil, in a horrid shape, vomiting flames of fire, had seiz'd him just as he entered the door, and was carrying him that way, as he believed to his infernal region; but, upon saying his prayers, the Dæmon quitted his hold, and vanisht in a clap of thunder, that had singed his beard.

His fear being a little dissipated, the pickle he was in, made not only himself, but all that were about him uneasie, till they had put him into a bucking-tub under a pump, and scrubbed him into somewhat a more sweet and cleanly condition; and then he flounced out of his tub, like Lazarillo de Tormes when he was show'd for a monstrous sea-fish. Newey being thus revenged on his master's severe vapulations, when he next went home, he would go to school no more, for having learnt to write and read, he told his parents that was learning enough for him, who was to be put out to a trade, so being then about 15 years of age he was bound an apprentice to a butcher in the City of Gloucester; but getting his master's maid with child, he ran away, and came up to London, before he had serv'd 3 years of his time. Here he got to be a footman to one Captain Palister, whom he robb'd of above 150 pounds in money and cloaths, and stealing also his commission, he scratch'd out his masters name, and put in his own, from which peice of impudence he ever after stil'd himself Captain.

Then he fled to Scotland where he resided till his master, Captain Palister, went to the West-Indies, where he died in Barbadoes; and the news thereof coming to Newey's ears, he came into England again, where he lived altogether upon bullying and gaming; but the income which accrued to him from the reversion of women of the town, being not sufficient to support him in his most exorbitant extravagances, to supply his irregular courses he took to polygamy, and accordingly married any body, were their portions great or small; insomuch that in a short time he had less than 9 wives, which he own'd to Sir Humphry Edwin at his tryal, for all whom he had such an extraordinary kindness that he would never see them want, by reason he left his spouses as soon as ever he had made them as bare as Esop's crow, when every bird had took it's own feather from her.

Farthermore, Newey had a sister living near Great Turn-stile in Holbourn, a glover, living in good credit and fassion, and from whom he had oftentimes several sums of money to supply his necessities; but at last craving 100 pounds from her, which she deny'd lending him, such was his ingratitude for all her former kindnesses, that he most villanously swore high-treason against her, in that she had counterfeited the current coin of the kingdom: But, not being able to prove his accusation, his sister indicted him for perjury, and being convicted thereof at the Sessions House in the Old-Baily he was fined 50 *l.* and stood in the pillory before his sister's door, at the May-Pole in the Strand, and at Charing-Cross. Then being a close prisoner in Newgate, he had in that prison several vicissitudes of fortune, as being sometimes confin'd in the Press Yard, and sometimes in the Master's-side, but most of all in the Common-side; where he was so fractious and quarrelsome with the officers of the goal, that many times they have been forced to put him for several days and nights together in the bilboes, or else in the condemn'd hold, where he hath been stapled down to the floor with sheers, or very heavy irons on his legs. Also whilst he was a prisoner there, one Mr. Allen the Ordinary of Newgate and he falling out, he sent several letters to the Lord-Mayor and Court of Aldermen, wherein he acquainted them of several irregularities committed by the Ordinary, in extorting money and cloaths from persons under sentence of death, by pretending he would procure them their pardons, and when he got what he could of them, they nevertheless were executed; which accusation against the Ordinary being plainly proved against him, not only by Newey, but also by several other prisoners, he was turned out of his office.

After 2 or 3 years imprisonment Newey's fine being remitted by the Sheriffs, to whom he was amerced, and he thereby restored to his liberty, he had no other way of living but by gaming; and having from one Ager, who formerly acted the part of St. George in Bartholomew-

Fair, and at Southwark, the sharping way of playing, he at length became as great a sharper as any at cards, especially French-Ruff, which was his master-piece. In this game, if you play at Forfat, that is to say, the rigour of the game, he that deals wrong, loses one and his deal, which was often lost by any that play'd with Newey by reason he generally kept a card in his hand private when his antagonist dealt. Also you are bound at this pastime to follow suit, and if you renounce or renege, you lose the whole game, if you so make it, otherwise but 1 or 2, according to agreement; But Newey's playing the greatest severities he always took the whole game in such cases. And to the end that unexperienced gamesters may be more wary at this play, when they light with sharpers, they are to note, that he that plays a Card that is trumped by the follower, if the next player, (for either 2, 4 or 6 may play at this game) hath none of the former suit, he must trump it again, although he hath never a trump in his hand that can win the former trump, and so it must pass to the last player. All the players round are bound to win the highest trump play'd if they can; and observe, that he who plays before his turn loses one unless it be the last card of all. At French-Ruff you must lift for deal, most or least carries it, according to the agreement of the gamesters. You must deal to all that play either 2 at a time first, or 3 according to pleasure, and he that deals, turns up trump; the King is the highest card at trumps, and so it is highest in all other cards that are not trumps the Queen is next, the Knave next, and next to that the Ace, and all other cards follow in preheminence according to the number of the pips, but all small trumps, win the highest of any other suit. Having turn'd up trumps, he that hath the Ace must take the trump turn'd up, and all other trumps which immediately follow that, if so agreed upon amongst the gamesters, laying out so many cards as he took up in liew thereof. After this they play; to win 2 tricks, signifies nothing, to win 3 or 4, wins but one; but to win 5, is the winning of five.

However, Captain Newey not thriving here by his sharping, he went over to Ireland, where falling out in a gaming-house, in Dublin, with a gentleman that would not be bubbled by him, they presently went into a back yard, and drawing their swords, Newey was killed on the spot in 1707, aged 30 years; and was so poor at the time of his untimely death that the parish was forced to bury him.

Cardonnel Goodman, *Esq; a Gamester.*

This memorable Esquire, was the son of a parson of Shaftsbury in Dorsetshire, where he receiv'd his birth, and having good education bestow'd upon him; came up to London, when he was about 20 years of age, where he was made one of the Pages of the Back-Stairs to King Charles II. Having been in this preferment about 3 years, his father died, who left him about 2000 pounds in money, but no real estate. Afterwards he became acquainted with the greatest rakes in town, and being very extravagant, as well as neglectful of his business, he lost his place, and in less than 2 years was as poor as Job.

Nevertheless, out of his extravagancy he had made shift to put himself into a very genteel garb; and as he was one day traversing the street, and gazing about him, the window of a certain tavern in the Strand opened, and a very fine woman looking out, whilst he turn'd his head that way, she made a courtesie and bowed her head, which he taking for a sign she had a desire to speak with him, made no delay to enter the house, and go up stairs, where she was ready to meet him at the door, and welcome him in, when looking wishfully on him, she feigned her self to be mistaken in the man, and began to make excuses; whereupon he would have retired, but she gently pulling him back with an amorous leer, said, Nay, since I have given you this trouble, and the gentleman I expected has past the hour he appointed, pray stay and take part of a collation, for 'tis pity good victuals should be spoil'd for want of company to eat it. Upon this she caused him to sit down, and filling out a glass of wine drank to him; he as kindly pledg'd her, and they talked of divers matters, till a very stately dish of fish, big enough to serve a dozen Dutchmen, upon this he began to enquire where were the rest of the company that were to participate of this banquet. She told him seeing they came not at their time, she would not stay, but entreated him to fall to with a hearty welcome; he did so, and they drank lustily, but eat not the tenth part of what was before them, so that the people of the house and their servants fared the better for it. The table being drawn, she entreated Goodman to stay, and asked him many questions, to which he answer'd so promtly, that she was manely taken with his conversation; then she sung very melodiously, but very low, as not to be heard by those in other rooms, and plied him with bumpers of Hock and Rhenish, that the wine and her singing lull'd him a sleep, so that not waking till it was dark, he found her still in the same place; and to his no small wonder a curious bed in the room, not there before, and as he after perceiv'd had been let through a trap-door in the ceiling, by cords and pulleys, for this it seems was the private nursery chamber of Venus. By this, Goodman was farther confirm'd in what she aim'd at, and could not be so uncivil as not to gratifie her desires in so pleasing a way; insomuch that she prevail'd with him to sleep in her arms for that night; but waking in the morning, he mist her, which did not a little startle him, for he then concluded her to be one of the Long-Cellar ladies, who had put the high game upon him, by emptying his pockets, which had not above 10 shillings in them, and had left him a large reckoning to pay; but fumbling in his breeches he perceived it far otherwise, he found his own money safe, and 100 guineas she left him in a silver wire purse; when thanking his good stars, he arose, and calling the landlord and demanding what was to pay, he told him not a farthing, but that there was a breakfast provided for him, which was likewise paid for. Goodman then enquired for the gentlewoman, but whether they knew her not or dissembled their knowledge of her, certain it is, from thence forward he saw her no more, nor could get any intelligence who this charming and liberal lady might be; but only supposed she wanted an heir to an estate, which otherwise upon her fumbling husband's decease might have parted from her to his relations.

Being flush'd by this lucky adventure, he lived as merry as a fox, that had stored his hole with the spoils of a hen-roost; but ill-got treasure is always wasting like snow in a thaw, or as the Dutchmen learnedly have it, Like butter stopping the crannies of a hot oven; for having revelled away the greatest part of it in expensive ordinaries, at last he was reduced to such extreme want, that he knew not where to be trusted for a farthing; and one day being in extreme necessity indeed for a dinner, and going by a cook's shop, where he saw a very good shoulder of mutton roasting, his hungry stomach obliged him to go in, and desiring six penny-worth, or more of that joint of meat, the cook was so civil as to bring him the whole shoulder to cut where and what he pleased, and he would reckon him accordingly, as not doubting his reckoning, because he was drest as well as a gentleman could be; but after Goodman had filled his belly to the tune of about twenty or two and twenty pence, for meat, bread and drink, calling for the landlord, who came up in an instant, and taking him aside, because there was other company at various tables in the same room, quoth he, Landlord, I have a great secret to deliver to you, which I would not have you to divulge for the world; then after many solemn oaths and protestations made by the cook that he would not reveal his secret, Goodman said, Why truly, landlord, I am a gentleman's son, come of a very good family, but through misfortunes I am at present reduced to a very mean state; and have not any money to pay for what I have called; but, as you said you would keep my secret, I hope you will be as good as your word, in saying nothing of it to any person. The cook thought it was a hard case to lose his reckoning thus, therefore, as Goodman was going out-a-doors, he calls him back again and giving him a good kick o'the breech, quoth he, You may go about your business now, but for the future, Sir, I would desire the favour of you never to declare any more of your secrets to me, for if you do, upon my word, Sir, I shall never keep them.

'Tis true, Goodman accepted of this kick of the breech quietly, to be excused from paying a twenty-penny reckoning or more; and afterwards getting to be an actor in the Play-house, he became very famous for the part of Alexander the Great, in the tragedy of the Rival Queens, written by Nat. Lee. He had good wages for his performances; but not confining himself to his gettings, he must attempt to clip and coin, for which being condemned for his life, a petition was delivered to King Charles the Second in his favour, praying that before he died, he might act the part of Alexander; which being granted, and his Majesty there present, he perform'd it so much to admiration, that his life was granted him; and afterwards the Dutchess of C——d taking a fancy to him, he was withdrawn from the stage, and at her Grace's sole cost and charges maintain'd without acting for the future.

Yet sometimes, for his diversion, he would play a part; as once in particular, in the solemn time of Lent, when some of the young actors were allowed a play for their own benefit, to do them a kindness, he promis'd to play Alexander for them gratis; and permitting them to insert his name in their play-house bills, that notice brought not only a great many persons of quality, but also Queen Catherine, who ordering the curtain to be drawn up, he would not permit it till the Dutchess of C——d was come; a second time he also refused acting till his Dutchess came, and a third time, some of the actors telling him that it was the Queen's express orders they should draw up the curtain, he swore several great oaths, That if the Pit and Boxes too were lin'd with Queens he would not act till his Dutchess was come; who being in this contest just enter'd, he perform'd his part according to his promise, to the great satisfaction of the whole audience.

Although Goodman had a good allowance to live upon from the Dutchess of C———d, yet was he a great gamester at cards, especially L'Ombre, at which 3 persons only can play; and though 2 of them do combine to make the third lose, yet are you to note that they all do their best (for the common good) to hinder any one from winning, only striving to make it Repuesto, which is when the player wins no more tricks than another, in which case the player doubles the stake without any ones winning it, and remains so for the advantage of the next player. But at length Goodman getting into plots and conspiracies and pretending so much goodness and candor to Sir John Fenwick, who was beheaded on Tower-Hill, as not to be an evidence against him, he fled into France, where he died of a fever, in the 50th year of his age, Anno 1699.

Beau HEWIT, *a Sharper and Gamester.*

THIS spark was the eldest son of an eminent linnen draper in Bristol, where he was born; and being sent up to London, was put apprentice to a chyrurgeon, whom he serv'd about 3 years, and his father then died; who leaving him an estate of about 210 pounds per ann. he bought out the remainder of his time of his master, and set up for a gentleman. He was a great admirer of the fair sex, whose hearts to make his own, he drest very nicely, and had a thousand singularities to distinguish him from other men.

By keeping company with the most chargeable jilts of the town he had almost confounded his patrimony in

less than 4 years; and one day paying a visit to one
Elizabeth Davis, a strumpet, debauch'd by a barrister
in Grays-Inn, there happen'd to be mention made of
Hampton-Court; and she pretending to be very desirous
of seeing that famous Palace, to which she had hitherto
been a stranger, he made an offer of his service to wait
on her thither, which she accepted and thereupon appointed a day, on the morning of which, he (as being
as punctual in the affairs of love, as a creditable merchant
is in the payment of money) waited on her at her lodgings,
and happen'd to surprise her in a disabile; but being
soon drest to the best advantage, he handed her down
stairs into a coach, and their made a thousand protestations of his love to her till they came to the water-side,
where a ravenous assembly of amphibious scoundrels,
some with their mouths full of bread and cheese and
onions, were ready to pluck them out of the windows
of their leathern sanctuary, before the driver could have
recourse to the door, to deliver them fairly into the vile
hands of the wrangling society. At length he pitch'd
upon a couple of red-cap Tritons, who handed them into
the wherry, and became on a sudden as complaisant
and as civil as if they had been bred at a boarding-school;
for 'tis certain that watermen quarrel about who shall
carry a fare, as lawyers do at Westminster about who shall
carry the cause. When Hewit had seated his mistress
on the right hand, the brawny slaves sat down to their
stretchers, and puffing and blowing at every pull like
a phthisicky man in a sweat, they row'd them onward of
their way, their ears being every now and then saluted
with a broad-side of scurrilous words and bawdy phrases,
which put the lady's pretended modesty to the blush,
and her spark to such a condfounded puzzle to defend
himself and her, that he was forc'd to exert his parts to
the utmost, and pelt their adversaries with the Billings-
gate dialect of rogue, taylor, whore, sempstress, cuckold,
mechanick, jilt, exchange-woman, and all the ill language
he could muster up, lest his mistress should think him
a blockhead. The time he proposed in exhibiting his

love to his fair companion, and preparing her heart for his design, with such mollifying endearments and prevailing dalliances, as were necessary to warm the inclinations of a female lover, he was forc'd to employ in ſtudying what to say to the next boat he met with, for the first word, like the firſt blow, was half the battle. In this manner, they smoothly slid along the slippery surface of the Thames, liſtning at spare-times to the whispering flags and osiers that adorn'd the pleasant banks, and gently bow'd their limber heads in becoming gratitude to the delightful breeze, that fann'd their verdant blades into so musical a motion. The weather prov'd so temperate and extreamly favourable, and the radiant sun shining forth with such an auspicious luſtre, that finer day ne'er bleſt a Lord Mayor's Show.

At length they arriv'd at Mortlack, and took a little refreshment at the old cuckold-making tenement the Garter; and to enliven their legs, which were almoſt benum'd for want of action, they walk'd to Richmond, where they order'd the boat to meet 'em, by which means they avoided a tedious circumference by water. They walk'd cross the fields, link'd arm in arm, as loving as any man and wife, and entertain'd one another's ears with unſtudy'd prattle, such amorous fuſtian as love popt into their mouths came simply out again without any amendment; so that had a couple of Bow-Street criticks been walking behind 'em, they might have had more diversion, than by hearing a dialogue in the Pit, between a beau and a mask, or the moſt elegant piece of courtship in the New Academy of Complements. When they came to the forementioned town of Richmond, they resum'd their places in the boat, and after an hours hard tugging againſt the ſtream, they arriv'd at the famous port to which they had design'd. Here Hewit having discharg'd the laborious drudges, and finding not above 18 pence left in silver in his pocket, he put his hand into his fob, to find what gold was lodg'd there; but to his extream mortification he found it as empty as a scull on an apothecary's stall, and presently he recollected, that over night he had taken out 5 guineas and left 'em in his closet-window; but thinking he had 'em about him, he came out and forgot 'em. This dishonourable misfortune made his heart broil with vexation like a mutton-chop on a grid-iron. He knew not what to do, nor how to come off handsomly; but at last concluded the best way was to make her acquainted with his disappointed circumstances; and after as many bashful hums and ha's as a bashful evidence makes when he speaks to a judge, he at last open'd his sorrowfull case, but as awkardly as a midwife talks Scripture, or a Quaker bawdy. He found by her countenance, that she was as much surpriz'd as he was daunted; and after a little pause I hope, Sir (says she) since you have brought me thus far out of London, you will contrive some way to convey me safe home: for indeed I did not take care, as I find I ought to have done, to bring money out with me, believing I could have no occasion for expences in the company of a gentleman, who has given me in words such assurances of his friendship. To which he made a suitable answer; begging she would remove all severe censures and reflections, though justly due to such inexcusable forgetfulness, and that she would be pleased to tarry but a little time in a tavern, till he stept to a friend at a small distance from Hampton Town, from whom he was assur'd of a supply: she seeming pretty well satisfied with what he propos'd, they accordingly went to an adjacent house, where he left her over a pint of Canary and a roll. He had now to go as far as Waltham upon Thames, which is at least 2 long miles, where a friend of his from London had resided about 6 weeks for his health; but adding mercurial wings to his feet, he outambled a chairman, and now and then put himself into a dog-trot, which made him sweat worse than a Penny-Post-man at Midsummer, and all to no purpose; for his friend was gone to London the day before. This disappointment upon the neck of the other was an insupportable grievance, and made him scratch his ears like a bilkt Hackney Coachman. But in returning he consider'd the matter, and found he had no other way left than to be a good husband, and leave his sword, which was silver-hilted, for the reckoning. So fixing upon this resolution he came back more like a running footman than a gentleman; and coming into the tavern, he receiv'd the ſtartling news that his lady was gone to London with the Lord M——n. These ſtrange tidings amazed him more than a blazing ſtar. Pray Sir (said he) unriddle this ſtrange myſtery to me; how, which way, after what manner, this business came about? Why, Sir, answered the other, I shew'd you and the lady into the beſt room in my house, which his Lordship always drinks in when he comes hither; I told his Honour, who had another person with him, that it was now taken up; he ask'd, By whom: I told him by a single lady; upon which they smil'd, and both went into the room to her; and after they had drank but one flask of wine, they left a crown for that, and the lady's pint of Canary, and handed her into a coach, to which she shew'd no signs of unwillingness, but rather seemed by her looks to be very well satisfied and this, Sir, says she, is all that I know of the matter; only that they ordered the coach for London. This intolerable usage made Hewit rave, fret, and vex like a horn-mad cuckold? to be thus jilted, fatigu'd, disappointed and teaz'd, he thought was enough to over power the philosophy of Epictetus, Seneca, or any other ſtoick.

In this vexatious condition he went down to the water-side, where by great accident he got a six-penny passage the same night, and was heartily glad to squeeze in amongſt trunks, boxes, baskets, and blew aprons; so that about 11 a clock at night he arriv'd safe at London, where he resolv'd to be as inveterate an enemy to all jilts, as he that had loſt his nose by encountering with the petticoat. And truly his resolution ſtood good, when according to the old proverb, Needs muſt when the Devil drives; for his subſtance being now exhauſted to nothing, he was forced to take to irregular courses; as

264

may be perceived by going one day to Tompion the watch-maker, and told him there was a uncle of his at Stroud in Kent, from whom he expected a considerable matter, had desired him to buy a watch, but he could not raise money enough to lay down for it. Now (quoth he) I don't desire you to trust me, but make a watch, and you may with your own hands deliver it to one Jack Try at Brown's Wharf, with a charge not to leave the watch, without the money be paid down. Accordingly the watch was made, and at the day appointed goes with his chapman and another to deliver it to the hoyman; which he did with the aforesaid caution, the hoyman promising to observe it, and at the next return he would produce either the watch or so much money; to which bargain the other two were witnesses. Now they had not parted from the hoyman an hour, before the two went back, and pretending there was something to mend in it, that it could not be sent before the next voyage, desired the hoyman to redeliver it, which he did without suspecting any fraud. When the hoyman came to town again, Tompion the watch-maker went, expecting either his watch or money, and therefore innocently demanded of the hoyman, whether he had dispos'd of the watch. But upon the hoyman's telling him that his friends had fetch'd it back before he went away, and that he ex-pected it to carry down the next time he went; the watch-maker began to smell a rat, and finding that the watch was irrecoverably gone, was resolv'd to get his money of the hoyman, and therefore arrested him; but he finding sufficient bail, stood tryal with him, and after several removes, and a great deal of money spent on both sides, Tompion got the better, and was allow'd costs of the Court; which the hoyman being not well able to pay, and having run in debt to carry his suit, was forc'd to leave off his employment, and take refuge in a troop of Horse-Grenadiers, in which a friend of his had bought him a place.

By the way also we are to take notice how he once serv'd a rope-maker. This ropemaker having a prentice who was a Yorkshire lad, whom he daily sent out to sell halters to inn-keepers, when he first came to him, and getting nothing by the matter, he was resolv'd to keep him at home, to make that dangerous sort of ware; but the young Yorkshire Tike liking gadding abroad better than a close confinement at home, quoth he, Master try me once more abroad with my goods, and I'll warrant you I'll vend 'em very well. The master next day sent him abroad again, with a pretty large basket full of halters, which covering and tying down very close from sight, he goes through London, crying Who will buy any Yorkshire Common-Prayer Books? Who will buy any Yorkshire Common-Prayer Books? The people admiring what sort of Common-Prayer Books they should be, call'd him almost at every other house, to see them; but quoth young Yorkshire, This being a sort of goods which no one sells but my self, by mess no body shall see them before they buy. The people then enquiring the price of his commodity, of which he had from the price of 2 pence to a shilling, the charge being no more at the highest, he took ready money for his goods before his customers saw 'em; but when they found how cunningly they were gull'd they heartily curst the seller and his Yorkshire Common-Prayer Books: however being an arch wag, he would somewhat pacifie their displeasure, by telling 'em, The Yorkshire people us'd no other sort of Common-Prayer Books, for truly they never make saying any prayers there till they came to the gallows, and the rope just put about their necks. So the boy returning home with an empty basket and full purse, to the great satisfaction of his master, he sent him out again with another basket full the next day, when being upon the same strain, Who will buy any Yorkshire Common-Prayer Books? Who will buy any Yorkshire Common-Prayer Books? Beau Hewit met him, and though he was one that us'd prayers as little as any body, yet being curious of seeing the Yorkshire way of devotion, and giving the Yorkshire Tike a shilling for one before he saw it, he no sooner beheld the halter, but he was inwardly vext at the trick put upon him; however, containing his anger, quoth he, Young lad, I have an occasion for a great deal of cordage of several sorts, therefore if you'll send your master to my lodgings to morrow I will agree with him about it. So telling Yorkshire where he liv'd, when he went home with a full purse again, he told his master of this customer, on whom he waited the next morning, and presently struck up a bargain for as much of his commodity as came to 30 pounds, which he presently fetch'd to his lodgings in York-Buildings, and receiv'd a Bank-Bill for the same. Then the rope-maker made the best of his way to the Bank of England for his money, and Beau Hewit made as much haste from his lodgings with his hempen ware, and found a chapman for it presently; but when the rope-maker went to Grocers-Hall to turn his Bank-Bill into ready specie, it being found to be a counter-feited one, he was secur'd for a cheat, and committed to Newgate, where it cost him a good sum of money before he got his liberty.

Another time Beau Hewit being in want of money, and using a certain ale-house in Fetter-Lane, which puts out for it's sign, 3 of those wooden horses on one of which the poets usually feign Bacchus to sit striding, or else it is the painters fancy to draw that jolly God so, he knew the victualler to take great delight in bird-catching; whereupon wheadling him out of 4 or 5 guineas, for informing him in what place in the County of Cumberland a couple of white linnets had built their nests, he thought his money very well bestow'd for the news of a rarity equivalent to, if not exceeding, this in Juvenal the Satyrist.

Rara avis in terris, nigroque simillima cygno.

To get these rare birds he prepares for his journey, and rid with all expedition into Cumberland, where having refresht himself for 2 or 3 days after a fatiguing journey of 200 miles, he went to the very field, in which, as Beau Hewit had directed him the 2 white linnets constantly resided; but after a long search among the hedges, and harmonious whiſtling, much exceeding the charming songs of the Syrens, which allur'd men of Ulisses, to drown themselves in the sea, finding no linnet of that colour, he made some enquiry among the country people about the matter, who perceiving the fellow foolish, although he was born as far north as they, told him the 2 white linnets had left that ſtation about juſt a week, whereupon Nick and Froth curſt his fate for not making more haſte than he had by riding poſt ; for had he caught but those white linnets it had been the making of him and his family for ever.

When Hewit had play'd a great many of these cheating tricks upon the town, insomuch that he was liable every day to be apprehended and sent to jayl for 'em, he play'd at hide and seek for some time, and then thinking he was forgotten, he began to appear abroad again, and turn'd gameſter ; but at firſt being a very great loser, he moſt assiduously ſtudied the use of the Geometrical Playing-Cards set forth by Monsieur Des-Cartes, the famous French philosopher and mathematician ; but finding the demonſtrations of that great man to be founded on no certainty, he was resolv'd to try his luck at dice ; but also not finding out the art of at how many times one may undertake to throw 6 with one dye, or at how many times one may undertake to through 12 with 2 dice, or with how many dice one can undertake to throw 2 sixes at the firſt caſt, according to the 10th, 11th, and 12th, Propositions of Hugen's treatise, *De ratiociniis in ludo Aleæ*, and finding his rules of calculating chances moſt false and erroneous, he damn'd that authour for as great a blockhead as he was a fool, in loosing his money upon such conceited whims ; therefore learning the more profitable and sureſt way of tricking both at cards and dice, in which the adversary could make no calculation of chances, he became so expert in the dexterity of slipping cards, or cogging a dye, that in 4 years time he was worth 6000 pounds : But at laſt playing at Hazard with one Sir Edward Payne, of whom he won 560 guineas, the losing gentleman finding some siniſter practices in his play, which created a quarrel, they fought a duel the next morning, in which Beau Hewit was kill'd in Hyde-Park, in 1702; and so there was a deserved end of the gamester.

Appendix

The three following descriptions are taken from the
1721 Edition.

BASSET, a French Game.

THIS game, amongst all those on the cards, is accounted
to be the most courtly, being properly, by the under-
standers of it, thought only fit for Kings and Queens,
great Princes, Noblemen, &c. to play at, by reason of
such great losses, or advantages, as may possibly be on
one side or other, during the time of play.

It is in its nature not much unlike our late *Royal Oak
Lottery*. And as that, by the lottery-man's having
five figures in two and thirty for himself, must certainly
be a considerable profit to him in length of time; so
here the dealer that keeps the Bank, having the first and
last card at his own disposal, and other considerable
privileges in the dealing the cards, has (without doubt)
a greater prospect of gaining, than those that play.
This was a truth so acknowledg'd in France, that the
King made a publick edict, that the privilege of a *Talliere*,
or one that keeps the Bank at Basset, should only be
allow'd to principal *Cadets*, or sons of great families,
supposing that whoever was so befriended, as to be
admitted to keep the Bank, must naturally in a
very short time, become possessor of a considerable
estate.

But all others, for fear of ruining private persons and
families, are confin'd politickly to a Twelvepenny
Bank tho' here they have the liberty of staking what
they please.

Appendix

The Terms of the Game are these.

Talliere,		The Pay,
Croupiere,		The Alpiew,
Punter,		Sept-et-le-va,
The Fasse,		Quinze-et-le-va,
The Couch,		Trent-et-le-va
The Paroli,		Soissant-et-le-va, &c.
The Masse,		

The Explanation of the Terms.

1. THE *Talliere* is he that keeps the Bank, who lays down a sum of money before all those that play, to answer every winning card that shall appear in his course of dealing.

2. The *Croupiere* is one that is assistant to the *Talliere*, and stands by to supervise the losing cards; that when there are a considerable company at play, he may not lose by over-looking any thing that might turn to his profit.

3. The *Punter* is a term for every one of the gamesters that play.

4. The *Fasse* is the first card that is turn'd up by the *Talliere*, belonging to the whole pack, by which he gains half the value of the money that is laid down upon every card of that sort by the punters.

5. The *Couch* is a term for the first money that every punter puts upon each card, every one that plays having a Book of thirteen several cards before him, upon which he may lay his money, more or less, according to his fancy.

6. The *Paroli* is a term explain'd thus, that having won the couch or first stake, and having a mind to go on to get a *Sept-et-le-va*, you crook the corner of your card, letting your money lie without being paid the value of it by the Talliere.

272

Appendix

7. The *Masse* is when you have won the couch, or firſt ſtake, and will venture more money upon the same card; which is only pursuant to the discretion of the Punter, who knows or ought to know the great advantages the *Talliere* has; and therefore should be subtle enough to make the beſt of his own game.

8. The *Pay* is when the Punter has won the couch, or firſt ſtake, whether a shilling, half-crown, crown, guinea, or whatever he lays down upon his card, and being fearful to make the Paroli, leaves off, for by going the Pay, if the card turns up wrong he loses nothing, having won the couch before, but if by this adventure Fortune favours him, he wins double the money that he ſtakes.

9. The *Alpiew* is much the same thing as the Paroli, and like that term us'd when a couch is won, by turning up or crooking the corner of the winning card.

10. *Sept-et-le-va* is the firſt great chance that shews the advantages of this game: as for example, if the Punter has won the couch, and then makes a Paroli, by crooking the corner of his card, as is said before, and going on to a second chance, his winning Card turns up again, it comes to Sept-et-le-va, which is seven times as much as he laid down upon his card.

11. *Quinze-et-le-va* as next in its turn, is attending the Punter's humour who perhaps is resolv'd to follow his fancy, and ſtill lay his money upon the same card, which is done by crooking the third corner of his card, which coming up by the dealing of the Talliere, makes him win fifteen times as much money as he ſtak'd.

12. *Trent-et-le-va* succeeds Quinze-et-le-va, and is mark'd by the lucky Punter, by crooking or bending the end of the fourth corner of his winning card,

which coming up makes him purchaser of three and thirty times as much money as he laid down.

13. *Soissant-et-le-va* is the highe&t and greate&t chance that can happen in the game, for it pays sixty seven times as much money as is &tak'd, and is seldom won by some lucky Punter, who resolves to push the extream of his good fortune to the height. It cannot be won but by the Talliere's dealing the cards over again, which if his winning card turns up, pays him with such a prodigious advantage.

And as I sometimes have seen at the Royal-Oak Lottery (before mention'd) a figure come up, that by some guineas laid on it in full, by the winning eight and twenty times as much has broke the keeper of it; so by the courage and extraordinary luck of some pushing Punter at this game, some great &take with Soissant-et-le-va may turn up, and by that means break the bank.

But this very rarely happens; the Talliere, like the Lottery-Man, being a great deal more likely to break the game&ters than they him. The sense of this great advantage which the dealer has (several families having been ruin'd by playing at it) has caus'd this game to be modell'd to a Twelvepenny Bank in France.

The Order of the Game is thus.

They sit down round a table, as many as please, the Talliere in the mid&t of them, with the bank of money before him, and the Punters each having a book of thirteen cards, laying down one or two, three or more as they please, with money upon them, as &takes; then he takes the pack altogether in his hand, and turns them up, the bottom card appearing is call'd the Fasse and pays him half the value of money laid down by the Punters, upon any card of that sort as has been said before.

The Manner of the Play is thus.

After the Fasse is turn'd up, and the Talliere and Croupiere have look'd round the cards on the table, and taken half the advantage of the money laid on them, he proceeds in his deal and the next card appearing, whether King, Queen, Ace, or whatever it be, wins for the Punter, who may receive, if he has laid money on such a sort of card the value, or making Paroli go on to a Sept-et-le-va, as has been said, the card after that wins for the Talliere, who takes money from each Punter's card of that sort, and brings it to his bank.

The Talliere's manner of expression in playing the game is thus: If the winning card be a King, and the next appearing after it be a Ten, then he says (shewing the cards that appear to all the Punters round) King wins, Ten loses, paying the money to such cards as are of the winning sort, and taking the money to supply his bank from those that lose; that done, he goes on with the deal, as, Ace wins, Five loses, Knave wins, Seven loses, and so every other card alternately winning and losing, till all the pack be dealt out but the laſt card.

The laſt card turn'd up (as I hinted before) is an advantage to the Talliere; because by the rule of the game, which was contriv'd for his benefit, tho' it be turn'd up, and the Punter may happen to have ſtak'd upon one of the same sort; yet it is allow'd as one of his dues, in relation to his office, and he pays nothing.

The Punter 'tis certain, who is luckily adventurous and can push on his Couch to a considerable ſtake, to Sept-et-le-va, Quinze-et-le-va, Trent-et-le-va, &c. if he have the fortune to arrive at that pitch, muſt in a wonderful manner, multiply his Couch or firſt ſtake; but that is so seldom done, considering the frequency of the Punter's losses, in comparison to the bank's advantage, that the dimmeſt eye may easily see, without a pair of spectacles, how much and considerable the design of this court game is in the favour of the Talliere.

The liberty that is used by our English pushing adventurers at this game, makes it of quite another kind than it is in France; for they (as has been said) are compell'd by the sovereign authority to ſtint the prodigal humours in Punting, and are only to play at a Twelvepenny Bank, where the losses or gains cannot be ruinous, nor so extravagant as to make a desolation in a family: But here in England, the Punters being oblig'd by no such confinement, have the liberty to ſtake one, two, three guineas or more upon a card, as I frequently have seen some of the nobility do at court, which, the Couch being Alpiew'd or Paroli'd to Sept-et-le-va, Quinze-et-le-va, Trent-et-le-va, &c. (which does sometimes happen) muſt needs redound extremely to the Punter's profit, who by the advantage of the multiplication, muſt undoubtedly raise his Couch, or ſtake (if he be so couragious to make it valuable) to a very extraordinary sum: And if he be so befriended by Fortune, to bring it to Soissant-et-le-va, he is very likely to break the bank, by gaining a sum so bulky, that 'tis probable at present the Talliere is not able to pay.

But this (like snow in summer) is a rarity that happens very seldom, 'tho it sometimes has been, and therefore is indeed only a decoy for the Punter to urge him to venture his ſtake boldly: the Talliere's certain advantage, for all this specious demonſtration of the Punter's probability of winning being plainly obvious and unanswerable, as shall further appear.

Suppose Ten, or any other card wins for the Punter, if another Ten comes up juſt after, in the winning card's place, it does not win for him but for the bank, but if it comes up three or four cards after that, it wins for the Punter: If Ace or any other card wins at firſt, and afterwards comes up again, in the next winning card's place, it does not go; but by a term they have for that part of the game, is said to *retire* till the next opportunity, because by the rule of the game, it muſt go for the bank before the Punter.

But then in return of this and subtilly to gain the eſteem of all the young adventurers, who are apt to set their mony briskly, if the card happens to come in the next losing place, it does not lose, because it has not gone for the Punter, but also retires without paying the bank, having won a Couch, which the Talliere saves, and should have paid.

To conclude, this game, as the aforesaid Royal-Oak Lottery was formerly, is of so tempting and decoying a nature, by reason of several specious multiplications and advantages, which seemingly it offers to the unwary Punter, that a great many like it so well, that they will in some coffee-houses, and other publick places, play at small games rather than give out, and rather than not play at all, will punt at a Groat, Threepenny, Twopenny Bank, so much the hopes of winning the Quinze-et-le-va, and Trent-et-le-va intoxicates them; but the judicious whose love of gaming does not exceed his governable understanding, will not engage at it; or if he does, will play so warily as not to be drawn by the seeming profitable glosses, since 'tis most certain, that it cannot be upon the square, and that the *Talliere*, if he pays you twenty pound in one night's play, only gives you opportunity in another to lose an hundred.

The Ingenious and Pleasant Game of BRAGG.

THE person appointed to have the eldest hand, deals with the whole pack about the table, to those that sit and are desirous to share in the gain and diversion. As many play at it as the cards will hold out to supply, he dealing three apiece to each of the gamesters at one time, turning up the last card all round, belonging to every one there.

Each gamester is to put down three stakes, one for each card, as much or as little as the humours of the company will consent to ; whether three Guineas, three Crowns, three Shillings, three Sixpences, or what other stakes, according to their qualities and purses, is thought convenient: and this being done, the manner of playing the game, is as follows :

The best card turn'd up in the dealing round, in its

degree, beginning from Ace, King, Queen, Knave, and so downwards, through all the cards of the persons sitting, wins the firſt ſtake, and the person who has the luck to have it dealt him, is to demand it from the reſt, who pay it accordingly; unless the Ace of Diamonds be turn'd up amongſt them, which if shewn by a superior authority in the game, is to be prefer'd, and wins the ſtake. And note besides, that tho' the eldeſt hand that has an Ace carries it from the reſt, by a kind of descent; yet the Ace of Diamonds, by the aforesaid authority, even in the youngeſt hand, which is the laſt card that is dealt, wins the ſtake from any other that is turn'd up before.

The next principal matter, and the main thing by which the second ſtake is to be won, is called the *Bragg*, which by the ingenuity of its management, gives the game its name. The nature of it is, that you are to endeavour to impose upon the judgement of the reſt that play, and particularly on the person that chiefly offers to oppose you, by boaſting of cards in your hand, whether *Pair Royals*, *Pairs* or others, that are better than his or hers that play againſt you; the beſt cards you can have really to bragg of, are a Pair Royal of Aces, the next of Kings, Queens, &c. A Pair Royal of any sort, winning from any Pair of the beſt sort, as a Pair of any sort, wins of any other cards that are not Pairs.

But here you are to observe, that the witty ordering of this Bragg, is the moſt pleasant part of this game; for those that by fashioning their looks and geſtures, can give a proper air to their actions as will so deceive an unskilful antagoniſt, that sometimes a pair of Fives, Treys, or Deuces, in such a hand, with the advantage of his compos'd countenance, and subtle manner of over-awing the other, shall out-bragg a much greater Pair Royal and win the ſtakes with great applause and laughter on his side, from the whole company.

The Knave of Clubbs, is here a principal favourite, as at Pam, and makes a Pair with any other card in hand, or with any other two cards a Pair Royal, and is often in this game very necessary to advance the credit of the Bragg, to him that has the assurance of imposing upon the company, and by such convenient confidence, the advantage of winning the second stake.

The third stake is won by the person that first makes up the cards in his hand one and thirty, each Ace, King, Queen, Knave, &c. going for Ten, and drawing from the pack, as is usual in that game; or in lieu of the one and thirty, if his fortune will not oblige him, the nearest to it may win, he having the privilege to draw or not to draw as he pleases, according as he finds it convenient, by the cards that are in his hand; for if he draws out, he loses his third stake.

Some very nice players at this game, make the Nine of Diamonds a second favourite card, with the Knave of Clubbs, to make a Pair Royal of Aces, so that those two joyn'd with one Natural Ace, shall win from any Pair Royal of Kings, Queens, Knaves, or any other cards, but a Pair Royal of Natural Aces.

The person that is so lucky to win all the three stakes, is to be rewarded by the whole company of gamesters round the table, with three stakes more, if they play the strictness of the game, which necessarily makes the winnings and losings amount to a considerable sum of money; but very often our modern gamesters wave this particular, and out of a decent regard to their pockets, content themselves with the satisfaction of the pleasure of the Bragg, rather than trust to the uncommon good fortune of winning the three stakes, from the rest of the disappointed company.

The deal is to go round from person to person, and by the different management of the Bragg, you may find very great diversion, some doing it so awkardly, with so little cunning, and so ill an address, that the defects or value of their game will presently be discover'd, whilst others with a more comical assurance, and by their subtle management, will wittily banter and impose upon their adversaries, and seldom fail of their design'd profit.

Appendix

It is not fair for any of the gamesters, that sit near him that makes the Bragg, to peep into his hand, or by any mute sign or token to give the opposer any knowledge of the cards, that he has in his hand; because it may chance that the oppositions, natural to this game, may draw on a considerable sum of money to be stak'd down, each of the two that are concern'd, valuing his own cards, and lessening those of his antagonist, as he thinks he has reason.

A very notable damage, occasion'd by one person peeping into another's hand, I once my self chanc'd to be spectator of. Some gentlemen and ladies, were casually one evening playing at this game, when one of the gamesters, who it seem'd was of the sort of those who were very skilful at the game in general; but particularly so, at the subtle management of the Bragg, and by his artful method and cunning manner of behaviour, had induc'd his competitor to believe that he resolv'd to out-bounce him upon very low and insignificant cards; but it was the gentleman's good luck at that juncture to have in his hand far otherwise than he imagin'd, having been dealt two Natural Aces and the Knave of Clubbs, which joyn'd with the other two, made the greatest Pair Royal that could then possibly be dealt; and consequently proper to win also the greatest stake that could be laid, he kept his countenance demure, and with a gesture neither overjoy'd nor desponding, made a Bragg of half a crown; the other who had in his hand a Pair Royal of Kings, and, as afterwards was discover'd, had, through the imprudence of the dealer, casually seen an Ace or two given about to other gamesters, thinking himself also as secure as possible, answers with a crown; his antagonist then sets an angel and the opposer immediately twenty shillings, they still raising the stakes every time, and vying with each other till the same amounted to seven pounds, when ill fate for one of them would have it, a too curious impertinent of the female kind, who sat next to him that had the Aces, having a furious itch upon her to know whether his repeated Bragg was

280

upon a sure foundation or no, could not forbear covertly peeping into his hand, and at the view was so surpriz'd, that on a sudden she gave a violent shriek, and by that indiscreet and rash noise, gave the gameſter with the Pair Royal of Kings, warning of his unavoidable loss, giving him reason to cease the Bragg, and hinder the other's winning the further intended ſtakes, which he declar'd he design'd to raise and go on with, till it came to a hundred pounds. If in drawing for one and thirty, to win the laſt ſtake, upon showing the cards, any two or more of the gameſters should happen to have the same cards, they are permitted to draw again, till they get either the one and thirty a better game, or lose it by drawing out. And this is all I know significant, in the ingenious and pleasant game of Bragg.

PRIMERO, a Spanish Game.

THIS game was anciently, amongst the graver sort of Spaniards, held in very great eſteem, but it continued not long so; for since the late ingenious invention of the Spanish game, call'd L'Ombre, the reputation it had is quite diminish'd, and the other in extraordinary requeſt, as having a very divertive addition, which the ancient Primero was defeive on.

The main difference between the two games, is, that Primero is play'd with six cards, and L'Ombre with nine; but as to the terms or appellations that they bear, they are much the same, Spadillo or the Ace of Spades, being here as there counted the beſt card; and two or three may sit down to play as they do at that.

They have, as L'Ombre has, Basto the Ace of Clubbs, Punto for the Ace of Trumps, with Manillio the Seven of the red cards, or Deuce of black; also Matadors, being Sequents of the firſt three beſt cards.

There is also another variation between the games, which gives this we are mentioning its appellation, and that is, as at L'Ombre, when any one has a sure game, and plays for the Voll, Spadillo, Mallillio or Kings, that are as good as Trumps, with the aforesaid Matadors, intitle him to win; so here, he that has Cinquo, Primero, which is a sequence of five of the beſt cards, assiſted with Spadillo, or any other valuable Trump, is sure to be successful over his adversary.